VILLAGES OF THE MEO

Aspects of their His

The villages of the Meon Valley.

VILLAGES OF THE MEON VALLEY

Aspects of their History

PETER R. WATKINS

SWANMORE BOOKS

Published by Swanmore Books
7 Crofton Way
Swanmore
Southampton SO32 2RF

ISBN 978-0-954-1566-3-3

Peter Watkins is also the author of:

Swanmore since 1840 (2001)
ISBN 978-0-954-1566-0-2

and

Bishop's Waltham: Parish, Town and Church (2007)
ISBN 978-0-954-1566-2-6

Design, typesetting and production by
John Saunders Design & Production, OX13 5HU
Printed in Great Britain by the
MPG Books Group, Bodmin and King's Lynn

Contents

Illustrations

Source of illustrations, author and where known owners of copyright are indicated in brackets. In the text only titles of the illustrations appear.

Cover: Meonstoke church (The Innes Marlow Collection)

Frontispiece: The villages of the Meon Valley (Neil Gibbons)

1. Wall from the Roman villa at Shavard's Farm, Meonstoke now in the British Museum Gallery 49 (Trustees of the British Museum).
2. Roman and Saxon sites at Shavard's Farm, Meonstoke on 1870 OS map (HCC).
3. Graves from the Saxon cemetery at Droxford (HFCAS Vol.35 p.111).
4. The Meonstoke disc brooch (HFCAS Vol.63 p.129).
5. Saxon earthwork near Marlands farm West Meon.
6. Parochiae in the Southampton area (P.H.Hase).
7. Corhampton church built c.1020 print c.1850 (The Innes Marlow Collection).
8. The Saxon north door at Corhampton church, now blocked up (Peter Ewence).
9. Twelfth century inscription in the south porch of Warnford church (Peter Ewence).
10. Domesday Book: part of the entry for Meonstoke Hundred – Land of the Bishop of Winchester, transliterated and transcribed into modern English (Phillimore and Co Ltd Chichester).
11. Tournai font in East Meon church.
12. Plan of the moated complex and manorial fishponds at Wickham Place (HCC).
13. Manor house at Wickham as it may have appeared in the fourteenth century (HCC).
14. William of Wykeham bishop of Winchester 1367–1404 (Warden and Scholars of Winchester College).
15. The Court House, East Meon before restoration (English Heritage NMR BB78/10152).
16. The Court House at East Meon after restoration (*Country Life 8th May 1937*).
17. Interior of the Hall, East Meon (*Country Life 8th May 1937*).
18. Great Funtley Farmhouse (English Heritage NMR BB95/03422).
19. The Gatehouse at Place House built by the 1st Earl of Southampton (The Innes Marlow Collection).
20. Thomas Wriothesley 1st Earl of Southampton (1505-50) by Robert Cooper (National Portrait Gallery, London).
21. Henry Wriothesley 3rd Earl of Southampton (1573-1624), patron of William Shakespeare by Daniel Mytens (National Portrait Gallery, London).

To Sheila and Graham, my sister and brother,
who may not share my enthusiasm for history but with
whom over the years I have shared many other things.

Acknowledgements

I wish to record my gratitude first to those who once loved the Meon valley and researched and wrote the history of one or more of the villages including Frances Collins (1899–1984), John Hurst (1908–2005), Charles Millen (died 1963), Frederick Standfield (1916–2004), Bruce Tappenden (1930–2002) and Kenneth Ward.

Many people have lent or given me books or documents, answered questions, lent photographs, reminisced, told me about memorable teachers or parsons, shared stories and myths, and directed me to fascinating people and places. The list is long and includes: Adrian Abbott, Arthur ApSimon, Jacqueline Arcedeckne-Butler, Margaret Ball, George Bartlett, Norah Blyth, Annie Bower, Sir Simon Cassels, Louise Clay, David Crossley, Matthew Dampier, Arabella Edmonstone, Peter Ewence, James Foley, Rosemary Frere-Cook, John Freemantle, Olga Groombridge, Ken Groves, Olive Hathaway, Clare Hooper, Gordon Hope, Bruce and Gillian Horn, Anthony Hulbert, Alan Inder, John Larrett, Terry Louden, Jenny Mallett, Den Marriner, Barrie Marson, Harry Martineau, Chris Maxse, Minnie Montagu, Martin Morris, Rod Passingham, Brian Patten, Sir Richard Pelly, Barbara, Lady Pelly, Ann Pendred, Royston Pratt, Humphrey and Joy Prideaux, Dr Mike Rogers, Andrew Sellick Peter and Vera Short, Stephen Short, Ruby Snell, Tony Thorpe, Peter Usher, Tony Williams, Rupert and Catherine Younger and contributors to the two volumes published by the Titchfield History Society

I am particularly grateful to George Watts, formerly senior counsellor at the Open University, who read my first draft, made many valuable suggestions for improvement and drew my attention to sources which I had not fully exploited. I am also greatly indebted to Innes Marlow who restored many photographs, put them on disk and took the cover photograph of Meonstoke church. Members of my family have once again helped in a variety of ways.

I have been fortunate to be able to visit many of the large houses in the Meon valley which are still in private ownership. I am again grateful to the staff of the Hampshire Record Office for locating documents and photographs with exemplary efficiency, to the Archaeology Department of Hampshire County Council, the British Museum, the Library of *Country Life*, the National Monuments Record Centre at Swindon, the National Portrait Gallery, the National Railway Museum at York, the Warden and Scholars of Winchester College, and Wickham Parish Council, also Peter Ewence, Innes Marlow, and Stephen Short, all of whom gave me permission to use illustrations which belong to them.

If I have succeeded in capturing something of the fascination which the history of the villages has for many of those who live there, the enjoyment I have derived from discovering and writing will not be the only reward.

Preface

All the villages in the Meon valley have a written history, some little more than book-lets, some full-length studies. Most were published at least 20 years ago, some nearer 40 years ago, most are no longer available and unlikely to be reprinted. Some villages have in addition books of photographs or publications containing recollections of older people. In some parishes the church guide is an authoritative introduction to the village as well as the church. All are listed in my bibliography.

I have not set out to replace any of the written histories – it would have been pre-sumptuous to do so – but I have drawn on all of them to bring together material which illustrates what was happening in the villages of the Meon valley, related to both the Hampshire and the national scene, highlighting similarities and contrasts. If I am accused of plagiarism I can only plead guilty and argue in mitigation that painstaking research deserves wider circulation. Some topics previously covered cursorily or not at all such as the Water Meadows, the Workhouse and Knowle Hospital have been included.

In addition to published histories I have used original documents and other sec-ondary sources some of which have become available since the earlier histories were written. Parish records were kept until the 1970s in the Parish Chest, the joint respon-sibility of the incumbent and the churchwardens and were not catalogued. They are now deposited in the Hampshire Record Office at Winchester, have been catalogued and some transferred to microfilm or microfiche. I have corroborated and occasionally corrected what was written earlier where subsequent research has cast new light on old problems. I have also made use of reminiscences oral and written.

An attempt has been made to steer between scholarly monograph and popular history aiming to be both academically accurate and accessible to the interested reader. Local history ought in my opinion to be a good story. It should illuminate the lives of ordinary people as well as recording the achievements of the great and the good – farm labourer and villager as well as squire and parson. Anybody unfamiliar with the geog-raphy of the Meon valley should consult the Ordnance Survey Explorer Map number 119 entitled *Meon Valley*. The frontispiece of this book is a much simplified diagram designed to show the relative positions of the Meon valley villages.

One further gloss: the recent past is often as much a foreign country as the remote past and so worth recording for the sake of posterity. As in my previous forays into local history the story has been brought up-to-date. Readers will find only brief reference to the pre-history of the Meon valley or to Roman occupation though there are abundant indications of both. My story begins with the Saxon invasions and subsequent settlement in the valley which took place somewhere about 450 AD since when the villages have a continuous history. My final chapters are devoted to life in the villages in the twentieth century and there is a postscript on the various ways some chose to mark the beginning of the third millennium. The book is written in rough chronological order but combines this with a topical approach finishing a story even though it ends outside the period under consideration.

May I finally record the help of many people who know far more about the history of one or more villages than I could ever hope to. I have greatly enjoyed exploring the Meon valley and the lanes around the villages which form the subject of this book.

Peter Watkins
Swanmore
April 2010

Introduction

❧

The Course of Tichefeld Water. This ryver risith about Estmayne a x. miles by north est from Tichefeld. It cummeth from Estmaine to Wikeham or Wicombe a praty townlet on the right hand a 5. or 6. miles lower, where the water brekith into 2. armelettes, and goith under 2. wodden bridgges soone cumming to one streame agayne. Thens [a 3. or 4. miles] to a wood bridge by Mr Wriothesleys [house], leving Tichefeld toun on the right [rype, and] a little beneth goyth under Warebridge of tymbre. Hither it ebbith and flouith. Thens withyn [a] myle it resortith into the wa [ter of] Hampton [haven].

> *From 'the Laboriouse Journey and Serche of Johan Lelande for Englandes Antiquitees. Given to Henry VIII as a New Year's present in the 37th year of his Rayne.*[1]

ONLY THOSE who live in Hampshire are likely to have heard of the River Meon. It cannot compare with the Thames, the Severn or the Trent or even with the Itchen, the Avon or the Test, better known Hampshire rivers. Yet to those who live in the villages through which the Meon flows it is a precious part of the scenery, providing cohesion to what would otherwise be entirely separate communities.

The Meon is a chalk stream emerging at a constant temperature of 50 degrees (10 Celsius) from springs at South Farm, in a fold in the Downs in the parish of East Meon. If it does not everywhere appear to have the translucent quality of other chalk streams in Hampshire this is because it is broad, has a very gradual gradient, is often slow flowing and in many places now has a deep layer of silt over the chalk. Until the Portsmouth Water Company was allowed to extract water the river was deeper, wider and faster flowing than it is today.

Its 22½ mile course takes it first north to run through the village of East Meon in a culvert deepened in 1955 to avoid the earlier danger of flooding in the streets. The river then turns north-west to reach West Meon through the deserted medieval settlement of Westbury. From there its route takes it west to Warnford where it is enhanced by the numerous springs which rise there, then south under the road at The Grinch, to run through Exton and Corhampton, then under the road once more to Meonstoke and on to Droxford. Further south the river crosses under the road yet again on its way to Wickham. It flows on to Titchfield and so into the sea at Titchfield Haven.

The only poetic reference to the river Meon is in a 'Poetical Essay' entitled *Titchfield* by the minor eighteenth century poet John Missing.[2] It contains the lines:

The solemn River parts the vary'd Meads,
And glides along majestically slow;
Nor murmurs as it passes; 'till, anon,
Down the abrupt Descent it rushing foams;
And roars, and thunders to the adverse Hills;
Again becalmed; adown the Vale it flows,
And reaches soon the much resounding Main…

Apart from the river there is one thing which all the villages have in common – a parish church. In some cases from the Saxon period but certainly from Norman times each village had its church, probably the only stone building in the village, as well as the most prominent and usually at the village centre. The ancestors of the village were baptised here, their marriage often blessed by its rites and they were buried within its confines. Only in the second half of the twentieth century did this cease to be true for most inhabitants. But the buildings have endured even though they are no longer the focus of village life. The first bishop of the West Saxons was Birinus (634–650) and by 660 the bishopric was based at Winchester. Throughout the middle ages and much later Winchester was the richest bishopric in England. It included the churches in the Meon valley until 1927 when the new diocese of Portsmouth was carved from it.

All the villages of the Meon valley contain memorable buildings. Place House (once Titchfield Abbey) may have been demolished in 1781 but it was originally a Premonstratensian Abbey founded in 1232. Attached to it was a fifteenth century barn and ponds once stocked with fish for the monastery. It was later the mansion of the Wriothesley family. Today it bears the marks of both abbey and great house and is well worth a visit. At Titchfield too is a church first built in the seventh century, with a Saxon porch, the oldest standing building of southern England.

Wickham is described by David Lloyd as 'the finest village in Hampshire and one of the best in the South of England'.[3] But long before the present square was laid out in 1268 it boasted a manor house opposite to St Nicholas's church. At Corhampton there is a Saxon church built almost a thousand years ago with mid-twelfth century wall paintings and a yew tree in the churchyard as old as the church. In Warnford Park are snowdrops in profusion though nobody knows how or when they originated. East Meon church is a small masterpiece, described as 'one of the most thrilling village churches in Hampshire'.[4] The Meon valley has its own deserted village in Lomer abandoned in 1551.

Running down almost the whole valley is a railway line built at the beginning of the twentieth century, closed after little more than fifty years but still much loved by those old enough to remember when it was still running and valued by many more as the route of a long distance walk.

These are a few of the highlights. Every village contains houses first built in the sixteenth century though their age is now often disguised by later modifications and modern frontages. All have remained villages, even Titchfield, which lies between the urban sprawl of Fareham on its east and Southampton on its west.

The villages of the valley are easily identified: the river flows through or close to each of them. Not so the parishes of which they form part. Until the nineteenth century many were very large, covering much more ground than they do today. The ancient parish of Titchfield for example was one of the largest in England with an area of 24½ square miles stretching along the coast of the Solent as far as the Hamble estuary and five miles inland to the boundaries of Wickham. During the nineteenth century it gave birth to five new ecclesiastical parishes: Sarisbury with Swanwick 1837, Crofton 1871, Hook with Warsash 1872, Lock's Heath 1893 and Lee-on-the-Solent 1893. In 1894 each became a separate civil parish.

Droxford was another large parish which consisted of four tithings. In 1829 the tithing of Shidfield (as it was then called) gained a chapel of ease and in due course was separated from Droxford. The tithings of Hill and Swanmore with a small portion of the parish of Bishop's Waltham formed the ecclesiastical parish of Swanmore when St Barnabas's church was built in 1845. As a result of the Parish Councils Act of 1894 these too became independent and the cord which bound them to the mother parish was broken.

Meonstoke too was a large parish. It included the chapelry of Soberton which did not become a separate ecclesiastical parish until 1897. Before then a new church had been built at Newtown in 1851 to serve the southern part of Soberton and part of Hambledon. Both West and East Meon were large parishes which straddled the A272. West Meon included Privett which became a separate parish in 1877. East Meon included the chapelries at Steep and Froxfield which became independent in 1868 as well as Langrish where a church was built in 1877. I have not been entirely consistent in my treatment of these parishes. The core of the book is the village rather than the parish.

The Meon flows through an area rich in prehistoric remains. At the mouth of the Meon is the well known Palaeolithic site of Rainbow Bar exposed at low tide (SU531021)[5] The chalk downs have many long and round barrows, burial places of the remote ancestors of the Meon valley. Above Meonstoke is the great Iron Age Hill fort of Old Winchester Hill. There are Roman remains at Warnford, Meonstoke, Wickham and elsewhere. But the continuous story begins with the arrival of Saxons and Jutes in the fifth century following the withdrawal of the Romans. Since about 450 there have been settlements in what were later to become the villages of the Meon valley

The valley is overlooked on both sides by hills. On the east is Old Winchester Hill. On the west is Beacon Hill above the villages of Exton and Warnford. On a clear day the view from Beacon Hill extends over the whole valley from Privett church, a prominent landmark in the north, to the Solent and the hills of the Isle of Wight in the south. The Meon valley is of incomparable beauty and of great historic interest.

1

From Rainbow Bar to the Normans

☙

T HE EARLIEST evidence of habitation in what later became the Meon valley comes from the Old Stone Age, perhaps as much as half a million years ago, before the Solent river flooded making a new coastline and Britain an island. Rainbow Bar was discovered in 1951 by Chris Draper, an amateur archaeologist and indefatiguable enthusiast. It lies off Meon Beach and is only exposed at low tide but flint tools and flakes found there provide evidence of the existence and something of the life style of our remotest ancestors.[1]

Further north the oldest route across the Meon valley formed part of the long distance route called the Ridgeway between the Sussex coast and Salisbury Plain. Old Winchester Hill, standing guard over the Meon valley, is its best-known landmark, inhabited in the Middle Stone Age, as long ago as 5000 BC. Much later, perhaps about 2000 BC, New Stone Age people made burial mounds called Long Barrows along the Ridgeway, one of which lies outside the western entrance of the later earthwork and another on the hillside to the south. About 1500 BC Bronze Age people made a cemetery of Round Barrows on the top of the hill which can still be seen. (On Beacon Hill on the other side of the valley there is a similar but smaller cemetery.) Another millennium passed and about 500 BC the Iron Age Hill fort, the best known landmark on Old Winchester Hill, was constructed, its ditch and banks the most prominent feature today, though originally the bank would have been surmounted by a timber palisade.

So for about 7000 years people have lived on or close to Old Winchester Hill. During the Second World War it was used for training by the armies preparing to invade Europe in 1944 and there are still notices warning of unexploded shells. Today it is part of the South Downs Way and a prominent landmark seen from the Meon valley, a favourite place for local people to walk, with splendid views in all directions. Two caveats have to be entered: first, there has never been a full scientific excavation of the hill; second, the name remains a mystery, though a number of imaginative solutions have been proposed.[2]

* * *

The Romans arrived in England in 43 AD and established defensive posts locally at Chichester (Noviomagus), Portchester and Winchester (Venta Belgarum). The road from Chichester to Bitterne via Botley divided close to Wickham. The southerly route led to the port of Clausentum (probably Bitterne), the northerly route which led to Winchester can still be traced in parts, south of Wickham, at Cold Harbour and at Shedfield House. It crossed the river Meon at or near Wickham where there is a band of gravel in the river bed and where a Roman settlement was established.[3]

Roman remains in the Meon valley are frequent but do not provide enough to enable us to reconstruct a pattern of settlement. In 1906 a Roman villa was found in Lippen Wood in Warnford and excavated by A. Moray-Williams.[4] He was also responsible a little later for the excavation of another Roman villa, at Stroud south of the A272 in East Meon. Here masonry walls, a tessellated floor and evidence of a Roman bath were found.[5] Close by there was a Romano-British farm at Old Down Farm, East Meon discovered in 1976.[6] Most important of all a small villa at Meonstoke was unearthed in 1935 and fully excavated in the 1980s (see below)

Two Roman sarcophagi were found in the parishes of the Meon valley many years ago: the first discovered in 1880 in Brigden Field, Manor Farm, Soberton is now outside the parish church; the second was unearthed in 1917 in a field close to the Grinch in the parish of Corhampton. The skeleton which it contained was buried in the churchyard and the coffin, now used as a container for flowers, is at the entrance to Corhampton church. Both are substantial stone artefacts and must have been used for the burial of leading warriors.

*   *   *

The year 410 AD marked the end of the military occupation, when Roman troops were withdrawn to defend the empire. Somewhere about 450 Jutes invaded the Meon valley. The name by which they were known, Meonware, was taken from the river. The use of the suffix *ware* follows Jutish practice in Kent and provides confirmation of Jutish origin.[7] They were pre-literate so evidence has to be pieced together from place names, artefacts found in their settlements and cemeteries and the writings of a later period.

Barbara Yorke, an authority on the period, sees no reason to doubt Bede's statement that southern Hampshire was settled by Jutes.[8] Jutish territory extended from the New Forest on the west to Hayling Island on the east. Three Jutish place names provide further evidence: as late as the twelfth century the New Forest was still known by the Jutish name *Ytene* while *Yting stoc* (modern Bishopstoke) was near the northern boundary of Jutish settlement. A lost village in the later parish of East Meon also had a Jutish name *Ytredene*.[9] The Meonware were then a distinct group of Jutes occupying the eastern portion of the mainland Jutish province, close to the later Sussex border. They had a separate existence until about 660 AD when Wulfhere king of Mercia gave overlordship of their territory to the South Saxons. In 685 Cadwalla king of Wessex incorporated the Isle of Wight and southern Hampshire into his kingdom of Wessex.[10].

If the first question is who were the Meonware, then the second is what relation did Romano-British settlements bear to those of the newcomers? Findings during the

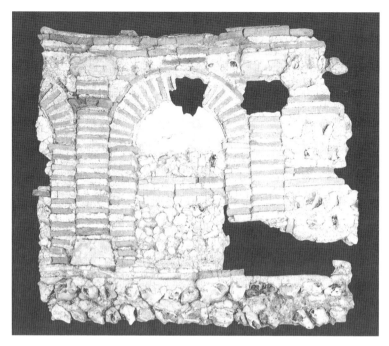

1. Wall from the Roman villa at Shavard's Farm, Meonstoke now in
the British Museum Gallery 49.

1980s at Shavards Farm, Meonstoke throw intriguing light on this problem though they do not solve it. During 1983, through the use of metal detectors, over 200 artefacts were recovered from fields at Shavards Farm and led to a four year research programme undertaken by the archaeology team at Hampshire County Council and King Alfred's College, Winchester (now part of the University of Winchester). A Romano-British villa, a Saxon cemetery and Saxon settlement were excavated. The resulting finds at Shavards Farm are the most important in the Meon valley.[11]

In 1935 in the course of the widening of the A32 a small Roman villa was found on the east of the road south of the Grinch. The rest of the Roman building lay under the road and to its west. At the time no full excavation was undertaken. In the 1980s a substantially complete wall which had fallen intact and been covered with soil for as much as 1700 years was found. Sealed beneath it was a coin dated 353 AD which established the date by which the wall had fallen.

The British Museum was informed and in 1989 the entire wall was lifted, boxed by the Royal Engineers and transported to London. A hole was made in the wall of the Museum and part of the Roman villa became a component of a display in the new Weston Gallery (room 49). It may not be as important as the adjacent Sutton Hoo Burial Ship but it placed the Meon valley and in particular Shavards Farm on the archaeological map of late Romano-British finds. The villa was a secular building but its likeness to early Romanesque churches raised the question whether this model originated in northern European vernacular architecture rather than in Italy as had previously been assumed.[12] Meanwhile the part of the Roman site which lay on the west side of the A32 in the grounds of Manor Farm, Exton was excavated and finds made clear that the Roman site had extended in this direction as well as further north of the villa.

Also at Shavards Farm, in a Saxon cemetery containing burials, on either side of Shavards Lane, at least 21 individual bodies were identified. Sixteen were adults and five children. Most of the adults were young or middle aged and only one probably older than this at the time of death. The Saxon settlement to the south produced a sunken floor hut, and a variety of artefacts including clay crucibles, antler horns, bone needles, pottery, reused Roman tiles and a fourth century Roman coin. The inevitable question, to which an answer is awaited, is when did the settlement move to the present site of Meonstoke and why was the church built to the south of the original settlement and by the river?

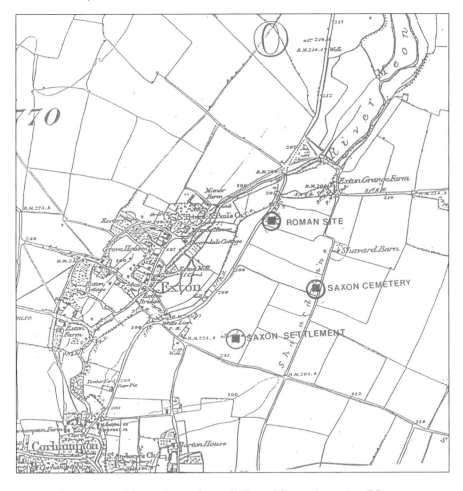

2. Roman and Saxon sites at Shavard's Farm, Meonstoke on 1870 OS map.

3. Graves from the Saxon cemetery at Droxford.

4. The Meonstoke disc brooch.

But Meonstoke is not the only parish in which there is evidence of early Saxon settlement. When the Meon Valley Railway was in course of construction at the beginning of the twentieth century a Saxon cemetery was discovered near Droxford station. For a time work on the railway had ceased because of shortage of labour so William Dale, a Southampton antiquary, was able to explore the site. He retrieved beads of glass, amber and terra cotta as well as bones and Saxon ironware. He was assisted by two navvies whom he described as 'more intelligent than usual and had a keen eye to business'. The finds were examined by Charles Read of the British Museum.[13] There was no further excavation of the site until 1973–4 when, under the direction of Fred Aldsworth, a professional archaeologist, 41 graves were examined dating from 450–600 AD, each taking four man days to excavate, record, photograph and remove. A variety of Saxon objects was found including swords, spearheads, shield bosses, belt fittings and brooches as well as beads, glass and pottery. They are now stored at Chilcomb House in Winchester. A Saxon settlement at or close to Droxford which the cemetery might have served has not so far been found [14]

Anglo-Saxon finds are still being made in the Meon valley. In November 2000 a copper alloy disc brooch was discovered near Meonstoke. It was dated about 600AD and was similar to that dug up at Droxford cemetery at the beginning of the twentieth century. Two years later in 2002 a square headed brooch was found near Exton also using a metal detector.[15] It seems likely that further evidence will reveal more about the early Saxon settlements in the Meon valley.

John Hurst identified what he thought might be the limit of Saxon settlement in the Meon valley in the ditch and double bank which, though now overgrown, can be traced over the top of the hill between West Meon village and West Meon Hut. It runs west to east from Marlands Farm down a bridle way, across the A32 then to the bridge over the now disused Meon Valley Railway in Vinnells Lane and along a field edge through Hayling Wood. A length has been lost between the wood and Heathfield Lane but from Heathfield Lane it can be followed in a strip of woodland as far as Peak Farm which is reputed to have been the site of a farm since the Saxon period though none of the present farm buildings are of any antiquity. The earthwork is shown on modern Ordnance Survey maps (SU646255 to SU667255).[16]

* * *

5. Saxon earthwork near Marlands Farm, West Meon.

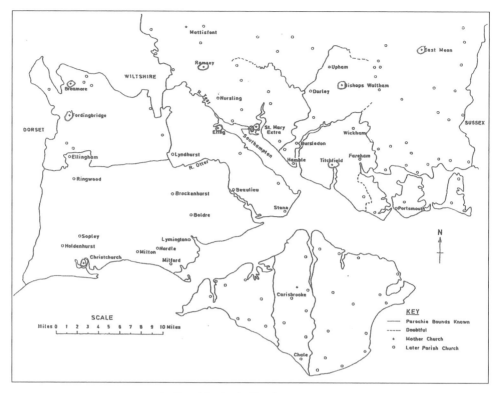

6. Parochiae in the Southampton area.

The Meonware were pagan when they arrived in England and remained so for over two centuries. Their conversion to Christianity, among the last of all the Saxon kingdoms, was the result of the work of Wilfrid (634–709) abbot of Ripon and Hexham and bishop of Northumbria while he was temporarily estranged from his northern appointments. Wilfrid was forced into exile three times and it was during the second of these, from 681–6, that he preached the gospel in Sussex, the Isle of Wight and the Meon valley. He is believed to have founded several of the churches in the valley, perhaps with Warnford as his headquarters. West Meon claims that Wilfrid preached at the village cross under what was called 'St Wilfrid's Yew' which survived until the end of the nineteenth century. Wilfrid is the first named person who can be identified with the Meon valley.

Churches, like most Saxon buildings, usually had a wooden frame and wattle and daub infill so it is not surprising that most of them have long since perished. Three stone built churches in the Meon valley contain architectural features dating from the Saxon period – Titchfield, Corhampton and Warnford.[17] Titchfield is the oldest, dating probably from 690 AD. The builders made use of Roman bricks which were brought up the tidal estuary of the Meon to Titchfield. The lower part of the west porch and part of the east wall of what was then an aisle-less nave have been dated to the late seventh century,

7. Corhampton church built c.1020 print c.1850.

8. The Saxon north door at Corhampton church, now blocked up.

one of the earliest in England. Similarity to Northumbrian churches of the same period is considered by some to be evidence of foundation by St Wilfrid. Titchfield church contains the oldest example of standing architecture in southern England.[18]

Corhampton is essentially a Saxon church built about the year 1020. The nave quoins, the external pilaster strips and the chancel arch were all worked in Quarr stone from the Isle of Wight. Later additions include the porch, a Victorian buttress and the east wall, the latter rebuilt in brick in 1855 following collapse when the foundations were undermined by road widening. The main church has many of the characteristics of Saxon architecture – long and short quoins on the south-west and north-west corners, to the left of the porch pilaster strips, surmounted by a stone string course. To the east of the porch is a Saxon sundial which divided the days into eight tides rather than twelve hours. The two doorways, that on the north side blocked probably as early as the thirteenth century, have Saxon arches.[19]

9. Twelfth century inscription in the south porch of Warnford church.

Medieval Latin Fratres orate [p]r[e]ce v[est]ra s[an]c[t]ificate te[m]pli factores Seniores ac juniors W[u]lfric fu[n]davit bon[us]Adam[us] reno[rvavit].

Square brackets[ ] denote abbreviations used in the text. The last word renorvavit *is completed two lines above. It probably represents an attempt at Leonine verse in which the last word of a line rhymes with a word in the middle of the line.* See Frances Collins in Hurst et al 1969 p.19.

    Inside is a superb Saxon chancel arch also of Quarr stone. The wall paintings in the chancel probably date from the mid-twelfth century and were uncovered in 1968. Their theme is the legend of St Swithun, the ninth century bishop of Winchester. In the chancel is also what is probably the original altar with five consecration crosses and a stone seat. Simon Jenkins comments: 'Even today there is a shyness to this church, hiding behind a massive yew tree above a mill stream. It is a place of antique calm.'[20]

    At Warnford the foundations of the earliest stone-built church dating from the eighth or ninth century were last uncovered in 1906 and parts of the Saxon wall are visible above the western arch of the nave.[21] There is also a Saxon sundial at Warnford: circular on a square stone with five crossed lines in the lower half to mark the middle of the Saxon three hourly tides. The existence of this Saxon stone sundial, says Frances Collins, confirms the existence of a stone Saxon church since a stone sundial is unlikely to have been attached to a wattle and daub building. Below the sundial is a not easily read twelfth century inscription in Latin which can be translated '*Brethren bless in your prayers the founders of this temple both old and young. Wulfric founded it, good Adam restored it*'.[22]

*   *   *

The names of many of the villages appear in writing for the first time in Anglo-Saxon charters and the parish boundaries of the present day are often identical with or close to the original estate boundaries. Some parishes are small, some very large all based on grants made by Saxon kings. The river Meon is described as early as 786 – *flumen quod appelatur Meonea* ('The river which is called the Meon') In 826 King Egbert (reigned 802–39, crowned and buried at Winchester), in gratitude for becoming the first King of all England, gave 20 hides of land at 'Drocenesford' to the Priory of St Swithin, the

In dñio hñt . III . car . 7 v . uilłos 7 VIII . bord 7 . VII . feruos
cū . III . car . T.R.E . uałb x . lib . 7 poſt . VI . lib . Modo VII . lib 7 x . foł.

40 c
IN MENESTOCHES HVND.

Ipfe eps ten *MENES* in dñio . Sep fuit in epatu . T.R.E.
fe defd p . XX . hid . modo p XII . hid . Tra . e . XIIII . car.
In dñio funt . III . car . 7 XXV . uilti . 7 XVII . bord . cū
XI . car . Ibi æccła cū una hida . 7 VIII . ferui . 7 II . mo
lini de . x . folid . Ibi . x . ac pti . Silua . de XL . porc,
7 in Winceſt . VIII . hagæ reddentes . VI . fol.
T.R.E . uałb . XX . lib . 7 poſt . XVI . lib . Modo XXX . lib.
Tam reddit de firma . XL . lib . fed diu ñ poteſt pati.
Æccła . reddit . L . folid.
Ipfe eps ten dimid hidā in cõ de Meneſtoche . Sep eps
tenuit in dñio . T.R.E . 7 m̃ fe defd p dim̃ hida . Ibi hт
dimid car . 7 uñ uiltm 7 uñ moliñ . Vał 7 ualuit . XXV . fol.
De æccła de Meneſtoche hт eps . XX . folid . *IN MENE*,
Ipfe eps ten in *MENE* . VI . hid 7 unā v cū æccła *HVND.*
Tra . e . IIII . car . In dñio . e una car 7 dim̃ . 7 XI . uilti
7 VIII . bord cū . III . car . Ibi . II . ferui . 7 uñ moliñ de
XXX . denar . 7 IIII . ac pti . T.R.E . poſt uał . IIII . lib . M̃ c . fol.
Ipfe eps ten *STOCHES* in dñio . Sep fuit in epifcopatu.
T.R.E . fe defd p . X . hid . modo p . VII . hid . Tra . e . IIII.
car . In dñio funt . II . car . 7 II . uilti 7 VIII . bord cū una
car . Ibi . VI . ferui . 7 IIII . ac pti.
De hac tra huj cõ ten Goiſfrid de epo . IIII . hid . quas
prius uilti teneb . Ibi hт . I . car . 7 II . bord . 7 VI . feruos.
7 IIII . acs pti . Æccłam huj cõ ten Malgeri . Vał . XV . fol.
Totū cõ uałb T.R.E . x . lib . 7 poſt . VIII . lib . Modo qd
eps ten . VII lib . Qd Goiſfrid . IIII . lib.

They have in lordship 3 ploughs;
5 villagers, 8 smallholders and 7 slaves with 3 ploughs.
Value before 1066 £10; later £6; now £7 10s.

In MEONSTOKE Hundred

11   The Bishop himself holds (West) MEON in lordship. It was
     always in the Bishopric. Before 1066 it answered for 20
     hides; now for 12 hides. Land for 14 ploughs. In lordship
     3 ploughs;
          25 villagers and 17 smallholders with 11 ploughs.
          A church with 1 hide; 8 slaves; 2 mills at 10s. Meadow,
          10 acres; woodland at 40 pigs; 8 sites in Winchester
          which pay 6s.
     Value before 1066 £20; later £16; now £30; however, it
     pays £40 of revenue, but it cannot bear it for long.
     The church pays 50s.

12   The Bishop himself holds ½ hide in the manor of MEONSTOKE.
     The Bishop always held it in lordship. Before 1066 and now
     it answered for ½ hide. He has ½ plough;
          1 villager;
          1 mill.
     The value is and was 25s. The Bishop has 20s from the church
     of Meonstoke.

In (East) MEON Hundred

13   The Bishop himself holds 6 hides and 1 virgate with the church
     in (East) MEON. Land for 4 ploughs. In lordship 1½ ploughs;
          11 villagers and 8 smallholders with 3 ploughs.
          2 slaves; 1 mill at 30d; meadow, 4 acres.
     Value before 1066 and later £4; now 100s.

14   The Bishop himself holds STOCHES in lordship. It was always
     in the Bishopric. Before 1066 it answered for 10 hides; now
     for 7 hides. Land for 4 ploughs. In lordship 2 ploughs;
          2 villagers and 8 smallholders with 1 plough.
          6 slaves; meadow, 4 acres.
     Of this manor's land Geoffrey holds from the Bishop 4 hides
     which the villagers held before. He has 1 plough;
          2 smallholders and 6 slaves.
          Meadow, 4 acres.
     Mauger holds this manor's church. Value 15s.
     Value of the whole manor before 1066 £10; later £8; now,
     what the Bishop holds £7, Geoffrey £4.

10. Domesday Book: part of the entry for Meonstoke Hundred – land of the Bishop of Winchester
transliterated and transcribed into modern English.

Old Minster at Winchester. The boundaries are identifiable as those of the parish of Droxford as it was to remain until Shedfield and Swanmore were created parishes in the nineteenth century.

Drockensford (variously spelt) – the name used throughout the middle ages – consists of two words. In addition to 'river crossing' the word 'ford' can mean 'a settlement near a ford'. Gordon Hope, the historian of Droxford, identifies this as the ford which carried the road (now B2150) from Hambledon to Winchester near Brockbridge before the bridge was built. He has photographs showing large flat stones on the bed of the river which may have been the foundations of a ford. The word Droce or Droke can, he says, mean *combe* of which there are several nearby. If he is correct Droxford would mean 'the river crossing place close to the droke or drokes'.[23]

The southern boundary of Droxford as described in 846AD contains the first mention of Wickham – '*and thonnae git oth Wic haema Mearce*' ('and then it goes as far as the boundary of the people of Wickham')[24] The boundaries of West Meon are found in a charter of 932 and of Exton in 940. Only the parishes of Meonstoke and Soberton have no known Anglo-Saxon charter perhaps because they were already royal estates.[25]

The name Titchfield is in a Charter of 982 as Ticcefelda, 'open land associated with Ticcea' – probably a man's name or possibly 'field of the kids' (little goats).[26] Warnford and Wickham appear for the first time in Domesday Book. There is no written reference to Corhampton until 1201. It is believed to mean 'corn estate' but the suffix *hamtun* is usually associated with a place of significance and it is hard to think this can ever have fitted this small village. The name Exton occurs in 940 and means East Saxon tun (*Essesaxtunate)* so suggests that it may have been at first in Saxon rather than Jutish territory. Meonstoke means 'cattle farm by the Meon' and also appears in the Exton charter of 940.

* * *

Before the Norman conquest each village probably had its church (though Wickham may not have had a church until later) and one or more mills on which its livelihood depended. The ecclesiastical parishes with which we are familiar were established in the century before and after the Norman conquest. Before that going back perhaps to 700 AD there were large parishes referred to by scholars as *parochie* – the area served by a mother church. They were founded by kings of Wessex and served to enhance royal authority as well as to spread the gospel. The Meon valley formed part of the territory of three *parochie*. In the south was the *parochia* of Titchfield which included Wickham. In the north East Meon *parochia* included within its boundaries the churches of the upper Meon valley from West Meon to Meonstoke. To the west was the *parochia* of Waltham whose eastern boundary is not certain but may have included Droxford. Attached to each *parochia* were communities of priests and lay brothers. The buildings were *monasteria* or minsters. This does not mean monastery as we understand the word but the place where a group of priests lived a communal life and from which they went out to preach, teach and baptise throughout the *parochia.*[27]

The ancient *parochia* of Titchfield with its community of monks and priests survived well into the twelfth century, perhaps until the foundation of the Premonstratensian monastery in 1232. Alverstoke became a separate parish about 948 and Fareham between 963 and 975. This removed about one third of the *parochia*. The loss of Fareham put Titchfield on the edge of its *parochia* since the boundary between Titchfield and Fareham lies only twenty yards from the churchyard wall. Wickham became a separate parish early in the episcopate of Henry of Blois (bishop 1129–1171) who granted it independence but on condition of the payment of the substantial sum of 20 shillings per year to the mother church. (Wickham continued payment to Titchfield until 1929.) After Wickham there was no further break up and Titchfield remained until the nineteenth century a very large parish and about half of the area of the *parochia* in the time of Ine (King of Wessex 688–726).[28]

The second feature of each village was one or more mills. Water mills were the result of new technology which became available between about 950 and 1050. The King's Mill at Titchfield is first mentioned in 982. By the time of Domesday Book there were at least 30 mills on the river Meon. The building of a mill required considerable engineering: mill stones must be brought to the site, trees felled to provide wood, a weir constructed as well as the provision of mill stream, leats, sluices and the mill buildings. Mills remained a crucial part of the economy of the Meon valley for close on 1000 years.

*   *   *

We do not know how the natives of the Meon valley heard news of the landing of William of Normandy at Pevensey in October 1066, nor of his subsequent victory over Harold near Battle. Their first practical experience of the Normans was probably the advance of an ancillary army up the Meon valley plundering and pillaging as it went. Domesday Book records pre-conquest values and compares them with the value in 1085. At Droxford for example there had been a reduction of 26% from £26 to £20. This may have been the result of the devastation of the invading armies but there are other possible reasons.[29]

William I spent Christmas 1085 at Gloucester and it was in the course of discussion with his council that the idea of Domesday Book was born. Commissioners were sent out to collect information from each village, enquiring in particular who held the land and how much it was worth.[30] Digests of the information were sent to Winchester and there collated. There are errors and omissions but it is an impressive record of contemporary royal administration. No other country in the early middle ages has anything like it. As Frances Collins points out, the makers of Domesday were not 'historians, economists or sociologists but hard pressed civil servants who could not waste time or parchment.'[31]It was not until the tithe maps produced for each parish about 1840 that information about land ownership was again collected on such a scale.

The material which had been collected was rearranged under landholders. The manors in the Meon valley were divided between the king, the bishop of Winchester and Hugh de Port, one of the king's leading tenants-in-chief. (The same family as the de Port who is credited with restoring Warnford church). The king held Meonstoke and Soberton and East Meon. He also held Titchfield which is described as an outlier of another royal manor, that of Meonstoke. The king does not seem to have kept the manor of Titchfield in his own hands since by 1100 it was in the possession of Paganus de Gisors. The bishop of Winchester held Exton and West Meon as well as Meon and Brownwich in Titchfield Hundred. Hugh de Port was lord of Wickham, Corhampton and Warnford. He also held from the bishop the sub-manor of Benstede (St Clair's Farm) in the parish of Droxford. Churches are listed at Crofton, Corhampton, Droxford, Exton, Lomer and East and West Meon but oddly not at Titchfield one of the oldest nor at Soberton or Wickham. Even though they are not mentioned in the Domesday Book there were by now probably churches in most if not all the villages.[32]

Much further information can be gleaned from Domesday, for example Crofton had a *saltern* (from which salt could be produced) and Titchfield was the only place in the Meon valley which had yet been granted a market perhaps reflecting, says George Watts, its key position as a port.[33]

*   *   *

11. Tournai font in East Meon church.

The Normans who ruled from 1066–1154 were great builders. Castles, cathedrals and episcopal palaces, built almost a 1000 years ago, are still to be found in many parts of the country, many now in ruins. The palaces which Henry of Blois (bishop 1129–71) built in Hampshire include Bishop's Waltham, Farnham and Alresford, though none in the Meon valley.[34]

Many of the churches in the valley bear evidence of Norman construction. Saxon churches built of wattle and daub were now replaced by stone buildings. At Titchfield there is a Norman doorway with unmistakeable zigzag mouldings, added to a Saxon structure. A Norman south aisle was also added but it was unfortunately destroyed in the course of nineteenth century restoration. At Droxford the church was first built in stone by Norman builders and the nave and chancel arch remain as well as the north aisle and north chapel added later in the twelfth century. Little remains at Soberton of the aisleless nave of the Norman church. There are scant remains of a Norman south doorway at Exton and a Norman doorway with original capitals at Wickham. At Warnford 'the tower is assertively Norman, broad and sturdy' says Pevsner.[35]

The jewel of the Meon valley churches is East Meon. It includes a Norman tower of about 1150 but its main claim to fame is the black Tournai marble font dated to about 1130–40 with its superb carvings of the creation on the north side and on the east the expulsion from Paradise with the story of the Temptation and Fall amid a host of dragons, birds and beasts. [36] It is one of only seven such fonts to be found in England, four in Hampshire, brought from Tournai in present day Belgium, by Bishop Henry of Blois and described by Simon Jenkins as 'a Bayeux tapestry in stone'.[37] To the medieval villager the church with its complex iconography was not chiefly an artistic experience but the means by which a pre-literate society learned the gospel embellished by stories of the saints some of them apocryphal and made sense of an existence which was often brutish and short and in many cases cut off inexplicably by sudden death.

2

The Later Middle Ages

❧

Tнᴇ ɴᴏʀᴍᴀɴ ᴋɪɴɢs hunted and so did almost all medieval monarchs. By the early twelfth century no less than eleven royal forests had been established in Hampshire, where game was protected and the forest law enforced. The best known is the New Forest but the Forest of Bere covered almost as large an area, originally from Romsey in the west to the Sussex border in the east. Though no longer a royal forest, Bere still includes 100 square miles of land between Eastleigh and the Sussex border with the Meon valley close to its centre. The name first appears in 1168 as *La Bera;* in 1237 it is *foresta de Ber.* The name is derived from an Old English word meaning 'swine pasture'. Mislingford on the border of Soberton parish may owe its name to a forgotten word for beech-mast, a favourite food of pigs.[1] The name was spelt in a variety of ways; on the tombstone of Richard Watts, an eighteenth century keeper of the forest, in Soberton church yard, for example the word is spelt *Bear.*

The forest was administered from two places, the eastern part which stretched from the river Meon to Denmead was Bere Portchester so named because its headquarters were at Portchester Castle. Each 'walk', had its own keepers, that for the west walk was based at West Lodge, now a private house. The purpose of the forest was then to provide hunting for royalty. The last king whom we know to have hunted in the forest was Charles I in 1628. In recent centuries the emphasis has shifted to the production of timber for the navy whose ships were constructed of wood far into the nineteenth century. The Forest of Bere was conveniently close to the naval town of Portsmouth.[2]

*   *   *

Nothing now remains above ground of Place House, Wickham, the Meon valley's first stately home. In the early 1970s a bypass of Wickham east and north of the village was proposed with a start date of 1977. It would have swept across the site occupied by successive manor houses from the twelfth to the eighteenth century burying it for good. As a result a thorough archaeological excavation was planned and took place in the late 1970s, by which time the projected bypass had been first postponed then abandoned on account of cost. The excavation had by then taken place and the results were published.[3]

Wickham was originally a linear village running from the church of St Nicholas and the manor house past the mill and then to the Dairymoor. The manor house was

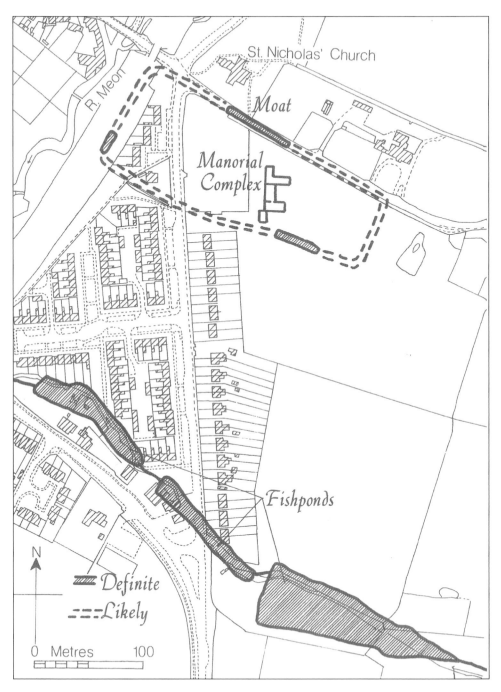

12. Plan of the moated complex and manorial fishponds at Wickham Place.

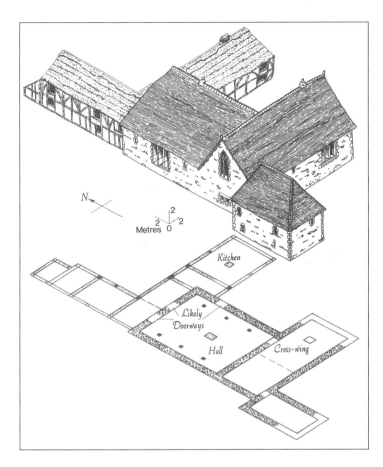

13. Manor house at
Wickham as it may
have appeared in the
fourteenth century.

opposite the church and straddled the much later road to Southwick. In the late
twelfth century a timber building was erected by the De Port family who had held the
manor since the Norman Conquest and were one of the leading Norman families
several members of which became sheriffs of Hampshire. They also owned St John's
House at Warnford. Though much had to be deduced from little firm evidence, excavation revealed shallow post-holes which established the general shape of the building.
The house was constructed round an aisled hall with a central hearth open to the sky.
No remains of internal partitions were found though there were two narrow wings,
one aligned north-south and one east-west and these were each divided into smaller
rooms of which one may have been the kitchen.

In 1268 Wickham was granted a royal charter for a market and fair.[4] At the same time
the village was enlarged by the addition of the Square – one of the largest in the country
– with a burgage plot behind each house.[5] Place House too was renewed. The hall was
rebuilt with flint walls and to the south two new ranges with masonry superstructure
were provided. At about the same time there were important additions. A moat was dug
which probably ran round the whole complex though because of subsequent house

building it was possible to excavate only part. The second innovation was the provision of fishponds the remains of which are still visible. The motive for both innovations was in part at least status. The De Scures, who now owned Wickham were, like their predecessors the De Ports, leading citizens of Hampshire and wished to remain in the forefront of architectural fashion. They continued to be lords of the manor until the death of John de Scures (the younger) in 1381. His sister Sybil married into the Uvedale family who remained lords of the manor until the eighteenth century.

*　　*　　*

In the course of the middle ages 15 religious houses were founded in Hampshire of which three were in Winchester – the cathedral priory of St Swithun, the abbey of St Mary (the nunnery and former Nunnaminster) and Hyde Abbey (which began life as the Anglo-Saxon New Minster and had moved in 1110 to the northern suburbs).[6] Almost the last foundation, the only Premonstratensian house and the only religious foundation in the Meon valley was Titchfield Abbey founded by Peter des Roches, bishop of Winchester (1205–1238). In 1232 he invited canons from Halesowen Abbey in Worcestershire to build a house at Titchfield. The Premonstratensian Order had been founded as recently as 1121 by Norbert of Xanten (1080–1134) at Premontre in France. St Norbert came from an aristocratic German family.[7] The canons lived a strict and simple life according to the Augustinian rule and wore a white habit hence the name White Canons. There were never many canons in the house – only 13 for example when a visitation took place in 1478.

One hundred and fifty years after its foundation the abbey was landlord of 15 manors which contained 60 villages and 500 tenants.[8] Some were within easy reach of Titchfield – Portchester, Stubbington, Funtley and Swanwick for example. Some were further afield – Corhampton in the Meon valley as well as Inkpen in Berkshire.[9] The abbey had an immediate impact on Titchfield which was already a substantial town, one of the few which had a market recorded in Domesday. The abbey constituted a magnet for trade. The coastal region of Hampshire was already richer than the chalk lands further north. George Watts points out that Titchfield was one of the five rich areas of Hampshire according to the lay assessment of 1333–1334 and was one of the most heavily assessed parishes according to the ecclesiastical grant of 1340. 'There was an inducement', he says' for the wealthy up-country peasant to saddle his horse and make the overnight journey to Titchfield, to enquire at the Abbey and in the market and taverns about vacant holdings or the possibility of a sale'.[10]

The abbey lasted for just over 300 years until it surrendered to the king's representatives in December 1537. From its foundation until the Reformation the canons owned the rectory and provided the vicars of Titchfield and Lomer and the chaplains of Crofton. After the Dissolution the site of the abbey building became the property of Thomas Wriothesley (see below chapter 4).

The abbey's main claim to fame was its library with some 326 volumes comprising

1000 individual books, most of them manuscripts painstakingly copied in Latin by the canons. It was catalogued as early as 1400 and has been described as, 'one of the finest examples of a monastic catalogue'. Sadly few of the books survived the Reformation but the index is still in existence and is in the British Library.[11]

To the south west of the abbey (and the subsequent Place House) is a barn 46 feet wide by 157 feet long with a floor area of 7000 feet, an impressive monument though sadly no longer in any sort of use and now semi-derelict. It is often described as a tithe-barn but there is no evidence that it was ever used to store tithes in kind collected from tenants. Nor is the date of its construction documented though dendrochronologists suggest that it was built in 1409–1410. 'There can be little doubt', writes Edward Roberts, 'that it is the finest surviving medieval barn in the county, not only for its near complete state of preservation but also for its sheer size and for the elaboration of its magnificent roof'.[12]

The monks constructed a number of ponds needed to ensure a good supply of fish required on the many fast days when fish was the only food allowed to the canons and required for their guests who on occasion included the king. Remains of these too can still be seen. Every few years the ponds needed cleaning out and so a diversion channel was constructed so that the fish could be caught and the ponds subsequently restocked. When Richard II was entertained there in 1394 swan was on the menu in addition to the more usual fish.[13]

The monks were also responsible for building Place House Cottage almost certainly as a grammar school, on the other side of Titchfield Lane, in what looks today like a modest eighteenth century cottage. The building can however be dated to 1447 using dendrochronology applied to the remaining timbers. No documents establish the existence of a school but it probably survived the Dissolution of the Abbey and lasted until the Civil War. It appears on a map of 1753 as 'School House'.[14]

*   *   *

The population of England grew steadily from about the year 900 AD to reach a peak soon after 1300. There was a move from pasture to arable to provide the extra food needed by a rising population. Land, some of it marginal, was brought into cultivation with marl, manure and legumes used to increase productivity. The early years of the fourteenth century saw a number of disasters. The poor harvests of 1315–17 led to a higher than average death rate when perhaps 10% of the population died. These years provided a foretaste of the much greater disaster caused by the arrival of the Black Death in Hampshire in the summer of 1348. It began a long-term decline of population and must rank as the seminal event of the later middle ages in Hampshire as it did in the rest of the country. Its effects were dramatic in both the short and the long term. 'Life was never quite the same again' is the judgement of Tom Beaumont James, the author of the *The Black Death in Hampshire*. 'We now know that the plague caused huge mortality and that there were many fewer people in Hampshire after 1350, they lived in a more complex society than before the arrival of the Black Death and were more comfortable, questioning, self-assured and wealthy'.[15]

The Black Death (though the name does not appear before the sixteenth century and may refer either to the sudden onset of the disease or to the dark discolouration of the skin which accompanied it) originated in Asia. It entered England in the late summer of 1348 at several points along the south coast of which the port of Southampton was one. In October 1348 Bishop Edington referred to 'the unprecedented pestilence'. The plague was at its worst in the Spring of 1349 and the number of deaths began to fall in May and June. At Corhampton six of the eleven villain tenants died. At Crofton 40 tenants remained in 1377 and 37 had died. The hamlet of Quob in the parish of Tithfield lost all its inhabitants in the Black Death though the village was repopulated afterwards. The Pipe Rolls of East Meon, a parish which belonged to the Bishop of Winchester, indicate the scale of deaths. Many holdings were left unfilled since the peasants had died and there was nobody to inherit. Deaths in the parish of East Meon have been estimated to represent at least 28% of villagers.[16] At Droxford, another manor belonging to the bishop, the total amount payable in fines by those taking land which had previously been held by people who had died rose from £4.50 per annum to £46.62 whilst receipts from corn sales fell from between £15 and £20 to £6. Sales of oxen, cattle and sheep rose substantially since there were insufficient people left to feed, drive and eat them.[17] In 1348 Bishop Edington filled 12 vacant parishes, in 1349 no less than 300 parishes needed a new parson.

The plague returned to Hampshire in 1361 and at Titchfield between a further 12% and 18% of tenants are estimated to have died. It is impossible for us to imagine the impact of the plague. Nobody can have known whether deaths would stop at 50% or whether the whole population would be wiped out. A population which had reached about four million by the early fourteenth century did not do so again for 200 years. Land was no longer scarce, marginal land was taken out of cultivation, wages rose and labour services were increasingly commuted to money payments. Sheep which needed less labour replaced arable as the demand for meat and wool rose. The late fourteenth and fifteenth centuries were a golden age – if you had survived.[18]

*   *   *

Between the Black Death and the mid-sixteenth century many villages were depopulated and deserted. There are at least 120 deserted villages in Hampshire, half of them on the high chalkland. Lomer is one of these. Unlike all the other villages in the parishes of the Meon valley it did not lie close to the river but over 500 feet above the valley on the chalk downs to the west of Beacon Hill, a mile or so from Exton and close to both branches of the South Hampshire Ridgeway. It is first mentioned in a Saxon charter in 962 which refers to *Lammaere* meaning Loamy Pond, probably the pond, vestiges of which still lie to the north-east of the site. In a charter of Ethelred II (reigned 978–1016) it was granted to Hyde Abbey in Winchester in whose ownership it remained until the Dissolution of the monasteries though it was leased to a tenant who as late as 1392 paid an annual rent in wine. Lomer and its church appear in Domesday when the lessee was named Roald. The total population in the eleventh century was probably between 50 and 80 people.

In 1243 Geoffrey de Lomer granted the right of presentation of a vicar for the parish of Lomer to Titchfield Abbey together with 40 acres of glebe. The church was thereafter served by canons of the abbey and enjoyed full parish status including the right to baptise and bury.[19] Its manorial landlords in the middle ages were members of the De Lomer family.[20] According to the tax assessment of 1334 Lomer bore comparison with nearby villages – Meonstoke which was assessed at £4.11.0, Warnford £3.3.0. Lomer £1.2.2, Exton £1.2.0.[21] The church was still in use in 1527 but when in 1551 Lomer was abandoned there were probably only four houses still occupied.[22] It had existed for at least 600 years. Since then the site has never been cultivated but used only for pasture. Though it has been investigated several times there has never been a full excavation.[23] Lomer was always a small settlement. The only stone building was the aisle-less church. The 1684 estate map of Preshaw names 'Chapple Yard' north of Lomer Cottage which suggests that the church lay there and not as had previously been assumed in the middle of the village.[24]

Lomer depended for its water supply on a well, lined for a few feet, but then dug into the chalk to a depth of about 200 feet which in the middle ages would have taken it below the water table.[25] An investigation conducted about 1970 concluded:

> In the village there is no clear pattern of streets and buildings … Peasant houses were built of timber or of wattle and daub on a flint foundation or on posts driven into the ground. They had no chimney, no second floor and were small in size. They have vanished and their positions are marked only by the darker grass of the hut floors and the strong growing patches of nettles in the adjoining middens. The housing of poor quality was easily destroyed by wind and weather, in fact peasant dwellings had to be rebuilt every 20 years or so.[26]

When the monasteries were dissolved there were new secular owners. Existence must always have been precarious. There is no single cause for the demise of Lomer. A few bad harvests, uncertain water supply and the rising price of wool which reached a new high in the decade 1537–1547 and led to a demand for sheep pasture, all contributed. In 1551 the Countess of Southampton received a royal command to amalgamate Lomer with Corhampton and it was subsequently referred to as 'Corhampton Detached'. So the parish ended its separate existence and any treasures which the church may have possessed were transferred to Corhampton. The few remaining villagers moved into the valley. In 1894 Corhampton Detached was transferred to Exton.[27]

*   *   *

No Prime Minister has come from the Meon valley, neither born there nor sitting for

14. William of Wykeham bishop of Winchester 1367–1404.

a Hampshire constituency, but in the later middle ages a man of comparable rank came from Wickham and for close on 40 years was bishop of his home diocese of Winchester.[28] William of Wykeham was born in September 1326 probably in the parish, though we do not know where. He was the son of John and Sybil Le Longe – the name was not a surname (there were as yet no hereditary surnames) but may have referred to his father's stature or ironically to his lack of it. The family were yeomen or upper peasant class.[29] William attended school in Winchester, lodging with a family and being taught in French, still the language of instruction.[30] Nothing is known about his early post-school career though it seems likely that the route from obscurity to recognition came through William Edington (bishop of Winchester 1346–66). In 1356 Wykeham entered royal service as clerk of works and later that year assumed overall responsibility for the royal building programme at Windsor – the largest of the whole middle ages costing £51,000.[31] The year 1361 saw him move from being in charge of building projects to becoming a senior official in the royal chamber with daily access to the king. The 1360s were his decade. In 1363 he became Keeper of the Privy Seal, in 1367 Chancellor. In October 1366 Bishop Edington died at Bishop's Waltham Palace and Wykeham was his designated successor though it was not until October 1367 that he was consecrated bishop in St Paul's cathedral and only on 9th July 1368 was he enthroned in his cathedral at Winchester.

Ordination does not seem to have been part of his original career intentions and unusually for somebody who became a bishop, he took orders only in his late 30s, becoming an acolyte (a minor church order) late in 1361 and priest in June 1362 already aged 37. His rise in the church hierarchy was 'nothing short of dazzling'. Within five years of his ordination to the priesthood he was bishop of the richest diocese in England and one of the richest in Christendom. He had meanwhile accumulated a remarkable collection of livings – no less than 18 in the year 1361 alone – mostly from the king. Almost all were cathedral prebends, with an enormous geographical spread – in Wales and Ireland as well as northern and southern England. When in 1366 Pope Urban V required pluralists throughout Europe to report their holdings Wykeham's income from his benefices was £872-6-8, a staggering figure which placed him top of the list and in the multi-millionaire class – the second name on the list had £270. The bishopric of Winchester was worth £4,000 per year.

Wykeham's later career was not as universally successful as his earlier years. In 1371 he ceased to be chancellor in response to parliament's request that the post should be held by a layman. In 1376 he fell out of favour with the king for reasons which are obscure and in 1377 he was temporarily deprived of the temporalities of his see. Under Richard II who became king in that year he was pardoned and in 1389–91 was once more chancellor, a post from which he resigned at his own request though he remained a significant figure until the end of his life.

Wykeham's passion was building. His career took off when he became surveyor of the royal castles. He began the rebuilding of the nave of Winchester Cathedral and built extensively at most of his palaces for example at Bishop's Waltham Palace where he was described as its second founder. He is best known for the founding of a school in Hampshire and a college at Oxford. The college dedicated to St Mary became known as New College, founded in 1379 and opened in 1386 whilst he obtained a royal charter for Winchester College, his school for '70 poor scholars', in 1382 and it opened in 1394.

Wykeham reached what in the middle ages was the great age of 80 and died on 27th September 1404 at his favourite residence, Bishop's Waltham Palace, where he had lived since 1401. The last ordination of his episcopate, though he was by then not able to preside in person, was held in the parish church of St Peter, Bishop's Waltham on Saturday 20th September 1404, a week before he died. Despite lavish expenditure he was still enormously wealthy and left no less than £10,000. He was succeeded as Bishop of Winchester by Henry Beaufort, the king's half-brother – the contrast between the background of the two men can scarcely have been greater.

*   *   *

None of the palaces owned by the bishop of Winchester were in the Meon valley. The bishop did however own three manors there, one at Droxford and two at East Meon. In East Meon alone his lands totalled 19,000 acres.[32] At East Meon the bishops owned

15. The Court House, East Meon before restoration.

16. The Court House at East Meon after restoration.

what has been described as 'a country residence'. The house was perhaps first built by Walkelin (bishop 1070–98) and the Victoria County History describes it as his favourite residence.[33] It may have been the favourite residence too of Henry of Blois (bishop 1129–71) since it was he who gave to the church at East Meon the black

17. Interior of the Hall, East Meon.

Tournai font. In 1211–12 the house was used for the entertainment of King John. In the next 180 years necessary repairs and some embellishment took place. It was however completely rebuilt by William of Wykeham but not until the 1390s, by which time he had ceased to be chancellor.

Edward Roberts found clear evidence in the pipe rolls of the rebuilding of the house and hall at East Meon between 1395 and 1397.[34] Planning had begun in 1385–6 when Wykeham had over 1000 cartloads of flints collected from the fields for later use. The house which he built consisted of a Great Hall with a cross wing at the north end which included at ground level buttery and pantry and at first floor level the Great Chamber off which was the garderobe (lavatory). The works were supervised and perhaps designed by William Wynford the master mason employed by Wykeham in many of his other projects.

Why, since he seems to have spent no time there, should he have rebuilt the Hall at East Meon? He was an old man by the time the house was built and he preferred the Palace at Bishop's Waltham close to the village of Wickham. The Hall at East Meon was neither a farmhouse which, says Edward Roberts, would have been timber framed, nor a palace such as Wolvesey or Bishop's Waltham but something in between. The steward, for example, who stood at the head of manorial administration for all the bishop's estates, used it when he came, twice each year, to preside over the manorial court. The bishop may have made it available to his friends, it was after all a pleasant rural retreat where hawking and hunting were available not unlike the holiday lets of modern times. William of Wykeham was in any case a compulsive builder and perhaps this is the reason why he rebuilt the Hall at East Meon.

Wykeham's successor as bishop probably did not visit East Meon in the early years of his episcopate still less stay there for any length of time. He was like Wykeham, a great builder and in the 1440s he added not only new ranges at Bishop's Waltham and St Cross in Winchester but also undertook work at East Meon and perhaps inserted glass into windows which had originally had only the shutters typical of earlier periods. William of Waynflete (bishop 1447–86) also visited the Court House in the 1450s and 60s.

*   *   *

In the Winchester diocese continuous lists of clergy can be compiled from the episcopate of John of Pontoise (1282–1304), the first bishop whose records survive. Before that there are occasional references in papal documents or episcopal charters.

We are greatly indebted to Frances Collins for her research on the medieval incumbents of three of the parishes in the Meon valley. Using papal letters and charters, the Registers of the bishops of Winchester and the archives of Winchester College she sheds light on the medieval incumbents of Meonstoke and Soberton, West Meon and Warnford.[35] She demonstrates that the livings of these parishes were often held in the middle ages and later by non-resident pluralists – men who held more than one living at a time and consequently were unlikely to live in the parish. They were occasional visitors employing nameless curates to serve the parish. This was a well-known phenomenon and one of which the papacy disapproved but seemed powerless to stop. Some bishops too inveighed against it but turned a blind eye and themselves sometimes benefited from it. What Frances Collins has confirmed from the records of three parishes was probably true of others in the Meon valley as well as elsewhere.

Why was there such widespread and long-lasting abuse? In the middle ages the clergy were usually literate in both English and Latin and this skill was at a premium. They were needed at the king's court, they constituted the civil service at all levels from clerks to chancellor of the realm and the diocesan bureaucracy depended on them too. From the time when the universities of Oxford and Cambridge came into existence early in the thirteenth century (Cambridge 1209, Oxford a little earlier) the clergy were often also fellows of colleges. The Winchester diocese was the richest diocese in England, its bishops high ranking royal officials and the diocese was conveniently situated for both London and Oxford so it was natural that the bishop should provide the best livings for his staff. Writing about pre-Reformation West Meon Frances Collins concludes:

The rectors of West Meon seem to have been …men of affairs attached to the court, the person of the bishop or the university. The work of the parish was undertaken by a curate: generally a man of humble birth, without security of tenure and very poorly paid. He might, if he were fortunate in his rector, live in the rectory on sufferance; the alternatives, a cottage or the village inn; the inn would at any rate provide company for a lonely bachelor. He was expected to teach in the parish despite his lack of learning, to visit the sick and to relieve the poor with parish alms. His salary was miserable and at the whim of the rector, in spite of a minimum of five marks (£3.6.8) laid down in 1346.[36]

Meonstoke was in the gift of the Bishop of Winchester and was a well-endowed parish. Walter de Cumbe for example who was appointed in 1292 was Archdeacon of Surrey, rector of Farnham and a canon of Lichfield. Though he drew 60 marks from the rectory of Meonstoke it seems unlikely that he spent much – or indeed any – time there. William of Exeter rector from 1330 to 1336 had permission to study abroad, probably in Italy, was a canon of Exeter, physician to Philippa of Hainault, wife of Edward III, was interested in botany and something of a financier, able to lend the king £100. He would have found residence at Meonstoke uneventful and tedious.

A century later Christopher Bainbridge (1464–1514) was a pluralist on a considerable scale. Meonstoke, of which he was rector briefly from 1497–9, was simply a source of further income. He was a man of great energy, fearsome ambition, a violent temper and many enemies. The posts he held included Provost of The Queen's College, Oxford, Treasurer of St Paul's Cathedral, Archdeacon of Surrey, Master of the Rolls, Dean of York and Dean of St George's Chapel, Windsor. In 1507 he became Bishop of Durham only to exchange his bishopric for the Archbishopric of York the following year. He was made a Cardinal by Julius II in 1511 and entrusted by him with a military expedition against Ferrara He was poisoned in 1514 probably by one of his Italian chaplains. When he died he had been intending to return to England as papal legate and was still under the age of 50. He was succeeded as Archbishop of York by his arch-enemy Cardinal Wolsey.[37]

*   *   *

What then did the typical medieval village church look like? The porch was not only the entrance to the church but a place where parish business was transacted. At the entrance to the church was a holy water stoup: at Warnford still to be found outside the west door. On the walls were paintings of Biblical incidents from Creation to Apocalypse as well as legendary scenes from the lives of the saints. Sculptures and stained glass told the same story. Between nave and chancel was the rood screen usually in stone though the rood itself – the figure of Christ on the Cross – was made of wood. In order to reach the rood there was a staircase in the thickness of the east wall of the nave. Most were blocked off at the Reformation when the rood itself was demolished.

The door which led to the screen can still be seen at Soberton. At Droxford the stair-case and the doorway leading to it were discovered and opened up in the course of early twentieth century restoration.

Stained glass too was broken up at the Reformation though one small piece, the arms of Cardinal Beaufort (bishop of Winchester 1404–1447) can be seen next to the squint in the chancel of Soberton church. Stained glass placed in churches by well meaning Victorian restorers serves only to make churches darker than they would otherwise be. Wall paintings were whitewashed over and so can sometimes be restored though not to their medieval glory. The remains of wall paintings have been restored at Corhampton and Soberton. At Corhampton they include part of the story of St Swithin. At Soberton the wall paintings have been identified as the Virgin Mary as a child, St Anne, St Katharine and St Margaret of Antioch.

At the east end of the church was a stone altar with its five consecration crosses. Many of these too were destroyed at the Reformation and replaced by wooden tables. On the south side of the chancel would be piscina (for washing the vessels used in the Mass) and threefold sedilia providing seats during mass for priest, deacon and subdeacon. On the north side of the chancel stood the aumbry where the Mass was reserved. At Droxford three piscinas built into the south wall of the sanctuary and both chapels as well as an aumbry in the north chapel which were found during the same early twentieth century restoration, had been concealed during the Reformation. The floor was made of earth and there was neither seating, heating nor lighting though from the twelfth century candles were placed on the altar to provide light in what was often a very dark building.[38]

3

The Era of Reformation
1500–1642

I N E N G L A N D the Reformation is often attributed to the desire of Henry VIII to replace, the now no longer young, Catherine of Aragon by the nubile Anne Boleyn in order to sire a male heir and ensure the succession. This may have been the occasion but the causes of the Reformation were deep seated, both religious and political and not confined to England. Events in England in the 1530s were strongly influenced by two new men. Thomas Cromwell became the king's closest adviser. When the aged Archbishop of Canterbury, William Warham, died in 1532, he was succeeded by Thomas Cranmer, a man of 44, with no episcopal experience, married and a Protestant sympathiser.

The Reformation began in England in the 1530s with Henry VIII's repudiation of papal authority. In the Meon valley its first effect was the dissolution of Titchfield Abbey in 1537 (see chapter 4). The first consequence for parish churches was the placing of the Bible in English in every church in 1538. Change accelerated with the reign of Edward VI (1547–53) who despite his youth was a convinced Protestant. Worship was to be in English and the first English Prayer Book was introduced in 1549. Stone altars were broken up and replaced by wooden tables, stained glass with images of the saints was smashed, wall paintings were defaced and sculptures destroyed.

The brief reign of Mary (1553–8) meant a return to papal allegiance and catholic worship and the departure into exile of Protestant bishops and clergy. Finally the accession of Elizabeth (1558–1603) saw an attempt at accommodation, what has been called the *via media*. England would neither return to papal allegiance nor adopt a Reformed pattern of church government. The Church of England retained the three-fold ministry of bishop, priest and deacon and aspects of catholic worship alongside services in English, a married clergy and a Protestant Book of Common Prayer.

Two of Elizabeth's three Archbishops of Canterbury were men of this middle way – Matthew Parker (Archbishop 1559–76) and John Whitgift (1582–1604) In between the two came Edmund Grindal (1576–1583), a convinced Puritan and exile in Strasburg during the reign of Mary. At Winchester the last Catholic bishop, John White, was sent to the Tower of London in 1561 and replaced by Robert Horne (1561–80) who had spent the reign of Mary in Strasburg. He was the first married bishop of Winchester and was a Puritan intent on removing from his diocese all remnants of papal allegiance.

In the early years of Elizabeth I there was an acute shortage of clergy. In 1561 the Archbishop of Canterbury, Matthew Parker, at the behest of the queen asked all bishops in the southern province to provide information about their clergy. The replies of Bishop Horne give us a snap shot of many aspects of clerical life in the Winchester diocese at the beginning of the reign of Elizabeth I. Questions included whether clergy were married: the queen disapproved of clerical marriage but had little alternative but to accept it. Clergy were asked where they lived, were they permitted to preach in their own parishes, how many livings did each possess and were they 'hospitable' – was this an expectation derived from monastic hospitality?[1]

In the Meon valley there were eight parishes. Only one cleric was married – William Overton rector of Exton – the remainder were *non conuigatus*. Most lived in their own rectories though some who were also prebends of the cathedral lived in Winchester for at least part of the year. Three held other livings – Stephen Cheston was incumbent of West Meon, Overton and Kingsworthy but he had appointed a curate at West Meon whose name was Franciscus John, a man 'moderately learned' who resided in the parish, had no other cure and was not licensed to preach. William Overton was incumbent of Nursling and Upham as well as Exton whilst George Flower rector of Warnford lived *in rectoria sua de Hideborne Worthy* (in his rectory at Headbourne Worthy).[2]

Meonstoke was a rich living. According to the *Valor Ecclesiasticus* (a survey of clerical income ordered by Thomas Cromwell in 1535) it was worth £46.13.4 one of the richest in the diocese at a time when not much over £5 was considered an adequate income for an incumbent whilst a curate deputising for a non-resident parson averaged between £3 and £5.[3] The rector of Meonstoke from the last years of Henry VIII to the last year of the reign of Mary was William Medowe (1545–57). He was a catholic by persuasion but from 1549 obliged to read the service in English as the Soberton Register makes clear: 'This tyme began the Ingles service in the time of King Edward VI'.

His successor was John Brereton who was appointed in the last year of Mary's reign and continued in office until 1581. An ex-catholic priest he was unmarried, lived in the parish and was allowed to preach at Meonstoke despite his lack of a university degree. His catholic sympathies showed and in 1569 together with the rector of Droxford, John Williams, he was brought before Bishop Horne for failing to preach against the pope. Both of them were ordered in future to preach against 'Papistical depravity, the usurped jurisdiction of the pope and the private mass'. [4]

When John Brereton died the bishop was able to appoint somebody whose theology and churchmanship were close to his own. Lawrence Humphrey rector from 1581 to 1588 was described by Frances Collins as 'one of the most stiff-necked Puritan divines in the reign of Queen Elizabeth'. He had spent the years when Mary was on the throne in Zurich and Geneva, had visited Basle and Frankfurt and knew many the leading Puritans in the English church. In his early years he had objected to wearing a surplice. He was an academic. While he was rector of Meonstoke he was also Regius Professor of Divinity at Oxford and President of Magdalene College and in 1580 became also Dean of Winchester where he substituted bread for wafers at Holy Communion. He was the first married rector of Meonstoke. Though the marriage was not a happy one there were no less than 12 children. If he visited Meonstoke at all during his incumbency it would have been occasionally and briefly.[5]

By now Meonstoke scarcely expected its rector to reside and had become used to the ministrations of curates. The next three rectors were also non-resident. Henry Cotton (1589–1600) was already a prebendary of Winchester which entitled him to a house in the Close and in 1598 he was appointed Bishop of Salisbury. He was followed by Hugh Gray (1600–1604) who was Gresham Professor of Divinity a post which required his frequent presence in London. He was also a prebendary of Lincoln cathedral. His death was recorded in the Meonstoke Burial Register on 20th July 1604 though he died in London. Nicholas Love who was rector for 26 years (1604–30) was also during that period headmaster of Winchester College (1601–10), President of the College (1613–30) and from 1615 rector of Wonston. He too visited his parish only occasionally.

The Reformation saw an attempt to control clerical pluralism and non-residence. Under the Pluralities Act of 1529 men with more than one benefice were expected to reside on one of them and by the Canons of 1583, 1597 and 1604 they were required to live in each 'for some reasonable time in every year' and to supply a curate to perform duties in the parish during their absence.[6] The legislation was a counsel of perfection rarely achieved. Many parishes were run by poorly paid and often nameless curates. We do however know the name of curates at Meonstoke though they probably served the chapelry of Soberton which lists them on its board of incumbents. When Nicholas Love and his successor John Harris (1631–57) were rectors of Meonstoke and Soberton the curate was George Gold. His daughters were baptised in 1617 and 1620. He died a widower and a relatively poor man in 1647 leaving a will and an inventory of his possessions. He left 40/- to the poor of the parish, owned £5 worth of books with table, desk and bookshelves and perhaps farmed in a small way since he had two cows and a pig in the yard, six sheep on the common and a yearling foal in the stable.[7]

*   *   *

Arthur Plantagenet was one of the most high ranking people to live in the Meon valley. Born in 1462 his life straddles the Wars of the Roses and the early Tudor period. He was the illegitimate son of the 19 year old Edward IV, Yorkist king from 1461–83, by Elizabeth Lucy Wayte a member of a family whose forbears came from Funtley.[8] He was brought up at court until he was 10 years old. As half brother of the princes in the Tower – the short-lived Edward V and Richard of York – he kept his head down in those perilous times. His mother's family had migrated to Soberton where his grandfather and great-grandfather were well-to-do woollen merchants. The Wayte family owned property in many of the parishes of south Hampshire.[9]

The accession of Henry VII in 1485 and his marriage to Elizabeth of York, Arthur's half-sister, marked a change of fortune. Henry VIII referred to 'cousin Arthur', accepted him as a kinsman and he became a member of the king's bodyguard. In 1511, now aged 49, he married Elizabeth Grey the daughter of Edward Grey, Viscount Lisle, and in 1519 she became Baroness Lisle. When she died in 1523 Arthur Plantagenet was himself created Viscount Lisle. They had three daughters, Frances, Elizabeth and Bridget and lived at Segensworth. When Elizabeth died in 1528 she was buried at Titchfield Abbey. One of the Lisle letters from John Husee, who described himself as 'your lordship's own man bounden', addressed to Lord Lisle in Calais asked 'whether your lordship will have my Lady Lisle now removed and laid in the parish church at Titchfield'. So her body was removed from Titchfield Abbey to Titchfield church.

After the death of his first wife Arthur married again. In 1532 he and Honor Grenville, his second wife, were invited to meet Francis I, king of France, at Calais. The following year Arthur was appointed Deputy Governor of Calais, still an English possession. He was later arrested and put in the tower by Thomas Cromwell for alleged complicity in a plot to betray Calais to the pope and Cardinal Pole. In 1542 he was declared innocent and 'restored to favour and liberty'. By now aged 80 years of age, he died before he could be released from the tower. 'His excitement was so great' wrote John Foxe 'that he died the same night'.[10]

*   *   *

Over 200 secular buildings erected before 1800 in the Meon valley are listed in *Hampshire Treasures* including farmhouses, cottages, shops, inns, stables, barns and dovecotes. Two of the earliest are the Court House and Hall at East Meon and Great Fontley Farmhouse in the parish of Titchfield.[11] The magnificent oak timbers used in

18. Great Funtley Farmhouse.

its construction were felled according to dendrochronologists between 1510 and 1538. Since the house would have been built of fresh timbers it can be dated to the early sixteenth century. It was a large house, the south front consisting of four bays jetted and close studded. At first it was thatched but early in its life thatch was replaced by tiles. The bricks used for the herring-bone nogging which can still be seen in places and for the magnificent chimneys may have been made in a kiln, remains of which have been found in a neighbouring field.[12]

We do not know for certain who built the house, probably James Hawkesworth who in 1532 'holdythe the syte of the manor of Fountley in the peryshe of Tychfeld'.[13] The Hawkesworth family 'who hovered between yeoman and gentry status' lived in the house until the early seventeenth century.[14] The survival of the house is remarkable and in the twentieth century was due largely to the work of Harold Dickson who bought the farmhouse and the farm with 250 acres in 1933 and whose daughter Jenny and her husband Nick Mallett (died 1995) inherited it and continued to care for it. It is a reminder of a vanished age.

*   *   *

From the fourteenth century onwards leading families commissioned funerary monuments and erected them in churches where they sometimes dominated the building or at least part of it. In three of the Meon valley churches there are spectacular tombs built within thirty years of each other at the end of the sixteenth century and the early years of the seventeenth century: the Wriothesley monument at Titchfield, the tomb built by the Uvedales at Wickham and the Neale monuments at Warnford (for the Wriothesley tomb see chapter 4).

William Neale bought the Warnford estate in 1577 and the family lived there for a century. The house which had been built by the De Ports was now in ruins and William Neale built a new one. He died in 1610 and the marble and alabaster monument on the north side of the chancel in Warnford church was erected in his memory. Was it the intention that he should be buried in the church? Despite the words *Hic requiescat* [Here lies], William Neale and both his wives are buried in the church of St. Bartholomew, Smithfield where he lived before coming to Warnford and where William had for many years been churchwarden. The epitaph on the Warnford memorial has about it a gloomy fatalistic note. The Latin inscription ends *Quid caro? Quid vita haec? Flos, pulvis et umbra?* [What is flesh? What is this life? Blossom, dust and shadow.]

It is William's son Sir Thomas who is commemorated in the much larger and more spectacular monument on the south side of the altar. He died on 18th September 1620 in the parish of St Clement Dane in London and was buried at Warnford on 3rd February 1620/1. On the tomb his first wife Elizabeth lies on his right and his second wife Mary on his left. Elizabeth bore him five daughters and Mary, whom he married on the death of Elizabeth, had four sons and one daughter. Below the three figures is a row of nine children (not ten) each kneeling on a cushion against a black marble panel [15] (For the Neales see page 140–2)

At Wickham the Uvedale monument of Derbyshire alabaster and marble, surmounted by the Uvedale arms, is the main feature of the church. It is now in the south transept though this was not its original position. It was commissioned by their son in memory of Sir William Uvedale who died in 1615 and his wife Mary who was the daughter of Sir Richard Norton of Tisted. The figures of William and Mary are half recumbent with their nine children kneeling in front of the tomb chest. John the eldest son appears on the tomb bearing a skull; he was baptised on the night of 15th April 1568 'being sicke'; he died and was buried two days later. The remaining children were three sons William, Richard and Francis and five daughters Catherine, Honor, Mary, Jane and Susan. The back of the canopy is crowded with ornaments and emblems, including numerous representations of skull and bones as well as a corpse. David Lloyd comments 'the designer was clearly afflicted with morbidity' – but then most tomb designers in the seventeenth century seem to have been so afflicted.[16]

It was the second son William, born in 1587, who commissioned the tomb. He was Member of Parliament for Hampshire in 1612–3 and for Petersfield in 1640 and 1643. As civil war approached he supported the king and was sent by Charles I to negotiate with parliament but he and his companions failed to prevent civil war. This second William died in 1652 and was buried at Wickham. His son yet another William died not later than 1663 and with his death the male line of Uvedales ended. In the Hampshire Hearth Tax returns which were made later in the decade it is Lady Uvedale, the widow of Sir William, who is living at Place House.

4

The Wriothesleys of Place House

❦

THE DISSOLUTION of Titchfield Abbey in December 1537 was the first and most spectacular evidence of the arrival of the Reformation in the Meon valley. It housed however relatively few canons – never more than 14 it appears. The abbey and its lands came into the possession of a young man aged 32, Thomas Wriothesley. (The family until then had been surnamed Wrythe and the name Wriothesley is pronounced 'Risley'). Members of the family were already royal servants: Thomas's grandfather Sir John (died 1504) had taken part in the coronation of Henry VII and his father was York Herald.

Thomas who had been at the royal court since the age of 18 became secretary to Thomas Cromwell and then from 1540 to the king himself and was Lord Chancellor from 1544–7. He was a power in the land with a portrait painted about 1535 by Hans Holbein the Younger, now the property of the Metropolitan Museum of Art in New York. It shows a rakish and determined figure capable of the ruthlessness which would have endeared him to both Cromwell and the king. He was one of the chief beneficiaries of the dissolution of the monasteries in the south of England acquiring Quarr Abbey in the Isle of Wight, Beaulieu and Titchfield Abbeys and later Hyde Abbey in Winchester. He gained 22% of the grants of land in Hampshire made as a result of the dissolution of the monasteries and he and his family were to be leading figures in the county until the male line died out with the death of the 4th Earl in 1667.[1]

Thomas seems to have anticipated the surrender of Titchfield Abbey and made plans for a great house which he would construct from it. He began at once to make the dissolved Abbey into a stately home, known as Place House and completed the transformation remarkably quickly. The great gatehouse, created by Thomas, 'inserted into a gap torn through the church' symbolises, says John Hare, 'the violence and revolution' of the Reformation as well as being a symbol 'of continuity and of the aspirations of the laity of the court of Henry VIII and of the new nobility'.[2] In 1542 he gained permission to crenellate the house and at the same time pardon for having already done it. Apart from the gatehouse the earl used mostly brick, at that time becoming fashionable, for the new parts of his house.

Thomas was a friend of John Leland the Tudor antiquarian and topographer – they had been fellow pupils at St Paul's School in London – who described the house in his itinerary through Hampshire in 1542: 'Mr Wriothesley hath buildid a right stately house embattled and having a goodly gate and a conduit castled in the middle of the

19. The Gatehouse at Place House built by the 1ˢᵗ Earl of Southampton.

court of it, in the very same place where the late monastery of the Premonstratensians stood called Tichefeld'.[3] Leland also noted the 'gramer schole propter ripam flumina' [near the bank of the river] and the park 'the ground whereof is sumwhat hethy and baren'. Thomas Wriothesley was knighted in 1540, became Baron Titchfield in 1544 and in 1547 the new king Edward VI made him Earl of Southampton. He died only three years later on 30ᵗʰ July 1550 at the early age of 45. His family was however to remain powerful in Titchfield for over a century and the house he fashioned out of the erstwhile monastery is today an impressive ruin.

Four generations of Wriothesley Earls of Southampton owned Place House. After the first earl, all inherited the title while they were still young and all died young, though the fourth earl reached 59. It is however the first and the third earls who made most impact on Titchfield. Thomas was succeeded by his son Henry, then a boy of five. He later became involved in a scheme to marry Mary Queen of Scots to the Duke of Norfolk and spent several years of his short life in the Tower of London for complicity in a Catholic plot. In that violent age he was fortunate to escape with his head. He died in 1581 at Crondall, 40 miles from Titchfield in north Hampshire, aged only 35, and was brought back for burial at Titchfield. The accounts of the costs for his elaborate funeral procession have survived.

In his will dated 29th June 1581 the 2nd Earl left instructions for the erection of 'two faire monuments', to include 'portraitures of white alabaster, one for my lord my father and my ladye my mother and one for mee'. Only one monument was erected but it was and remains the glory of Titchfield church. The contract for the work to be undertaken by Gerard Johnson the elder, a Flemish refugee, was signed in 1594. The monument has three effigies. The first earl and the countess, originally buried in St Andrews, Holborn, were exhumed and reburied at Titchfield. The second, third and fourth earls were all later buried in the vault under the monument. On the top of the tomb is an effigy of Jane, first Countess of Southampton who died in 1574. Below on either side of her are her husband, the first earl, dressed in robes of state with the garter insignia and her son the second earl wearing plate armour. David Lloyd describes the resulting tomb as a 'magnificent monument'.[4]

It was however the 3rd Earl, also Henry, who succeeded to the title at the age of seven, who made most impact on Titchfield. He grew up to be a handsome and cultured courtier and the patron of William Shakespeare, seven years his senior, who dedicated *Venus and Adonis* (1593) and *Lucrece* (1594) to him. Suggestions that Shakespeare may have visited Titchfield, that his plays may contain allusions to events in the village, that there was a gay relationship between the two men, or that his widowed mother was the Dark Lady of the Sonnets, can be neither proved nor disproved. Like his father the third earl spent a short period in the Tower at the end

20. Thomas Wriothesley 1st Earl of Southampton (1505–50) by Robert Cooper.

21. Henry Wriothesley 3rd Earl of Southampton (1573–1624), patron of William Shakespeare by Daniel Mytens.

of Elizabeth's reign, for his alleged part in the Earl of Essex's rebellion of 1601. He was condemned to death but the sentence was commuted to life imprisonment and he was released by the new king James I in 1603.

Now in his thirties the 3rd Earl embarked on a series of projects in Titchfield for which he is rightly remembered. He also employed his considerable energies in exploration in North America and improving the defences of the Isle of Wight. At Titchfield he was responsible for building Stony Bridge over the Meon north of the village, creating the ironworks at Funtley and erecting the Market Hall in the Square at Titchfield. He undertook a survey of the estate which resulted in the map of 1610, the original of which no longer exists but copies make clear how valuable and ambitious a project it represented. He died of fever at the age of 51 fighting in the Netherlands and his eldest son died with him. Both burials are recorded in the Parish Register on 28th December 1624 (see page 47).

Before moving on to the 4th Earl of Southampton three of the 3rd Earl's achievements need to be considered. First, he has been credited with the building about 1611 of the Titchfield Canal from the village to the Solent shore which is often described as one of the oldest canals in England. Until recently this was the orthodox view. More recently an alternative has been canvassed and the result is a hotly contested controversy.

An entry in the Parish Register for 24th June 1611 reads: *The same day Titchfield Haven was shut out by Richard Talbot under god's permission at the cost of the right honourable the Earle of Southampton'.* From this it has been assumed that the canal was built soon afterwards by the Earl but no documentation exists to support this view Using a number of later documents John Mitchell argues that the 3rd Earl was not responsible for shutting off the mouth of the Meon so causing the end of seaborne trade reaching the village nor for the construction of a canal. 'Titchfield Haven' was he claims one of two channels of the Meon 'shut out' in order to improve the flow of water in the other channel. The failure to find any reference to the building of a canal is because no canal was built then or later. The watercourse called the New River was, he claims, constructed early in the eighteenth century in order to convert reclaimed pasture on the western side of the estuary to water meadows.[5] The debate will no doubt continue until conclusive proof emerges to settle the issue one way or the other.

Second, iron working at Titchfield was initiated by the 3rd Earl. He began in 1603 using ironstone from Hengistbury Head which was shipped to Funtley where is was converted into wrought iron. By 1620 the Earl possessed the first tin plate mill in England. Further developments took place after his death. By 1647 John Gringo was responsible for a second mill, at Wickham, as well as the mill at Funtley and the family remained in charge until 1773. The Gringo family became members of the Society of Friends and one is named on the plaque recording burials in the Friends Burial Ground at Swanmore. Henry Cort took over the mill at Funtley in 1775 and it was here that he developed the techniques of puddling and rolling which made Titchfield one of the cradles of the Industrial Revolution.

22. Titchfield Market Hall before removal in 1971.

23. Titchfield Market Hall re-erectd at the Weald & Downland Museum.

The Market Hall is a building which Titchfield owed to the 3rd Earl. Many towns had such a building erected in the later middle ages or the sixteenth century though few have survived collapse or later rebuilding. The Titchfield Market Hall had a timber framework and herringbone brick infill. On the ground floor was an open arcade

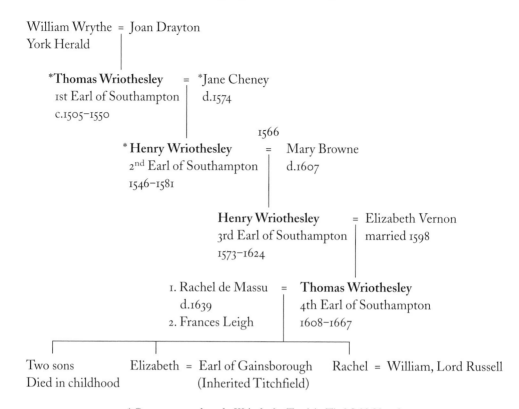

William Wrythe = Joan Drayton
York Herald

*Thomas Wriothesley = *Jane Cheney
1st Earl of Southampton   d.1574
c.1505–1550

1566

* Henry Wriothesley = Mary Browne
2nd Earl of Southampton   d.1607
1546–1581

Henry Wriothesley = Elizabeth Vernon
3rd Earl of Southampton   married 1598
1573–1624

1. Rachel de Massu = Thomas Wriothesley
   d.1639   4th Earl of Southampton
2. Frances Leigh   1608–1667

Two sons   Elizabeth = Earl of Gainsborough   Rachel = William, Lord Russell
Died in childhood   (Inherited Titchfield)

Commemorated on the Wriothesley Tomb in Titchfield Church

The Wriothesley Earls of Southampton

where traders could display their goods and on the first floor was a meeting room with an open gallery where the Manor Court probably met. By 1750 the Market Hall seems to have fallen out of use. About 1810 it was moved from its central place in the Square to Barry's Yard behind the Queen's Head Hotel, perhaps because the newly built turnpike road was bringing more traffic into the centre of the village and the Market Hall was an obstruction. Soon afterwards cells and a lock up were built into the ground floor. After that the historic market hall quietly decayed and by the late twentieth century it was described as 'a derelict shed partly covered with ivy'.[6] The local authority decided that it was dangerous and demanded its immediate demolition. It was however carefully dismantled, labelled and in 1972 re-erected at the Weald and Downland Museum at Singleton near Chichester where it was restored to its seventeenth century splendour. To anybody who recalled its last days in Titchfield its present state must be a revelation.

The 4th Earl of Southampton, Thomas, second son of Henry, was aged 17 when he succeeded to the title in 1624. Soon afterwards he entertained the recently married king Charles I and his queen, Henrietta Maria at Place House. It was the fate of the fourth earl to hold the title through the reign of Charles I, the Civil War and Commonwealth and to see the accession of Charles II. He hesitated at first over where his loyalty should lie between king and parliament but eventually threw in his lot with the king who escaped to Place House in 1647 where he was arrested and taken into parliamentary custody. Thomas is believed to have been with the king when he was executed and to have spent the following night with the body of the dead king. He was fined £6,466 for the part he had played on the side of the king in the Civil War. Despite his support for the king he remained at Titchfield throughout the period of the Commonwealth. When Charles II became king in 1660 Thomas was made Lord Treasurer but he died in 1667 disillusioned with the new king. His death too is recorded in the Parish Register though the

24 Thomas Wriothesley 4th Earl of Southampton (1608-67) after Sir Peter Lely.

clerk seems to have found spelling his name even more difficult than usual 'June the 18th ...Buried ...Thomas Royothizley Eirle of Southampton High Treasurer of England to Charls the 2'.

At the dissolution of the monasteries lands granted to the Wriothesleys included Bloomsbury and their London house was in Holborn. The 4th Earl had a manor house there in the early seventeenth century. It was demolished in 1657 and in 1660 a new Southampton House was completed and the land south of the house became one of the first London squares, known at first as Southampton Square but later as Bloomsbury Square.[7] Further west Great and Little Titchfield Streets derive their names from the Bentinck family whose subsidiary title was Marquess of Titchfield. The family owned the land now occupied by the BBC in Great Portland Street.

Both Thomas's sons had died in childhood and there were only daughters to inherit. Place House passed to Elizabeth who married the Earl of Gainsborough and they entertained Charles II there in 1675. Rachel, heiress to Bloomsbury, married William, Lord Russell who was beheaded in 1683 for implication in the Rye House Plot. The family was restored to favour by William III and descendants were Dukes of Bedford.[8] Place House was lived in for a time and survived for another century though its great days were over. The estate was divided by act of parliament in 1740 and the paintings in the house were removed. In 1761 the east range was pulled down and in 1781 material from Place House was used by the Delme family who were in process of rebuilding Cams Hall at Fareham. Sufficient of the house built by the 1st Earl remains to enable us to visualise the grandeur of its hey-day.

5

The Parish Registers

❦

T HE CLASSIC PERIOD of ancient parish government lasted for about 250 years, from the end of the sixteenth century, when the parish vestry was replacing the manor court, to the passing of the Poor Law Amendment Act in 1834. Between these years there were in each parish six officers all unpaid, all selected from the leading families and all obliged to serve their turn, normally for one year at a time, or to provide a substitute. There were two churchwardens, two overseers of the poor, a parish constable who acted as policeman and fireman and the surveyor of the highways, all appointed or nominated by the vestry over which the parson presided. This parish structure was overseen by the county Justices of the Peace, people of some consequence in the county and meeting in Quarter Sessions. Churchwardens and overseers were each empowered to raise a rate to fulfil their respective functions and the records to which these gave rise, together with a list of the officers themselves, have often survived.[1]

It is sometimes possible to reconstruct the names of the churchwardens for several hundred years. The West Meon Churchwardens' Accounts from 1694 to 1792 contain a list of the two churchwardens for all except three years (1714, 1728 and 1763). Although churchwardens were chosen for a year there are an increasing number of occasions when the same person served for several, sometimes consecutive, years. Women appear as churchwardens in West Meon only twice in almost 100 years – in 1695 and 1706 and both were widows. The Earwaker family provided churchwardens in 43 of the 98 years recorded in the book. They were, says Frances Collins, 'farmers, skilled artisans – generally carpenters or builders – or innkeepers; five families of them with fingers in every pie'.[2]

Churchwardens were responsible for the fabric of the church. Much attention was devoted to the bells which at West Meon were recast in 1722. They were rung to mark special occasions such as the annual celebration of the deliverance of the country from the Gunpowder Plot when, in addition, the service specified for the day in the Prayer Book, headed 'Gunpowder Treason', was held. This together with services for 30th January when Charles I was executed (King Charles the Martyr) and 29th May the day on which Charles II returned to England in 1660, remained in the Prayer Book until 1859. The bells of West Meon church were also rung to mark the burial of Mary II the wife of William III in 1695, the Coronation of Queen Anne in 1702, the news of Admiral Vernon's victory at Portobello in 1742 and the Treaty of Aix la Chapelle at the end of the War of the Austrian Succession in 1748. How did news of such events reach the isolated villages of the Meon valley? Perhaps by the coaches which by now passed through the villages daily to and from London. Church services reminded people of the outline of their history.

At Privett the 'Church Book' provides information about this small chapelry on the edge of the parish of West Meon. It was served by a curate who had a house next to the churchyard 'if he pleased to dwell therein', but who rarely stayed long. The church does not seem to have been heated until 1815 and not until 1864 was there an organ: services were accompanied by a bass viol. When the organ arrived it was probably a barrel organ with a set of well-known tunes and this sufficed until the new church was built in the 1870s.

*   *   *

In the middle ages there was no systematic recording of births, marriages and deaths. It was not until September 1538, during the reign of Henry VIII, that Thomas Cromwell, the king's chief minister, issued an edict that every parish priest was in future to record in a book, christenings, weddings and burials. The parish must provide a 'sure coffer' with two locks, one kept by the priest and the other by a churchwarden. Much later Jews and Quakers were exempted from the requirement but since there were few of either in the Meon valley the registers contain a full or almost full record of all who lived in the parish. Few parishes have complete lists back to 1538. 'Clergy showed a patriotic impartiality in their disregard of canon and state law alike' wrote Fearon & Williams.[3] Out of a total of 232 parishes and 80 chapels of ease in Hampshire only 20 registers date from 1538. By the early seventeenth century however most parishes were keeping records in registers which have survived to the present day and 'proof of laziness was removed by the destruction of the originals'.[4] Until the 1970s they remained in the 'sure coffer', by then referred to as the Parish Chest.

West Meon was the first parish in the valley to keep registers. A record of five burials apparently pre-dating Cromwell's edict has survived from 5th April 1536. Marriage entries date from 28th May 1538 and baptisms from 3rd January 1542. They are not however complete nor as originally kept. It seems that in 1598, perhaps in conformity with an order of that year that all records should be kept in a book, the entries were rewritten. The early records are all in the same hand and carefully spaced, suggesting that the clerk planned his work before he started. There are however omissions; perhaps the original paper entries had been lost.[5] The same appears to have been true at Meonstoke. Entries for the years 1599 to 1678 are in the hand of the then rector Dr Robert Mathews (died 1681, one of the few resident rectors of the parish) who copied out the early entries.

The registers vary; some of the early ones are in Latin, kept as was required, by the incumbent who was often the only person with sufficient command of the language, others are in English from the beginning. At Exton baptism entries and some

25. The Parish Chest at Titchfield.

marriages were recorded in Latin from 1603–5 and from 1607–22. (After 1733 Latin was no longer the language of official documents and registers were kept in English). The West Meon Register is in Latin until the Civil War. In the early years some parishes kept one Register for all three categories of entry, sometimes putting a letter in front of each entry C – christening, M – marriage, B – burial. Some wrote up their records monthly, perhaps from rough paper, with baptisms, marriages and burials each kept separately. Some are scarcely legible, spelling is idiosyncratic, some have been damaged by damp. The entries are not of course records of births and deaths but of baptisms and burials which usually took place a few days later though in the case of baptisms sometimes much later, a fact which may be noted by the parish clerk. Sometimes particularly in the eighteenth century baptism was private and the baby was subsequently brought to church.

In all the parishes of the Meon valley with the single exception of Warnford some or all of the parish registers have been transcribed by later historians and copies are available for study on the open shelves in the Hampshire Record Office at Winchester. The earliest copy seems to have been made in 1906 for the parish of West Meon by Dr Julian Rogers the local doctor who lived at *The Cedars* in Doctors Lane.[6] Some transcripts are indexed and annotated, others not. The first two Titchfield Registers covering the years 1589 to 1678 were transcribed professionally and are exemplary, of enormous value since the use of originals is fraught with difficulty.[7]

Soon after he succeeded to the throne Charles I visited Titchfield and this merited an entry in the parish register: 'King Charles and Queene mary came to Titchfield place the xxth day this moneth and the Queene stayed there five weekes and Three dayes'. ('Queene mary'is Henrietta Maria, the wife of Charles I who had arrived in England only on 12th June 1625. Their stay at Titchfield was a honeymoon).[8] In the following month two burials are recorded of members of the court – John Potter ' the xxvjth day follower to ye Court', and Jane Malborne 'a servant to the queens Court the xxvth day'. Three years later another momentous national event was recorded by the clerk: 'The Lorde Duke of Buckingehame was slayne at Portesmouth the 23 day of Auguste being sattersday Generall of all the fleete by sea and land whose name was George Villers Right Honerable.' Later clerks were less forthcoming and the Civil War, the execution of the Charles I and the return of Charles II were unrecorded.

Not surprisingly members of the Wriothesley family and their servants of Place House figure prominently in the Titchfield registers. The following are all entries relating to members of the household who were buried in Titchfield between 1607 and 1624.

October 1607 Teage Corey my Lord of Southamptons footman the vj day

November 1607 The xvj day the Right Honorable Marie Countess of Southampton

January 1613 Edward Quinby Esquire Steward to the Right honorable the Earle of Southampton the xxvij th day.

January 1615 The Lady Marie the daughter of the Right honorable the Earle of Southampton the xth day

December 1623 Christopher Sa'derson seruant unto the Right honorable the Earle of Southampton the vij th day

December 1624 The Right Honorable Henry Earle of Southampton Knight of the most noble order of the garter and one of his Ma'ties most honorable privy Counsel the xxviij th day. The Honorable Lord James Wryosley the eldest sonne of the sayd Earle the same xxviij th day.

In 1623/4 the villagers of Titchfield must have been surprised by the speed with which their vicar remarried. On 25th February ' Mris Elizabeth Blier the wife of Tymothie Blier Vicar of Titchfield was buried the xxvth day'. Less than two months later the register records the wedding of 'Mr Tymothy Blier and Mris Sara Tymberlake the xvj day'

Clerkship if not hereditary often ran in families. The second Titchfield register starts with the names of the clerks responsible for keeping it. 'This book was bought by Tho'Edwards & Rich'Trodd Churchwardens of Titchfield for the yeare of o'Lord god 1636 And Was Kept by Robt Willmott Clarke of ye same p'ish the same time 1636'. There follow the names of four later parish clerks of whom three come from the same family – William Moudy 1651, Stephen Moudy 1681, Stephen Moudy 1705. Only Peter Sexey 'who entered his Clarks place July ye 11 1658' (and whose name appears no less than three times on the same page) has no evident relationship to the Moudy family.

At Soberton a new clerk was appointed to coincide with the beginning of the registers towards the end of 1538. William Middleton, was clerk for 50 years, married twice

26. John Speed's Map of Hampshire 1610.

and baptisms of 14 of his children are recorded. As the baptism entries for the first five years of his first marriage have been lost it is quite likely that he and his first wife had two or perhaps three further children. After William Middleton's death in the year of the Spanish Armada (1588) there is no further named clerk until 1662 when John White had already held the post for 13 years. William Middleton noted the serious outbreak of 'English sweate' in 1564: ' The newe swette raynged over All Ingland'. He also described the birth of twins in what must have been an unconventional way: 'Halfe a child was crystened at home by ye mydwffe' and 'the other halffe chylld was crystened at ye churche'.

The first Droxford Register runs from 1633 for marriages and burials and from 1635 for baptisms and ends in the 1730s.[9] The period of the Civil War and Commonwealth, from about 1645 to 1660 provides evidence of discontinuity in many parishes. At Droxford the rector Nicholas Preston was replaced by Robert Webb an independent minister, in 1650. In the 15 years from 1635 to 1650 the average number of baptisms was 15 per year. In the 1650s the average was 6.8 dropping to as low as three in 1654, 1658 and 1659. We may speculate about the reason but cannot know. The record of the number of baptisms was unreliable in the 1670s with none in 1675 and 1676 and only three in 1677 – a slipshod clerk or a careless rector seem the likeliest explanation.

Dramatic fluctuations in the number of burials are usually a sign of epidemics in the parish. The average number of burials per year in the first Droxford register was just under ten. In the year 1655 there were 21 burials recorded. Seven members of the Strugnell family died in just over a year between January 1654 and March 1655/6. In 1676 there were 23 burials and in 1680 & 1681 there were 20 and 21. At Titchfield burials rose dramatically between November 1627 and February 1627/8. There were 51 burials with 22 taking place in December alone when the average per month was about four. A number of those who died are recorded as 'solgar' (soldier) all probably members of a local garrison camped on the Common. Eleven years later there was another dramatic rise in the number of burials in Titchfield: between August 1638 and April 1639 (nine months) there were no less than 106 burials an average of 12 per month compared with four or five in normal times.

Those who committed suicide and Roman Catholics were not buried in consecrated ground. At Titchfield 'Thomas Houghton the fifth day was buried in the fields for that he poisoned himself (January 1603). In September 1625 the Titchfield register records 'Dorothie Nash the vj day a recusant was buried out of the Christian burial between the butts without Comfort of minister or Clarke there'. At Droxford on 8th October 1705 Mary Knight of Swanmore who had 'hang'd herself and was found by the Jury non compos mentis was inter'd without Christian burial'.

Acts of Parliament passed in 1666 and more effectively in 1678 required burial in wool in order to encourage the wool trade. *No corpse … shall be buried in any shirt, shift, sheet or shroud or anything whatsoever made or mingled with flax, hemp, silk, hair, gold or silver…other than what is made of sheep's wool only … or to be put into any coffin lined or faced with…any other material but sheep's wool only.*[10] There were heavy penalties for non-compliance. An affidavit was required after each burial to the effect that the deceased had been buried in wool. In the Droxford Register the affidavit is recorded for each burial, the first one appears on 7th September 1678. When no affidavit was provided this too is recorded. On 19th December 1690 'Francis Morley, Esquire ' was 'interred … and noe affidavit was brought but the forfeiture paid'. A little later in 1695 a further act placed a tax on all baptisms, marriages and burials. It did not however last long. The Droxford Register records 1702 'the last year for the tax on burials'.

A further feature of parish life illustrated by the registers is the dominance in the parish of inter-related families At Droxford the Benstead family, though variously spelt, had at least five branches and rated no less than 60 entries in the first register. Other families who figured prominently in the register were Cleverly, Knight. Prouting, Strugnell and Cluer all spelt variously but recognisable. According to the contemporary Hearth Tax returns no less than ten families with the surname Cleverly were to be found in the tithings of Hill and Swanmore. At Hill there were five out of 19 families with the name Cleverly.[11] Some of the same names are to be found among those living in the Meon valley or surrounding villages in the twenty first century.

*   *   *

The eighteenth century brought further changes to the format of the parish registers. The first was the adoption in England in 1754 of the Gregorian calendar. Until then the year had begun on 25th March. For dates between 1st January and 24th March both modes are often found on gravestones, written for example 1685/86.

Second, in 1755 parliament passed Hardwicke's Marriage Act, 'For the better prevention of clandestine marriages'. In future there were to be separate registers of banns and marriages both containing pro forma which must be completed by the officiating parson. They are of great interest to historians. The banns books had to be signed by the person who called the banns and this provides the name of the person who took the service at which the banns were called, often the curate employed by the non-resident parson. The marriage register required the signature not only of bride and groom but of two witnesses. In the eighteenth century many brides, grooms and witnesses made their mark instead of signing and this provides an index of literacy on the assumption that if you couldn't write your name you probably couldn't write anything else nor could you read. It has also to be said that many of the signatures on marriage certificates suggest that writing was not an activity which participants performed frequently.

Frances Collins notes that in the parish of Meonstoke the later years of the eighteenth century and the early years of the nineteenth century saw a marked rise in the number of illegitimate children, recorded in the register as 'baseborn' or 'bastard child of …'. Between 1771 and 1780 there were seven, between 1781 and 1790 13 and by 1836 a further 23. The first child was often born less than nine months after the marriage and in one case baptism and marriage took place on the same day. No man could afford to marry a sterile wife since provision for old age depended on the benevolence of children. Children were regarded as legitimate if they were born within one month of the parents' marriage.

*   *   *

Both the name and the use of Briefs originated in the middle ages. From the reign of Henry VIII until their abolition by act of parliament in 1828 they came in the name of the sovereign. They were in some ways like 'The Week's Good Cause' but the sponsor was neither the BBC nor national charities. The object of a Brief was usually the repair of a church, for victims of fire or flood or in the seventeenth century in particular for the relief of foreign Protestants. Briefs were initiated by a parish but issued by the government and read from the pulpit on Sunday morning. Money was collected by the clerk after the service. Meonstoke was the subject of a Brief after the fire of 1719 destroyed 23 houses in the village. It hoped for £5,178 but we do not know how much the parish received.

In the Meon valley the parish of Exton has one of the most comprehensive lists of Briefs. They appear in the parish registers between 1675 and 1720 together with a few in 1726 and 1727. Loss by fire is by far the most frequent cause of appeals for help. The largest amount requested was £7,639 by an optimistic parish whose church had been destroyed by fire. The generosity of the Exton congregation was more likely to be called out by a catastrophe nearby: in 1689 the church at New Alresford was burnt down and the small parish of Exton contributed no less than £7-2-9 perhaps largely coming from one person who knew the parish of Alresford and had the means to give generously. Appeals for foreign Protestants were received sympathetically. Exton parishioners contributed to the relief of persecuted Protestants in the Vaudois in 1699, in Orange in 1703 and 'Reformed Episcopal Churches in Great Poland' in 1716.[12]

Between 1706 and 1751 the Wickham Register devoted no less than 52 pages to Briefs which it received. At Meonstoke 72 Briefs were received between November 1804 and June 1811, not long before they were abolished. Of these 45 were appeals for the building or replacement of churches and 18 for repairs after fires. Contributions were small; the largest 2/7 ½ and several produced as little as 3d. In some cases hope sprang eternal: Adderley Church in Shropshire requested help by means of Briefs on no less than five occasions. Meonstoke gave 1/-. Bloxwich church in Staffordshire asked for £1693-18-0 and received 6d. from Meonstoke.

*   *   *

Rose's act passed in 1812 required each parish in future to keep three separate registers for christenings, marriages and burials, in a 'dry well painted iron chest, in some dry and secure place either at the parsonage or in the church'. Finally in 1837 the Whig government introduced secular registration of births, marriages and deaths. The church continued to keep its own records but since Roman Catholics and Dissenters were no longer obliged to use the machinery of the Church of England parish registers are less complete though in the parishes of the Meon valley there were few who were not baptised, married or buried according to the rites of the established church.

Despite the brevity of early entries something of the tenor of daily life can be gleaned from the registers. Child birth was perilous – all too often baptism is followed in the same month by the burial of the child and sometimes the mother too. The birth of twins was particularly hazardous: rarely do both infants and the mother survive. In lists of baptisms kept in the seventeenth century it is the child's father and not mother whose name is usually recorded except where a child is born out of wedlock. Marriage was usually between two people from the parish and where the man comes from outside the clerk indicates whence he comes, rarely far away.

The Titchfield Registers contain occasional references to the crafts practised in the parish perhaps to distinguish them from people of the same name who performed another craft: 'BrickeMaker, Sirvayer of Water Woorkes at Meenelane end, schoole-master, The Shooe maker, Farryer, one of the forg men, a worke man to the Iremell', are examples

Until the publication of Dr Samuel Johnson's Dictionary in 1755 there seems to have been no such thing as correct spelling of even common words. Words were written as they sounded or as the clerk decided, sometimes differing on consecutive pages or even consecutive lines. This applies to the names of places and people as well as to common words. The first Titchfield clerk spelt the word 'marriage' in no less than eight different ways sometimes in consecutive entries. – weddid, married, mared, marryed, married, maryed, mar'yed, marryd. Capital letters too seem to be used or not without rhyme or reason. There is an engaging idiosyncrasy about the result and usually the meaning can be discerned though sometimes a degree of ingenuity is needed : the Titchfield Register in April 1601 includes under 'Buryed' 'Wm tealer by myscha'se Droned xxixth', (presumably meaning 'William Tealer drowned by accident on 29th'.)

*   *   *

For over 400 years the parish registers were kept in the Parish Chest maintained by the parish priest or under his supervision. But a trunk usually kept in the church was not the best place for the preservation of precious records. Under the Parochial Registers and Records Measure of 1978 all records over 100 years old and no longer in use were to be deposited with diocesan records though they remained the property of the parish. The need for this more systematic storage was amply demonstrated by a note in the Register of the parish of Soberton for the years 1813 to 1874: 'Whoever takes Charge of these Books should be careful not to place them in a Chest which rests on the ground as the Church is very damp and will decay the paper. Many old registers have been greatly injured and rendered useless through carelessness in this particular and persons searching for the Births and Burials for some legal purpose have been put to great inconvenience or Loss on this account.'[13]

6

From the Civil War to the Glorious Revolution

THE CHURCH OF ENGLAND's search for its own identity begun in the reign of Edward VI continued until 1660. Discrepant opinions were held with increasing vehemence and helped to cause the Civil War in the 1640s. By the early seventeenth century a high church party wanted to move the Church of England in a catholic direction. The stone altar – replaced during the Reformation by the Holy Table made of wood – was no longer to be placed lengthwise in the chancel but against the east wall and to be surrounded by a wooden rail. Liturgy and ceremonial became more elaborate. Three successive bishops of Winchester were high churchmen: Lancelot Andrewes (1619–28), Richard Neile (1628–32) and Walter Curll (1632–47).

At the other end of the spectrum Puritans, some inside the Church of England, some outside, became increasingly militant. The clash between the two sides helped to lead to civil war in 1642. Parliamentary success meant the abolition of bishops (in 1646), the sequestration of many parish priests, and the replacement of the Book of Common Prayer by a Presbyterian Directory of Public Worship as well as the suppression of un-Biblical feasts like Christmas. Between the outbreak of the Civil War in 1642 and the return of Charles II in 1660 Britain experienced a greater upheaval than at any time since the Norman Conquest. We have no means of knowing where the sympathies of most people in the villages of the Meon valley lay but it is reasonable to assume that more favoured the king than supported parliament.

The war reached the Meon valley early in 1644 in the run-up to the battle of Cheriton. The Exton Burial Register has this entry: 'A strange boy who followed the king's troupe (of London) was buried the 14th January 1644.' At the end of March Sir William Waller, the parliamentary commander gathered his troops at East Meon and part of the force moved to West Meon where horses were stabled in the parish church. The Cross which stood in the centre of the village was destroyed by parliamentary troops. Meanwhile royalist troops under Sir Ralph Hopton reached Warnford and there appears to have been a skirmish between the two sides there since the Burial Register records the death of two soldiers in 1644 though it does not say to which side they belonged nor whether they had been wounded in battle. A cannon ball, pistol ball and halberd are amongst the artefacts of war found locally. In the garden of the later school in East Meon cannon balls are frequently found.[1]

On 29th March 1644 the two armies met at Cheriton, the first battle to be won decisively by parliamentary forces and a defeat from which the royalists never recovered. Waller occupied Winchester and neighbouring towns. This in turn led to the bombardment of the Palace belonging to the Bishop of Winchester at Bishop's Waltham and the escape of Bishop Curll in a dung cart to his sister's house at Soberton perhaps sheltering, as legend has it, at Bishopsdown Farm on the way. Episcopacy (government of the church by bishops) was abolished in 1646. The following year Walter Curll died in London and his body was brought back to Soberton where it was buried in the churchyard though the place of his burial is not known. The Curll Chapel in Soberton church is named after a grandson of the bishop, Sir Walter Curll who was buried there in 1678 and Barbara his wife buried in 1698, both commemorated on a wall plaque.[2]

This was not however the end of the direct involvement of the Meon valley in the momentous events of the 1640s. In November 1647 Charles I himself may have ridden down part of the Meon valley. He escaped from house arrest at Hampton Court, hoping to be able to play parliament and the army off against each other. He and four others set off for the Isle of Wight, reached Bishop's Sutton expecting to change horses at *The Ship Inn* but found it occupied by the parliamentary committee for the county. So the king with one companion rode on to Titchfield where they hoped to be picked up by a boat from the Isle of Wight which had come to the mouth of the river Meon. John Hurst reconstructs a possible route bringing the king over Beacon Hill and Corhampton Down but he admits that there is doubt about the route south of Droxford. The king was taken to the Isle of Wight by the governor of the island Colonel Hammond who turned out not to be sympathetic to the king. Charles's stay there became incarceration first at Carisbrooke Castle then on the mainland at Hurst Castle 'cold, damp and dark', from which he was moved to London to trial and subsequent execution.[3]

As a postscript to the Meon valley's part in the events of the 1640s and 50s, Charles II came through Warnford after his defeat and escape following the battle of Worcester in November 1651. The king, on his way from Salisbury to Brighton where he boarded a ship for France, rode through Warnford and met guides on Old Winchester Hill above the village.[4]

*   *   *

With the defeat of the king in the Civil Wars parliament was free to remove those clergy of whom it disapproved most strongly. At Droxford Dr Nicholas Preston who had become rector in 1640 was sequestered 'by the tyranny of the late usurpers' and replaced in 'the yeere 1650' by Robert Webb, an independent minister. Dr Preston returned in 1660. Edmund Calamy gives an account, written much later, of what happened in Droxford when Charles II returned: 'The former incumbent came to take possession of this living and thrust out Mr Webb and his family in a rough and violent manner… The wife of Richard Cromwell, Esq. sent her Coach for them to a house of theirs. Poor Mrs Webb being big with Child fell into Labour in the Coach.

Mr Webb had a great Family and was very poor'.[5] The restored rector, Nicholas Preston, lived until 1664 and was buried in the south aisle of Droxford church, where the inscription reads ' By the tyranny of the late usurpers having spent his dayes in a pious and paynful ministry. Hee lived beloved and died desired'. It commends his 'eminent loyalty and zeal', which must indicate whose side the parish was on, just as Calamy's account of the treatment of Robert Webb indicated his sympathies.

At Exton Thomas Gawen (1612–84), a prebendary of Winchester, chaplain to Bishop Curll and tutor to his children was, not surprisingly, sequestered and replaced by John Ridge who in turn was removed in 1662 because he refused episcopal ordination. In the meantime Thomas Gawen became a Roman Catholic.[6] At Meonstoke John Harris was rector from 1631 to 1657 and also Warden of Winchester College. He was a royalist but survived through the Civil War and Commonwealth, living for part of that time at Meonstoke. His successor was his curate Robert Matthew (1657–81) whose wife bore six children all born in the rectory at Meonstoke. The Register records his burial in wool as required by the Act of 1678. At West Meon John Bludworth rector from 1640 was sequestered in 1652. The birth of his first child in the rectory in 1647 is recorded but the later children were born at Bray in Berkshire. He was replaced by an intruder, Mr Bonborne, who in turn departed in 1660 and was replaced by Abraham Alleyn (rector 1660–89).

Among clergy who were deprived of their living during the Commonwealth but later achieved prominence was the oddly named Accepted Frewen (1588-1664), rector of Warnford from 1626–45. He owed his unusual Christian name to his father John Frewen, rector of Northiam near Hastings, an ardent Puritan whose parishioners thought he was a dissenter. (John Frewen's second son was named 'Faithful'.) Accepted Frewen, despite his Puritan Christian name, took the opposite point of view from his father and was a follower of Archbishop Laud. He took his degree at Magdalen College, Oxford and soon afterwards became chaplain to King Charles I and a canon of Canterbury cathedral. He moved back to Oxford and was President of Magdalen College from 1626–43, twice serving as Vice-Chancellor. At the beginning of the Civil War he was responsible for handing over the university plate to the king and in 1644 was made bishop of Lichfield and Coventry. Soon afterwards he was deprived by parliament. His reward came when Charles II returned. For the last four years of his life from 1660–4 he was Archbishop of York.[7]

Nicholas Preston's successor as rector of Droxford was William Hawkins (1664–91) In 1678 he married Anne the daughter of Izaac Walton (1593–1683) who wrote *The Compleat Angler,* first published in 1653, sub-titled *The Contemplative Man's Recreation.* Walton was steward to Bishop George Morley first at Worcester and then at Winchester. He lived for part of the time at Farnham Castle now the main residence of the bishop, part in the Close at Winchester where his father in law had a house in his capacity as a prebend of Winchester. He was also on occasion his guest at Droxford where he was a friend of the curate John Darbyshire and of Sir Francis Morley, who leased the Manor House. He must often have fished in the Meon.[8] He died at Hawkins' house in the Close at Winchester during the severe frost of December 1683 at the great age of almost 90 and was buried in the cathedral. His famous book is read today not as a guide to fishing technique but 'as an idyllist and as such [it] is unmatched in English prose.'[9] In the south-west corner of the south transept of Winchester cathedral is the Izaac Walton window to which fishermen of England and America contributed and which was dedicated just before the outbreak of the First World War on 8th June 1914.

The later years of the seventeenth century saw the last attempt to enforce church attendance. The Droxford churchwardens for example reported to the bishop in 1684; 'John Perin, Thomas Cleverley and his wife, Simon Frye and his wife, Cutbert Reeves and Mary his wife come very seldom to church….Wee believe that there are severall persons above sixteene yeares old that doe not communicate according as is required'. What was almost as bad when Cutbert Reeves did come to church it was 'with his hatt on and kept it on all the time he stayed there'.[10]

*   *   *

On his return in 1660 parliament reckoned that Charles II needed £1,200,000 to run the royal household and the country in peacetime. After considerable debate parliament decided in 1662 that the king's government required additional taxation and hit on an idea not previously tried in England, a Hearth Tax, an annual levy of 2/- payable annually on each hearth or stove. It was collected in twice yearly instalments on Lady Day and Michaelmas. Despite its unpopularity the tax was levied until 1689 when it was abolished, one of the reforms which followed the Glorious Revolution.

For local historians the records of the Hearth Tax are invaluable providing the names of all householders in the late seventeenth century. Exemption was granted to those who did not pay the poor rate, the church rate or own property or occupy premises worth more than 20/- per year. The assumption was that the more hearths a house had the wealthier the householder. As a rough guide one or two hearths indicated poverty and ten or more affluence. The 'middling sort' possessed between three and nine hearths. Approaching two thirds of houses in the Meon valley had one or two hearths suggesting poverty and just over one third of all householders were not chargeable.[11]

The houses with most hearths and therefore probably owners with the most affluent life-style were George Mersh who lived at Place House, Titchfield which had 57 hearths, followed by Lady Uvedale owner of Place House, Wickham with 35 hearths and Thomas Neale of Warnford Park who paid tax on 20 hearths. Next came John Stewkeley who lived at Preshaw which had 17 hearths and Sir Richard Uvedale the owner of the Manor House at Droxford which had 15 hearths. Clergy were not exempt, but Dr Hawkins the rector of Droxford lived much of the year in the Close at Winchester where his house had 13 hearths. Although he was rector from 1664 to 1691 he does not appear in the Hearth Tax returns until 1674 when the Rectory had ten hearths. In 1684 the churchwardens comment 'the Minister of the place hath usually beene absent three partes of the yeare'.

7

The Poor Law to 1834

IN THE MIDDLE AGES responsibility for the poor rested with the church and in particular with the monasteries. In the sixteenth century the problem of poverty became urgent: the monasteries no longer existed and the first great price rise in British history took place between 1540 and 1640. The poor fell into two categories – those who couldn't work and those who wouldn't work, or to put it another way into the 'deserving poor' and 'rogues, vagabonds and sturdy beggars' who figure in much Elizabethan literature.

Late sixteenth parliaments passed innumerable statutes to control both but it was not until the end of the reign of Elizabeth I that the Poor Law of 1601 created the framework which lasted for more than two centuries. It placed responsibility for the poor firmly on the parish which, under an act of 1572, was already required to appoint two Overseers of the Poor. Their responsibility included assessing and collecting the poor rate and using it to meet the needs of the deserving poor either by distributing relief or by setting the poor to work. The Overseers were appointed annually and the county Justices of the Peace in Quarter Sessions supervised the system. Every contingency was covered: the old, widows, women giving birth to bastard children, orphan or pauper children, illness including epidemics and death. Records of the Overseers of the Poor are among the most frequently kept in the parish and provide invaluable information about this important section of the population. Only Warnford among the parishes of the Meon valley lacks records of the Overseers and records of the church-wardens have not survived either.[1]

In 1662 came the first of several measures establishing the law of settlement. This was designed to ensure that responsibility for the poor should rest on the parish in which they were born. Strangers could be removed unless they had rented a tenement worth £10 per year, held a parish office or could find someone who was prepared to be responsible for their upkeep. Until 1794 people could be moved on if they seemed likely to become chargeable; after 1794 they could only be sent back to their birth parish when they became chargeable. In 1749 the overseers of Soberton moved on Nicholas Harding, his wife Elizabeth and their six children aged 11, 8, 7, 3 and 18 months since they 'are lately intruded and come into the parish of Soberton and are likely to become chargeable … we adjudge that the place of their last legal settlement to be Southley in the county of Devon'. They were 'to be removed and conveyed from out of the parish of Soberton to the said parish of Southley'. Nor was this an isolated case. Removals under the law of settlement were frequent: the Overseers of East Meon returned William and Mary Pook to Soberton, the Overseers of Soberton sent Frances Painter back to Droxford, Charles Harfoot and family to Hambledon, Thomas Stones to Fareham and in return Widow Mary Hooker was returned to Soberton.

An act of 1722 allowed parishes to 'lodge, keep, maintain and employ' the poor and so children could be apprenticed and taught a trade. In Soberton the Overseers adopted this solution. In 1802 Thomas Upton, a boy of 14, was apprenticed to the Rector, Edmund Poulter 'with him to dwell and serve until he accomplish his full age of 19 years. He shall serve his master in all lawful business according to his Power, Wit and Ability and honestly, orderly and obediently, in all things demean and behave himself. The Rector shall provide and allow meet, competent and sufficient Meat, Drink, Apparel, Lodging, Washing and other things necessary and fit'. Hannah Strotten, a child of eight, was apprenticed to Giles Osborne 'to dwell and serve until she be 21 years or the time of her marriage', to be trained 'in the art, skill and mystery of Housewifery'. Ten year later Hannah appears in the records of Warnford when she and her expected child were allowed to settle there

The act of 1722 also authorised parishes to provide for the poor by setting up a work-house. East Meon had one of the early workhouses provided in 1727 by adapting a row of cottages in what is still known as Workhouse Lane. It remained in use until, like all similar parish workhouses, it was made redundant by the provision of a Union Workhouse, in this case at Petersfield. It remained in existence though disused until burnt down in a fire in 1910.[2] In the parish of Droxford the capital from four charities was used to buy four cottages in Horders Wood as a workhouse. In 1822 this was replaced by a rented house north of *The Hunters Inn* at Swanmore which was marked as the 'Old Poor House' on the tithe map in 1842.[3] At Wickham a building in the north of the parish was bought for £800 in 1798 to accommodate 27 paupers and a governor was appointed and paid £21 per year. The parish bought a loom and flax and wool so that the paupers could be engaged in productive work.[4] At West Meon the overseers required those in receipt of poor relief to wear a badge embossed with the letters WP which stood for 'West Meon Pauper', described as 'badging the poor'. The parish provided a poor house in a paddock between the end of what was later called Doctors Lane and the west of what became the embankment built to carry the Meon Valley Railway.[5] At Soberton a workhouse was opened in a building rented from Mr Minchin at Taplands Corner.[6]

From the end of the seventeenth century many villages provided a Pest House in order to isolate the victims, usually of smallpox in the eighteenth century and of cholera in the nineteenth century. The pest house was built or provided in an isolated place where victims were unlikely to pass on the disease. At East Meon a purpose-built pest house was provided at Stroud some distance from the village centre. It too became redundant when replaced by the isolation ward at Petersfield Union Workhouse. The house survives and is now called Mount Pleasant Farm.[7] At West Meon too the houses used to isolate the poor are still marked on the Ordnance Survey map and lie close to the A272 on the northern outskirts of the parish. Titchfield like other parishes had both a workhouse and a pest house.

Bastardy was a problem in Soberton as in most parishes. If possible the father of the child was identified and made responsible for the upkeep of the child. If he was single then he was made to marry the girl, if married then he must pay what we should call maintenance. In 1815 Martha Jones of Soberton gave birth to a girl and James Barton owned up to being the father. He paid 40/- towards the cost of the birth, 9/- for an order of filiation and was expected to pay 2/- per week thereafter whilst Martha paid 6d.per week to the Overseers as insurance in case she proved unable to look after the child. [8] Although the man responsible for the child rarely accepted responsibility at once, village gossip was often sufficient to identify him. In 1754 Elizabeth Lambert of Soberton was pregnant and the Overseers brought Thomas Quinton of Corhampton before the Justices. [9]

The responsibilities of the Overseers included payment from the poor rate for recruitment to the militia undertaken by the Parish Constable. In the second half of the eighteenth century Britain was frequently at war, usually with France, and the army and navy needed to be reinforced. Service was encouraged with financial inducements. Militia men were selected by ballot. They could provide a substitute or plead hardship and be excused. If they opted to serve, the family might receive support from the poor rate. At Soberton Mary Ann Jurd received 4/6 a week while her husband Richard was serving, though the payment would cease if she followed the regiment and left her children, unless she received a permit allowing her to do so.[10]

The Overseers interpreted their role generously, provided a welfare safety net for the poor of the parish and oiled the wheels of village life. Frances Collins points out that in the parish of Soberton they ensured a decent burial for the poor, for example providing beer at the funeral of Widow Burrell. They kept the pound in repair, paid Dame Webb for nursing the sick, mended the bridges at Rudley Mill and Cuttbridge and paid John Holland for repairing the church clock.[11]

In addition to the work of the statutory Overseers the parson and well-to-do laity continued to accept some responsibility for the welfare of the village and many boards erected in churches record money or land left to be invested and used for the relief of poverty frequently at the discretion of the parson.

*   *   *

In the second half of the eighteenth century the Poor Rate rose inexorably and the office of Overseer became even more unpopular. In 1771 the Vestry at West Meon agreed that every landowner 'shall take each his turn … and every Person (except widows), are to serve the Office themselves and not by Substitute or Deputy.' At West Meon the amount distributed in poor relief rose from £105 in 1763 to £276 in 1789 and to no less than £457 in 1802–3, a rise of over 400% in 40 years. A combination of factors accounted for the increase. Prices increased by about 60% whilst wages rose by only about 25%.[12] Mechanisation of agriculture meant that fewer people were needed so unemployment rose. Poaching which might have afforded some relief was illegal and this is the period when in order to protect their property the landed gentry had little compunction about using the notorious and vicious man traps. At the end of the Napoleonic Wars in 1815 there was a series of poor harvests, unemployment rose further and wages were depressed. Labourers lived in extreme poverty whilst the landed classes appeared to flourish causing deep resentment.

Agricultural labourers were driven to desperation and there were riots throughout southern England in 1830, often called the 'Swing' Riots, allegedly led by the mysterious Captain Swing, and caused by general distress. On large estates where quantities of grain had to be processed it made economic sense to invest in the new threshing machines and this in turn was a major cause of unrest in 1830. They were hated because threshing by hand using a flail might be inefficient but it provided work for farm hands during the winter months.[13] The aims of the movement were to increase wages to enable a man to support his family, to end the use of threshing machines and so increase the amount of work available, to achieve a guaranteed rate of poor relief, to force landlords to lower farm rents and sometimes to abolish tithes.

Trouble began in Kent in August 1830. It reached Hampshire and in November there were riots at Emsworth, Havant and Gosport. The men carried axes and sledge-hammers and destroyed threshing machines. On Monday 15th November farmers in Exton received menacing letters and by the end of the week there were threats against threshing machines and demands for higher wages at Warnford and West Meon. During the following week riots broke out at Wickham, machine breaking took place at Droxford and there were demands for higher wages at Titchfield.[14]

The ring leaders were arrested and brought before a specially summoned Commission of Assize at Winchester. There were 245 prisoners in Winchester gaol, mostly men under 35. Benjamin Harding of Corhampton was sentenced to death though the death penalty was later commuted to transportation for life to Australia. Two of the prisoners, James Cooke of Fordingbridge and Henry Cook of Micheldever, were hanged at Winchester gaol on 15th January 1831.[15] Nationally 19 men were hanged, 644 imprisoned and 481 transported.[16] The events of 1830 hastened the end of the old poor law.

The early 1830s were a grim period not least because of the fear of cholera. The recently appointed rector of Exton William Dunsantoy followed his predecessor's example in recording in the parish register his comments on current events. On Wednesday 21st March 1832 he wrote 'Set apart in this parish and all others throughout England and Ireland as a general fast day to supplicate the divine Majesty to remove from our land the most grievous disease called Cholera Morbus heretofore unknown among us; when a most suitable discourse was delivered on the occasion by the Revd. Able Chapman then Curate of this parish'.

Fifteen years later there was another public fast in Exton occasioned by the Irish potato famine. There was 'a grievous scarcity and dearth of divers articles of sustenance and necessaries of life' which during the last two years had been 'most severely felt [in Ireland] so much as to cause the Death of hundreds of its inhabitants and also thousands to emigrate to other parts of the empire in order if possible to evade this heavy judgement now around them.'[17] In England at least conditions were beginning to improve.

8

Church and School in the Eighteenth Century

❦

THE CHURCH OF ENGLAND in the eighteenth century has become, not without justification, a byword for laxity and complacency if not actual corruption. The diocese of Winchester established a tradition of inefficiency early in the century and successive bishops maintained the tradition. Reform began only when Charles Sumner became bishop in 1827.

The bishop, appointed by the Crown, carried out a Primary Visitation of his diocese soon after his arrival. The responses elicited to the preliminary questions addressed to incumbents by three bishops of Winchester have been published, for the Visitations carried out by Richard Willis (bishop 1723–34) in 1725, by John Thomas (bishop 1761–81) in 1765 and Brownlow North (bishop 1781–1820) in 1788. Despite many omissions and inadequacies they provide much information about the state of the church in Hampshire, including the Meon valley, in the eighteenth century.[1] The Droxford deanery was one of nine in Hampshire and included 32 parishes covering almost the whole of what in 1927 became the mainland part of the Portsmouth diocese. Of the three enquiries the one made in preparation for the visitation of Richard Willis in 1725 produced responses from all the parishes of the Meon valley. In 1765 the replies of only five Meon valley parishes have survived. In 1788 six replies are recorded, some of which were full and detailed others less so. In 1725 William Hailes the curate of Titchfield provided a good deal of information; others were less forthcoming: David Lewis the curate of 'Subberton' (*sic*) was one whose response was laconic. He wrote 'All things well'.[2]

Authorities in church and state were interested in the number of 'papists' and Protestant dissenters to be found in the parish, both categories regarded as potentially subversive if not actually disloyal. In the Meon valley there were few Catholics or Protestant Dissenters. At Titchfield in 1725 there were two women who were papists but 'they are of no estate or consequence'. Although there was no meeting house there were 'about 30 Presbyterians and Anabaptists, so called'. By 1788 there were in Titchfield no papists and 'not more than 8 or 10 persons supposed to be dissenters'. There was apparently a Roman Catholic chapel at Soberton and the number of papists 'about 39'. In West Meon in 1725 there were two Anabaptists and in East Meon 'one protestant dissenter who is of the Presbyterian perswasion' *(sic)*.

The Enquiry of 1725 provides information about the existence of schools for which the Church of England.was responsible There were it seems many fewer in the Winchester diocese than elsewhere.[3] At Titchfield there were two schools, one run by Clement Walcot who was paid £10 to teach 12 boys 'to read, write and cast accounts', whilst Dame Adams received £4 to teach the same number 'the English tongue'. There is no indication whether Dame Adams's pupils were boys, girls or both. At Wickham there was an unendowed school where Charles Ford taught 20 scholars. At Meonstoke and Soberton there was no school, but the rector Abraham Markland paid for the schooling of 12 children who were taught to read. Corhampton was well provided. Michael Ainsworth the curate of both Soberton and Corhampton must have had his hands full since in addition he was 'obliged to teach 8 boys to read and write and arithmetick'*(sic)*. There were apparently 'upwards of 30 scholars in the school' of whom 18 boarded with the master in his house, described as 'a mansion house'. (Mansion house was already archaic as the name for a dwelling house.) At West Meon William Chase, clerk of the parish 'instructs the children (few in number) to read, write and cast accompts'*(sic)*. In East Meon there was no 'publick school endowed' though at Froxfield, also in the parish, 'Robert Love of Basing Esq. Late deceased' had left £1000 for the endowment of a charity school.

No question about schools was included in the preliminary information collected for Bishop John Thomas's Visitation in 1765. The 1788 returns show little improvement in the provision of education in the previous 60 years. There may of course have been Dame Schools where some children received a rudimentary education for which their parents paid. The enquiry was only concerned with those schools receiving endowment from Church of England sources. At Titchfield there was an endowed school where Mary Petty, nominated by the churchwardens and the overseers of the poor, taught 12 poor children 'to read the English tongue'. At Soberton a schoolmistress was paid by subscription to educate seven poor children whilst at Corhampton there was a charity school where eight day boys were instructed in reading, writing and 'arithmetick'. The perpetual curate William Davis was also schoolmaster and in this dual capacity received £49 but there is no indication who, where or what he taught though he lived in a free school house near the church. The remaining villages – Exton, West Meon, East Meon and Steep – had no endowed school. We can reasonably conclude that it was only the few who received free education during the eighteenth century and then only for a short period.

Only in the Visitation of 1765 were questions asked about Sunday services. Each church held a morning service which consisted of Morning Prayer, the Litany and Ante-Communion as well as a sermon which might be composed by the incumbent or be drawn from a book of sermons published by a well known divine. It was expected to last between half an hour and an hour. The eighteenth century church was an auditorium with a more prominent place accorded to the three-decker pulpit than to the altar. The bottom tier was occupied by the clerk who led the responses and might 'line-out' the Psalms for a largely illiterate congregation. The second tier was occupied by

27. Meonstoke House, the Rectory of Meonstoke & Soberton to 1897.
Georgian with Victorian wings.

the parson from which he took the service wearing a surplice. For the sermon he would occupy the top tier of the reading desk and wear a black gown and bands, a reminder of the preaching tradition of the Protestant Reformation.

If there were a second service the parson was described as doing 'double duty' and the service would be Evening Prayer and sermon held, in country parishes usually in the afternoon and preceded or followed by catechising of the children. Hymns were illegal in the worship of the Church of England until 1820, so singing led by 'the singers' consisted of metrical Psalms to the tunes of *Tate and Brady*. Holy Communion took place usually three or four times a year – Christmas, Easter, Whitsun and some-times Michaelmas. – occasionally monthly, at the end of morning service.

The Articles of Enquiry in the Winchester diocese in 1765 included two questions about services: First, *Is divine service performed in your church twice on every Sunday? If not declare the reason for such omission.* Second, *Is the sacrament administered so often in each year that every parishioner may receive the communion at least three times?* The Meon valley churches provided scant evidence. The questions lent themselves to the answer

'Yes', with no further elaboration though respondents sometimes provided corroboration. At Titchfield there were two services on a Sunday, at Crofton one. At Corhampton 'once a fortnight during the summer season since the endowment is small' whilst the sacrament was provided 'once a year only'. At East Meon the sacrament was provided on five occasions during the year.

The returns for the county of Hampshire provide rather more information. One service a Sunday was sometimes justified on account of 'ancient custom' or because a curate was serving two parishes and held one service in each church or by the small endowment. Of incumbents who provide specific information just over half held two services, under half one and about 8% one service every two weeks. The usual number of Communion services in Hampshire churches was four each year. Twenty four churches held four, seven churches held only three and five held five. Nine churches held a monthly Communion most of them in the towns of Winchester, Southampton and Portsmouth.[4]

*   *   *

From the sixteenth century to the nineteenth century the concerns of the bishop were not only with the church building It was he who licensed lay men and women to undertake a variety of trades and professions. He was also the arbiter of morals and it was the duty of his emissaries to ensure that all attended church. There are many examples of the range of his powers in the villages of the Meon valley. At Corhampton in November 1734 John Upton was given a licence to teach at the Free School and on his death William Davis was licensed to succeed him. In September 1742 Elizabeth, the wife of John Newman, was licensed as a midwife. A century earlier the Uvedale household living at Place House, Wickham were allowed to eat meat during Lent – a privilege likely to be accorded only to the well-to-do.

If licences were required to perform a variety of functions then the bishop was also empowered to apply sanctions against offenders. Adultery and a variety of other sexual offences appear frequently in the bishops' registers. Joan Roach of East Meon had no fewer than five bastards. She had apparently often been presented but had not been punished. In the same parish Judith Mee never came to church. The curate of Privett had not preached the minimum number of four sermons in the year, another parishioner had refused to pay church rate and others had, it appeared, been working on St Bartholomew's Day.[4]

*   *   *

There was less church building in the eighteenth century than in any other. The amenity most often added was one or more galleries which made the building dark and sometimes threatened the stability of the structure. Most galleries were removed in nineteenth century restoration. There were two motives for the building of galleries.

The 'singers', predecessors of the choir, wanted to sit together so that they could sing the psalms, a fashion which spread from parish to parish and a move not always approved of by incumbents. The second motive was the desire of families to own a pew. Even if they didn't occupy it every Sunday they liked to feel that it was their property. At Droxford two galleries were built the first in 1766 at the west end of the church with seven pews and the second in 1788 constructed over the chancel arch for the singers. What it looked like or how it was reached we unfortunately do not know. Only three years earlier the Vestry had decided that it did not want an organ and had returned to the donor the instrument which they had been given. In 1789 the rector Dr Chelsum presented an organ and this time it was accepted though it was a barrel organ with two barrels and so would, unlike the organ of 1785, not require an organist.

At Exton the gallery had a short life. It was built in two parts: the first for the singers at the expense of the rector (John Baynes rector 1794–1831) in 1806. Three years later it was extended across the church partly at the expense of the rector and partly by Sir Thomas Champneys who also built the staircase.[6] In 1834 the next rector, William Dunsantoy (rector 1831–61) provided the church with an organ. In 1847 the church was closed for a year and largely rebuilt at the expense of two generous ladies – Mary Touchet and her niece Mrs Ffarington and the galleries were demolished.[7]

Burials in the church itself continued until well into the eighteenth century. At Droxford Dr Peter Nourse (rector 1701–22) was buried in the chancel and Dr James Cutler (rector 1746–82) in the south aisle.

9

Enclosure

THE OPEN OR COMMON field organisation of the countryside in the middle ages is one of the most popular themes of school history. Equally frequently taught is its replacement in the eighteenth century by enclosure initiated by act of parliament, when the landscape as we know it, with isolated farmsteads and small fields separated by hedges, came into existence. Both generalisations are broadly true but both need to be qualified. Open fields were typical of the midlands and central southern England of which Hampshire and the Meon valley were part, but not of the remainder of the country. There were a variety of organisations, particularly in large parishes where each tithing had its field system. Enclosure was a much more complex process taking place over a long period and by a variety of means than school generalisation allows.[1]

In the early middle ages peasant farmers lived in the villages of the Meon valley in dwellings made of wattle and daub surrounded by crofts where they grew crops for their own use. They went out each day to work on strips in large open fields, some of which belonged to the lord of the manor where they were obliged to labour for so many days per year. In addition each had his own strips allocated each year by the manorial court growing crops, usually barley and wheat, also uniform for the whole village. All had in addition rights of pasture on the commons and in forest, heath and moor. As the population grew from about 900 AD to about 1300 additional lands – assarts – were taken into cultivation and sometimes these too became open fields. It was a method of agriculture for subsistence rather than growth and before the end of the fourteenth century enterprising peasants favoured enclosure which would give them more freedom to capitalise on their land.

There were four ways in which enclosure could take place. If all parties reached an understanding then enclosure would happen by agreement. Second, the lord of the manor might obtain all the land previously held by his tenants and could enclose it. Third, there might be a formal agreement between all the landholders and the land be divided between them. The process was often a slow one taking place over centuries.

In the documents which remain we have only hints of the process of enclosure of arable fields before the eighteenth century. At Titchfield for example the arable fields were never formally enclosed, but by 1550 the open field system was in a state of decay. There were common fields it seems at Posbrook and Meon.[2] At Lomer in 1381 the parson's glebe was described, his 45 acres of arable was spread through six fields though much of it was consolidated in two blocks of 16 acres each – the beginning of enclosure it seems. He was also entitled to pasture one ox and 30 sheep.[3] Of the 61 formal agreements affecting parishes in Hampshire listed by Chapman and Seeliger, only one was in the Meon valley – for East Meon dated 1661.

There is however a further distinction to be made; between the enclosure of arable fields which took place earlier and the enclosure of commons which was accomplished mostly in the nineteenth century and nearly always by act of parliament. Almost all the enclosure acts affecting the villages of the Meon valley were passed in the middle of the nineteenth century and most of them in a single decade, the 1850s – East Meon 1845 and 1856, Droxford 1851, Meonstoke 1856, Soberton 1858 and Titchfield for which there are four awards all dated 1859. Alverstoke, once part of the ancient parish of Titchfield, is the last listed enclosure in Hampshire, dated 1887. With the exception of Corhampton, Exton and West Meon all the villages of the Meon valley were at some time subject to parliamentary enclosure. None of these was concerned with arable fields but with the commons which had remained unenclosed. The date is that of the passage of the enclosure act through parliament; the process of enclosure was complex and often took several years to complete.[4]

The fourth means of enclosure, parliamentary enclosure, was more complicated than the other methods but also more watertight. Until 1836 a separate act of parliament was needed for each parish. From 1836–45 enclosure could take place provided the owners of two thirds of the land agreed. From 1845 parliament resumed control. Inclosure Commissioners ('Inclosure' was now officially spelt with an I.) were appointed and operated under criteria laid down by parliament. Inclosure must pay for itself by sale of some of the land so as to defray costs, provision must be made for endowing the parish church and the school, recreation ground and allotments were provided for 'the labouring poor', roads must be provided and their width was specified in the scheme. By the 1870s there was concern about the loss of commons and open spaces and preservation replaced further enclosure.

Medieval field systems have now gone beyond recall. In the larger parishes each tithing once had its field system. In the ancient parish of Droxford for example there were separate field systems at Hill, Shedfield and Swanmore as well as Droxford itself. Many of the open arable field systems in the Meon valley had been replaced by enclosed fields by the Tudor period and almost all by the mid-eighteenth century. Evidence for the common fields survives in the names of fields and sometimes in the shape of small fields to be found on the tithe map made for each parish as a result of the Tithe Commutation Act of 1836. Long, thin, hedged fields were often derived from the enclosed strips in the open fields. In the parish of Droxford there are references to West Field and North Field in 1794 which Chapman and Seeliger say were then 'probably in process of informal enclosure'. At Midlington there was a common field in 1628 whilst Great Field and Mayhill Field are shown on the tithe apportionment of 1841. Exton was still in open fields in 1730. Common fields are named and some survived until the tithe map of 1841.

The nineteenth century saw the enclosure by commissioners appointed under the

General Enclosure Act of a substantial number of the commons in the parishes of the Meon valley.[5] Under the Droxford award dated 1851, 1199 acres was enclosed. This included much of Waltham Chase or Horders Wood, a huge area mostly falling in the newly created ecclesiastical parishes of Shedfield and Swanmore.[6]

Meonstoke Down was enclosed under an award made in 1856 though not implemented until 1863, for which Charles Pink was the valuer. About one third of the parish was enclosed, over 670 acres altogether most of it the less productive land in the east of the parish above the 300 foot contour. Land was allotted to 38 people three of whom gained substantial amounts. Henry Wooldridge held 391 acres and was allocated a further 152 acres. Laura Lomax who owned Stocks Farm comprising 284 acres was allocated a further 113 acres whilst Charles Sartoris, the owner of Warnford Park, bought 80 acres for £1000 with which the award was financed. The award appears to have benefited most the smaller copyholder: the largest were awarded about half of their present holding, medium landowners over half whilst the smallest holders were awarded about the same amount as they already owned or even more. The smallest awards were ¼ acre. Only copyholders were entitled to land so for example George Foster who farmed 72 acres at Stocks Farm, Warnford but did not own the land received nothing from the award. The award made provision for land for allotments 'for the labouring poor' and 4½ acres for a recreation ground as well as indicating the roads which were to be provided.

The four awards for the old parish of Titchfield ran in a semi-circle south-west and north-west of the village of Titchfield and included the substantial area of Titchfield Common as well as part of Swanwick Heath and Sarisbury Common, covering a total of 1150 acres leaving 140 acres unenclosed. It was the enclosure of the commons of the parish and the advent of a large number of smallholders which provided the stimulus for the strawberry industry in Titchfield and the neighbouring parishes (see pages 185, 205, 226).

*   *   *

The Forest of Bere was one of the last royal forests to be disafforested. A royal commission set up in 1785 reported in favour of the removal of Forest Laws from Bere Forest and this was accomplished by act of parliament in 1812. Land was sold to defray expenses and the remaining land allocated to commoners.[7] Thomas Thistlethwaite the owner of the Southwick estate was awarded 517 acres which still remain in his family. Today the largest block of woodland in the Forest is the so called 'West Walk' to the east of the A32 north of Wickham which is administered by the Forestry Commission. There are tantalising glimpses of the past for example a massive earthwork now hidden in dense undergrowth which was the dam of a medieval fishpond. There are ancient trees, for example the thousand-year old 'Bere Oak' its girth now almost ten metres and its height over 19 metres, thought to be an ancient boundary marker, or because of its location on the highest point in the forest, a tree connected originally with Anglo-Saxon ritual and perhaps where once a Saxon hundred court met.

* * *

Summarising the effect of enclosure Hoskins comments 'The enclosure movement in all its forms was the last great revolution in the English landscape, radically changing much of the countryside as it took place. It also gave us a landscape which is much more pleasing to most people'.[8] What Hoskins says about England as a whole is certainly true of the landscape of the Meon valley.

10

Workhouse, the Asylum and the Police

N O N I N E T E E N T H C E N T U R Y institution has left such a profound mark on the national consciousness as the workhouse. Established for unions of parishes in the late 1830s workhouses survived into the twentieth century though their rigour was gradually mitigated. Even today there are hospitals often in 'Union Road', originally built as workhouses, to which the stigma clings. Following the Reform Act of 1832 a Royal Commission was set up to investigate the Poor Law. The poor rate had grown astronomically, used to subsidise inadequate wages. Under the Poor Law Amendment Act of 1834 the poor law would no longer be administered by the parish. Instead three Poor Law Commissioners, 'the Bashaws of Somerset House', initially with Edwin Chadwick as their secretary, would administer a national scheme from London.

The country was divided into unions of parishes each required to provide a workhouse, nicknamed 'Bastilles', where the able bodied poor would receive relief. 'Outdoor relief' would be abolished and the test of 'less eligibility' applied -conditions were to be harsher in the workhouse than they were outside so as to remove any incentive to enter the workhouse. It was the greatest change in poor law administration for over 230 years and neither the poor nor many in the parishes from which they came liked it. But it could have been worse – Malthusians would like to have abolished the poor law altogether. By 1841 there were no less than 586 unions nationally and 320 new workhouses had been built.[1]

In Hampshire there were 27 unions of parishes and most of them built a new workhouse. The villages of the Meon valley came under three unions. The workhouse built at Droxford and opened in 1837 cost £5,837 and included five acres of garden. It served the Meon valley parishes of Corhampton, Droxford, Exton, Meonstoke, Soberton, Warnford and West Meon (as well as parishes which fell outside the Meon valley – Bishop's Waltham, Durley, Hambledon and Upham).[2] East Meon was served by a workhouse built at Petersfield whilst Wickham and Titchfield were part of the Fareham Union where a workhouse was built and opened in 1836. Today it is the only one of the three still standing, now part of St Christopher's hospital.

The first task of the newly appointed Poor Law Guardians, two for each parish, was to consolidate provision for the poor, closing parish workhouses and building one large enough to house all who in future would have access to relief only through the workhouse.[3] At Titchfield the Poor House in Mill Street was closed in 1836 and its remaining inmates transferred to the new workhouse at Fareham. The contents were

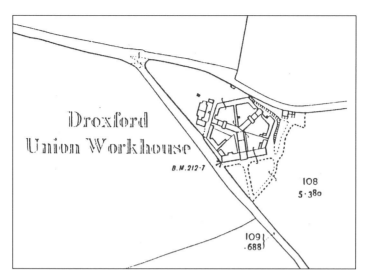

28. Site and plan of the Droxford Union Workhouse designed by Sampson Kempthorne on OS map 1908-09.

sold – 51 low bedsteads, an 80 gallon copper, a stone salt mill and intriguingly a man trap. [4] In East Meon likewise the familiar building in the road still known as Workhouse Lane was closed in 1836.[5]

The Poor Law Guardians of the Droxford Union met for the first time at *The White Horse* at Droxford on Christmas Eve 1835 and thereafter fortnightly, under the chairmanship of Robert Hatch Stares, a substantial landowner and farmer in Droxford who lived on the corner of North End Lane and the turnpike road to London.[6] The site of the proposed workhouse had already been selected and its current lessee Louis James Lovekin, a doctor from Droxford, had agreed to release for the purpose Gibbs Croft in what was later named Union Lane.[7]

There was much to be done. The new 'dietary system' laid down by the Poor Law Commissioners in London must be implemented in the existing workhouses from 1st January 1836. Decisions must be made about the future of the four parish poor houses – at Droxford, Soberton, Hambledon and Bishop's Waltham – which the Guardians inherited. It was decided to close the poor house at Soberton at once and to transfer the 19 paupers housed there to Hambledon. The remaining three houses would remain open for the moment but there would be rationalisation: children under 13 would be kept at Bishop's Waltham, the old (over 60) and those 'partly idiots' would be placed at Droxford and the able bodied would be accommodated at Hambledon.

In May 1836 the Guardians undertook further standardisation. They ordered 25 men's suits of grey cloth at 18/- per suit and 20 boys' suits at 13/- each, 100 pairs of half boots in various sizes at 5/- per pair and 100 yards of grosgrain at 7½ d. per yard, to be made up into dresses for female paupers. Even more macabre, coffins were ordered in bulk. For infants they paid 5/- per coffin, for children under ten 10/-, children between 10 and 15 12/-, and for adults 16/-.[8] Funerals were to be of the simplest. The cost of coffin and burial fee would be met by the Guardians but they would not pay for a pall over the coffin nor for the church bell to be tolled. In the following year they resolved to build 'a small hearse' pulled by one horse or by four men which could be used, depending on the distance involved,' to convey the dead to their respective parishes'.[9]

The new workhouse was put on hold because there was a shortage of bricks.[10] In any case the Guardians had contracted with the Fareham Guardians to accommodate 100 'healthy paupers' from the Droxford Union for a year from Michaelmas 1836 in their newly opened workhouse, a period later extended to October 1837 when the new Droxford workhouse was ready to receive its first inmates. Droxford and Bishop's Waltham poor houses were now to be closed. The master of the Droxford poorhouse, John Evans, and his wife were to be allowed to remain in the house and in future John would be schoolmaster and porter, paid 8/- per week and his wife 6/-. (By 1841 he was only porter.)

The Guardians were given two other tasks by the government. Under the Tithe Commutation Act passed in 1836 each parish was to be surveyed and the Guardians were to be responsible for arranging for this to be done. The year 1837 also saw the beginning of secular Registration of Births, Marriages and Deaths also to be under-taken by of the Guardians. They appointed a Superintendent Registrar for each of the districts into which the union was divided.[11]

The Guardians appointed Sampson Kempthorne architect of the new workhouse. He was responsible for designing a large number of workhouses and became the official architect to the Poor Law Commissioners. At Droxford he designed the work-house using the 'hexagon' model – a central hub from which three wings radiated. From the central hub the master could watch all the paupers when they were in the exercise yards although each class of inmate occupied its own yard – able, infirm, male, female, children and adults – segregated from one another at least in the early years. It was a system in vogue for prisons as well as workhouses. After a year's delay the new workhouse was at last built and the Guardians met there for the first time on 5th September 1837. Four parish poor houses had been closed and the new union work-house opened in little more than two years.

Conditions in the workhouse were Spartan. The Commissioners' permission was needed to increase the food allocation and in October 1837 they agreed to an increase in the amount of bread from 12 ounces to 16 ounces per day for men and from 10 ounces to 14 ounces for women.[12] In the early days men and boys slept in single beds in two tiers, women and girls shared double beds; only the sick and infirm enjoyed the luxury of single beds in a single tier. On admission all were stripped of their own clothes, examined by the medical officer, dressed in workhouse garments and assigned to a ward. A 'dead house' or mortuary was sited in the men's and boys' yard. Tobacco was prohibited to able-bodied men between the ages of 16 and 60.[13] Work included oakum picking and sack making. Like many workhouses the Guardians erected a bone mill which would facilitate 'bone crushing'.[14] It was however banned after the Andover workhouse scandal when famished paupers were found to be eating scraps of flesh on the animal bones which they were set to crush. The minutes record women with bastard children absconding from the workhouse leaving the children behind.

The workhouse accommodated mostly the old who had nobody to care for them and the very young. It provided for the poor for almost a century. Although built to accommodate 200 the Droxford workhouse was never full and often not much more than half full. In 1841 there were 114 inmates; 24 were over 60 and no less than 41 were aged 10 and younger. In a few cases a whole family was consigned to the workhouse. Sarah Kiln a young woman of 30 was there with 8 children: Rebecca (10), Charlot (*sic)* (9), Ann (7), Jane (6), Emma (5), James (4), Eliza (3) and Mary (1). What had happened to father – death or desertion? But whatever had happened the family was without support and the workhouse was the only recourse open to them.[15]

The workhouse was staffed by a master and matron (often husband and wife), cook, nurses and a gardner/handyman. There were schoolmaster and schoolmistress for the needs of the substantial proportion of the inmates who were of school age. The local doctor was medical officer and the rector of Droxford chaplain.[16] Men living at the workhouse cultivated the garden which supplied vegetables for the house whilst women helped with domestic chores. The kitchen was equipped with a range and a copper. Casual vagrants were provided with overnight accommodation but were required to work for two hours before leaving with bread and cheese provided for the day ahead – unappetising and often consigned to the hedgerow we are told.

There were no doubt examples of hardship or even brutality in some workhouses, particularly in the early years, but the harsh image of the workhouse owes much to the vivid pen of Charles Dickens. As time went on life in many workhouses was humanised. What should be the guiding principles of the workhouse was the subject of a perennial Victorian debate. They should be plain and austere thought some. There were critics of both 'pauper palaces' on the one hand and of 'bastilles' on the other. Sampson Kempthorne was thought to have got the blend right – he had avoided both extremes, providing neither prisons nor palaces for the poor.

At Droxford one family served as master and matron for a long period at the end of the nineteenth century. Alexander Lindsay was appointed schoolmaster in the work-house in 1880 and on the death of his father in 1884 he and Kate his wife became master and matron and remained in office until Alexander's death in August 1909 at the age of 52.[17] He was only 27 when he was appointed master and throughout his long reign enjoyed the confidence of successive Boards of Guardians. The regime over which the Lindsays presided did not conform to the usual image. Alexander was a considerable musician and formed a workhouse band, played the piano and organ, sang at home and at village concerts. There were flowers, photographs, pictures and attractive bedcovers. The workhouse may not have been luxurious but it was comfortable and homely. Alexander was also a keen gardener and there were roses and a fruit garden. Outings too by horse-drawn brake were arranged: to Hillhead and in 1897 to Stokes Bay to see the review of the fleet at the time of the Queen's Diamond Jubilee.[18]

The workhouse lasted until 1930. The problem of the poor became acute once more in the twentieth century but from 1906 there was an effective Labour Party and growing recognition that the plight of the poor was rarely their own fault. The early twentieth century saw the beginning of unemployment and sickness insurance which in effect reintroduced 'outdoor relief'. It was Neville Chamberlain, Minister of Health in Baldwin's Conservative government of 1924–9 who in 1929 introduced the Local Government Act which swept away 635 Poor Law Unions and transferred their buildings to the County Councils.

The Guardians of the Droxford Union held their last meeting on 11th March 1930 with no mention of their imminent demise. The Minutes simply remain unsigned.[19] Tenders for funerals were made to the end of March 1930 – for indoor poor they accepted a tender of £4-7-6 per adult and £2-2-6 per child and for outdoor poor £4-5-0 for an adult and £2-0-0 for a child. In March 1929 they agreed to buy 'shroud flannelette' at 7¾d. per yard, black cashmere stockings for £1-6-0 per dozen pairs, women's laced boots at 8/10½ per pair, men's grey shirts at 6/2½ each, men's cord

29. Alexander Lindsay Master of Droxford Union workhouse 1884–1909.

30. Old people in Droxford Union workhouse with matron and nurses.

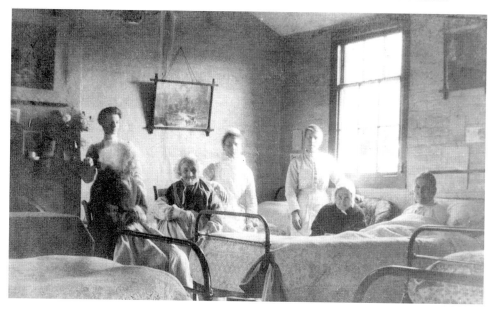

trousers at 11/8½ per pair, men's nail boots at 12/5 per pair and men's tweed caps at 11/6 per dozen. The new nurse to be appointed would be paid £45 per annum. All made it sound as though things would continue as usual.

After closure the Droxford workhouse stood for a further 40 years. Renamed Waltham House it fulfilled a variety of functions. It was it seems for a time an old peoples home run by the County Council. During the Second World War it was used to billet evacuees from bombing in Portsmouth and Southampton. It was later a store for civil defence equipment and then for Education Committee stock. Its last use seems to have been as a mortuary for victims of road accidents on the A32. In 1973 it was demolished without announcement, the ground sold by the County Council and houses built on the site[20] Had it survived only a few more years such cavalier treatment of a historic landmark would not have been possible. It would have been listed and like the asylum at Knowle an alternative use found for the building. Not surprisingly there are few photographs of the workhouse – neither inmates nor their relations wanted a memento.

*   *   *

An act of parliament passed in 1846 required each county to provide at least one asylum for 'pauper lunatics' as part of its responsibilities under the Poor Law. In 1851 there were three private asylums in Hampshire catering for 180 patients and many more pauper lunatics were kept in union workhouses.[21] The Hampshire Justices originally intended to meet their new obligation by building an asylum at Hollam Hill in Titchfield parish but local landowners objected. When a site at Knowle Farm was offered for sale the Justices bought 105 acres for £5,500 and erected a building at a further cost of £15,000, intended at first for 400 inmates. It had the advantage that its relative isolation meant that nobody need feel threatened by its existence.

It was known throughout the nineteenth century as The Hampshire County Lunatic Asylum and was one of the earliest asylums in the south of England as well as one of the largest. It is nonetheless perhaps the least known institution in the Meon valley. We should not today use the terms pauper, lunatic, idiot or insane, whilst the word asylum has acquired a different meaning, a measure of our greater sensitivity to tragic aspects of human need though that was not entirely lacking even in mid-Victorian England: White's *Gazeteer and Directory of Hampshire* describes the new institution in 1859 as 'this large and well-conducted asylum for those afflicted with the worst of human maladies'.[22]

The asylum was built on an attractive and isolated site on the edge of Wickham, healthy and high up with views to the south over the Solent to the Isle of Wight. It was constructed of red brick, well-proportioned and well-planned but with no unnecessary expense. In the early years for example the internal walls were not plastered. Its contours were soon softened by the creeper which began to cover the walls. The Hampshire County Lunatic Asylum opened its doors in December 1852 and in the first year there was an average of 153 inmates. It grew rapidly. By 1868 there were 619 inmates, by 1881 there were 825 and the asylum was overcrowded. The number reached 1000 in 1883 and a second block was built. It was not until 1921 that the county opened a second asylum, Park Prewett near Basingstoke.

The Medical Superintendent and his family lived on the premises. Two early superintendents served for long period. Dr John Manley appointed in 1854 was followed in 1885 by Dr Thomas Worthington who retired in 1906. The Revd George Hodgson Mason was chaplain. Appointed in 1855 he served for almost as long. He lived at Wickham and came to the asylum daily, usually on horse back travelling on the only direct road, known then as Asylum Lane (now Mayles Lane), until blindness prevented his continuation in office. In 1879 a church was provided but it soon proved to be too small and in 1901 a new church was built and remains, a listed building, where services were held until the hospital closed. Meanwhile a chaplain's house was built in 1897.[23]

There was strict segregation by sex of both staff and patients reflecting the contemporary practice in workhouses and elsewhere. Only the Medical Superintendent, the chaplain and members of the management committee – all men of course – visited both halves. Even the isolation unit was segregated and in the new church men and women entered by separate doors. Though admission to the asylum was the responsibility of the Poor Law Guardians who paid about 11/- per week for each admission, the asylum was administered until 1888 by the county justices. It was as far as possible selfsupporting and grew much of its own food on the adjacent farm. The asylum made its own clothes and later generated its own electricity. It was also one of the earliest buildings in the Meon valley (other than the large houses) to have piped water, lavatories and a sewerage system. Until 1888 beer was served with each meal and this too was home brewed. (Beer was then a much safer drink than water which could easily become contaminated.) Many of the inmates worked on the farm, a form of therapy which was believed to aid recovery. They were not paid: labour was part of their contribution to their keep at the asylum. There were recreational facilities, band and bandstands, football and cricket teams.

There was a high turnover of staff who were poorly paid (£25 per year for men; £15–£17 for women) and worked long hours (6am to 10pm). Most were untrained: training for nurses was in its infancy in the nineteenth century. The Minutes of the Management Committee in 1886 record dissatisfaction with the nurses who 'displayed little intelligence, interest in their patients or tact in their management and were not well acquainted with their duties'. Soon afterwards the training of nurses began and they could obtain the Certificate of Proficiency in Nursing. Rules were strict – there must be no bad language, no force was to be used and staff were forbidden to receive gifts from patients or visitors. Inmates were provided with clothes made on the premises, not a uniform but utilitarian. Many patients were admitted, later discharged and after a time readmitted perhaps several times. Few stayed long enough to become institutionalised. Many entered the asylum in middle life.

31. Knowle Hospital opened 1852 closed 1996. The Administration Building.

Until late in the century children were not generally admitted to the asylum but in 1894 an Idiot Childrens' Block was opened and attached to the female section. There were unmarried mothers but fewer than mythology suggests and there was more tolerance than we have come to believe, of what was later described as 'moral turpitude'.

The years of the First World War were fraught with difficulty. Other asylums were closed in order to provide for the needs of wounded soldiers and their inmates sent to Knowle. Patients from Greylingwell at Chichester as well as asylums at Portsmouth and Oxford came to Knowle and by 1916 the number of patients had reached 1350. Fifty members of the staff served in the armed forces and 13 were killed.

By the 1920s life at Knowle was beginning to change. In 1923 the name was altered to Knowle Mental Hospital and in the same year a cinema was provided. Ten years later 'talkies' were introduced, wireless had arrived in 1924 and in 1927 the telephone. Basket making began in 1923, the forerunner of occupational therapy. In the mid-1930s the Idiot Children's Block was converted into a nurses' home. The Second World War again brought overcrowding and in 1947 there were 1142 patients. The advent of the National Health Service in 1948 brought another change of name, this time to Knowle Hospital.

Knowle Hospital closed in 1996 when government policy was to treat mental patients as far as possible in the community. For a time the buildings were surrounded by barbed wire to save them from vandalism. In the year 2000 53 acres of the site became Knowle Village with a road built from a new 'island' on the A32 between

Fareham and Wickham. The buildings of the hospital have been preserved as part of the overall plan of the village as has the church. The war memorial commemorating members of the staff and patients who died in the two world wars has been returned to the church. So far 550 houses and apartments have been provided but it seems likely that the next decade will see substantial further growth.[24]

*   *   *

The establishment of the metropolitan police in 1829 by Robert Peel is well known, less familiar are two later acts which led to the establishment of police forces in the country. The Rural Police Act of 1839 was permissive but Hampshire was nonetheless one of the first counties to implement the act and the Hampshire police force was created in December 1839. In 1856 came the County and Borough Police Act under which all counties were required to establish a police force.[25]

White's Gazetteer of Hampshire 1859 describes the police organisation in the county. The Chief Constable was Captain J.H.Forest who was paid £350 per year with a further £100 allowance for his horse. There were 16 Superintendents paid between £85 and £105 per year, one Inspector who received £65, 24 Sergeants on 23/- per week and 256 constables who earned between 17/- and 21/- per week. The force at Droxford was commanded by Superintendent Dore. In 1858 a handsome building with a green plaque on the front of the building was built as the police headquarters in the Meon valley. It was capable of accommodating the constables, providing for the 'temporary confinement of prisoners' and accommodating a Petty Sessional court. In 1905 the station sergeant at Droxford was William Padwick. [26]

The police headquarters in the Meon valley continued in Droxford and so did the court until the 1990s when the court was transferred to Fareham and the police head-quarters to Bishop's Waltham, though the building in Droxford survives. In addition from the end of the nineteenth century every village had its policeman changed about every two years to ensure that he did not become so familiar with villagers as to reduce his efficiency in maintaining law and order.

11

Roman Catholic and Protestant Dissent

꧁

THE YEAR 1660 saw the restoration not only of king and parliament but also of the Church of England. Protestant dissenters had lost and for the next quarter of a century were persecuted. Roman Catholics too were proscribed by law. James II's actions and in particular the birth of a son who would be brought up a Roman Catholic and eventually become king led to the king's flight to France in 1688. William and Mary, both Protestants, became joint king and queen.

The Toleration Act passed in 1689 allowed Protestant dissenters to worship in their own way though they were excluded from public office unless they received Holy Communion in the established church. Roman Catholics remained throughout the eighteenth century a semi-persecuted minority. People were reminded of their potential disloyalty by the two Jacobite risings of 1715 and 1745. As late as 1780 the Gordon Riots in London were caused by attempts by the government to give some civic rights to Roman Catholics.

In the meantime the Book of Common Prayer, reissued in 1662, included orders of service for 5th November, 30th January –'being the Day of the Martyrdom of the Blessed King Charles the First' – and for 29th May marking the end of 'the Great Rebellion by the Restitution of the King and Royal Family'. John Foxe's *Acts and Monuments* the first English edition of which was published in 1563 and usually called by the popular title *Foxe's Book of Martyrs* helped to keep alive the memory of the Marian martyrs in the minds of ordinary people. It was not until 1828 that the Test and Corporation Acts were repealed and the following year the Catholic Emancipation Act extended civic rights to Roman Catholics.

*   *   *

Frances Collins cites, as the earliest reference to dissent from the teaching of the church in the parish of Soberton, an entry in the register of Thomas Langton (bishop 1493–1501). In 1496 the register records an unnamed man who believed that a priest in mortal sin could not consecrate the elements at Mass. This she points out was the teaching of John Wycliffe (c. 1330–84) and suggests that Lollards, (contemptuously so nicknamed meaning 'mumblers who talked nonsense') the followers of John Wycliffe, were to be found in the Meon valley. Perhaps Lollard Bibles (the first translation into English of the Latin Vulgate) were circulating in the district and the matter was reported to the bishop by the curate in the absence of the rector.[1]

It was not however for almost a century that there is evidence of dissent from the Church of England (though not yet so named) in the Meon valley parishes. In February 1570 Pope Pius V declared Elizabeth I both heretic and usurper and urged her subjects to depose her. The hunt for papists was on and was to continue for a century and more, though varying in intensity and rigour. People were obliged to attend church and to receive communion on pain of fines and imprisonment. There were two kinds of recusant: 'church recusants' would attend services but refuse to receive communion whilst others would not attend the services of the Church of England at all.

The Roman Catholic centre in the Meon valley in the late sixteenth and early seventeenth century was the Manor House at Exton. This is the era of priests' holes, some real, others imaginary, where priests and the vessels they used to celebrate Mass could be hidden behind false doors or between floors. Those caught harbouring priests might be fined, imprisoned or executed. John Goldsmith who lived at Exton House was gaoled in October 1580 because his wife Susan, a member of the prominent catholic Tichborne family was 'obstinate in her Poperie' and the Goldsmiths were known to give shelter to priests beginning to arrive in England from France in the 1580s. John Goldsmith was however released in February 1581 because 'he had the ear of the council'. In 1592 he was fined 100 marks (£66, an enormous figure at the time) for hearing Mass and so was his son Peter who lived at Corhampton. Peter later went to Douai, was ordained priest at St Owers in 1601 and returned to England. By 1627 it seems that the Goldsmith family had been reconciled to the Church of England; there are many appearances of the family in later Exton Registers.

There were also a number of Roman Catholics at Meonstoke, Exton and Soberton, where particularly women were summoned to appear before the bishop's court.[2] In 1646 five Soberton residents were fined at Quarter Sessions for recusancy whilst the rector of Exton, Thomas Gawen, was deprived of the living and subsequently became a Roman Catholic. Returns for the Droxford deanery in 1603 do not support the view that Roman Catholic recusancy was a serious threat in the Meon valley. The total of 'papists' for the whole deanery was only 32 of whom 13 were to be found in Meonstoke, Soberton and Exton.[3] In 1676 the Compton Census found ten papists in Soberton and seven in East Meon.[4]

Robert Buckley (1517–1610) was the last surviving priest of the Abbey of Westminster, professed by Abbot John Feckenham in 1558 when the Abbey had been restored by Mary and before it was again suppressed by Elizabeth I. Father Buckley spent most of Elizabeth's reign in prison but was released by James I only to be arrested again in the aftermath of the Gunpowder Plot. Set free once more about 1608, perhaps on account of his great age, he spent his last years at Punsholt Farm on the northern edge of the parish of West Meon. He died on 22nd February 1610 and was buried under the stone floor of the chapel, later the kitchen and today the dining room of the farmhouse.[5]

From the seventeenth century Southend Farm close to the south-eastern boundary of Soberton was the base of a Jesuit mission to which many Roman Catholics came for Mass. When the Jesuits were suppressed by the pope in 1773 the mission was carried on by secular priests and continued in existence until 1839 when it was closed, though the erstwhile chapel remained in existence until 1959 when it was demolished – said to be unsafe as either barn or cattle shed. The dining room ceiling at Southend Farm contains plaster mouldings including *fleur de lys* said to have been made by Napoleonic prisoners from Portchester, grateful for the ministrations of Catholic priests during their incarceration.[6] After 1839 Catholic worship was available only in Petersfield until the coming of the White Fathers to Bishop's Waltham in 1912.[7]

*   *   *

Protestant dissent – Congregational, Presbyterian, Baptist, Quaker and from the mid-eighteenth century Methodist – is often ignored or undervalued by local historians. Its chapels are rarely architecturally distinguished and many have closed. Its records are less accessible than those of the Church of England whilst local historians are more often Anglican than members of one of the free churches. The diocesan enquiry of 1603 found only 27 Protestant dissenters in the whole of the Meon valley and they were mostly at Wickham (6), East Meon and Froxfield (15)

Yet from the late seventeenth century to the twentieth century Protestant dissenting chapels found a place in village life even though their members often felt under the shadow of the established church and were no more than tolerated by Anglican clergy. The Compton Census of 1676 was partly initiated to enquire what had been the effect of the Conventicle Act and the Five Mile Act passed in the early years of Charles II to restrict the activities of Protestant dissenters. In the Meon valley Protestant dissenting meetings were identified in the parish of Droxford (20 people were meeting according to the census) where there was a Quaker meeting at Swanmore and Anabaptists at Hill. At Titchfield there were 47 dissenters.[8]

After the passing of the Toleration Act in 1689 Protestant dissenters were permitted to build meeting houses but needed a licence from the bishop to do so. There was a fee of 6d, raised in 1812 to 2/6.[9] In the archdeaconry of Winchester (covering the whole of Hampshire) almost 1500 licences were issued, 46 of them in the parishes of the Meon valley, most of these in Titchfield, East Meon, Meonstoke and Droxford. Only occasionally is the type of dissent specified though Independents, Baptists and Methodists are named on occasion. Most of the buildings were private houses where a room would be licensed for dissenting worship. At Swanmore, then in the parish of Droxford, a barn belonging to Charles Barton was licensed in April 1754. Some chapels were however built: at Titchfield for example in 1799 'a newly erected building on the east side of High Street' was licensed. Round about 1800 dissent seems to have been particularly active in the parish of Titchfield. Between 1821 and 1827 Dr John Shoveller a dissenting minister who lived at Portsea, is recorded as applying for licences for premises at West Meon, Droxford, Meonstoke and Warnford [10]

The eighteenth century saw the founding of a variety of Protestant dissenting meetings and by the middle of the nineteenth century almost all villages in the Meon valley had one or more meeting places, alternative to the parish church, which often attracted labouring people who preferred hymn singing, extemporary prayer and fervent preaching to the staid liturgy of the Church of England.

According to the Religious Census of 1851 Titchfield parish had a number of Protestant chapels: three Independent or Congregational chapels – one in High Street, Providence Chapel at Sarisbury Green and an Independent chapel at Warsash – as well as a Particular Baptist chapel near Bursledon Bridge. All of them had three services on a Sunday and the Independent chapels in High Street and at Warsash had congregations approaching 200 at one or more of the services on Census Sunday.[11]In 1892, a Plymouth Brethren chapel opened in South Street, Titchfield.

Wickham had one of only seven chapels in Hampshire belonging to the Wesleyan Methodist Association, a short lived breakaway from Wesleyan Methodism, formed in the mid-1830s. It became part of the United Methodist Free Church when this was formed in 1857. The church at Wickham was in use before 1800 so was probably originally a Wesleyan chapel. The minister of the church at Wickham in 1851 was William Hardcastle who lived in Gosport where he was also minister of the North Street chapel. At the northern end of the valley at East Meon there was an Independent chapel at Ramsdean between East Meon and Petersfield as well as one in East Meon itself.

In the villages of the central part of the Meon valley Protestant dissent was represented from the nineteenth century by Primitive Methodism founded by Hugh Bourne and William Clowes in 1811.[12] It reached the Meon valley from north Hampshire in the 1830s and the Bishop's Waltham Mission was started from the Micheldever Circuit. Horatio Hall was the first Travelling Preacher – the title used by Primitive Methodists to describe their ministers. The first 'preaching places' included Meonstoke and Warnford and in 1846 Woodlands (an outlying hamlet in West Meon) was added. The term 'preaching place' meant a house in which a member of the society lived and where services were held. There were as yet few Primitive Methodist chapel buildings.

In 1848 Meonstoke with 26 members and Warnford with 18 members were the strongest societies in the Circuit. Meonstoke's members included two local preachers, George Chalk and Charles Reeves. Local preachers were lay men and a few women who did their ordinary work during the week and on Sundays took services and preached, sometimes walking many miles to do so. Many were farm labourers, shepherds, carters and blacksmiths. There are records of baptisms conducted by Primitive Methodist ministers: Charles and Mary Reeves' daughter Mary was for example baptised at Meonstoke on 22nd August 1847.[13]

When the Religious Census was held on 30th March 1851 the only Primitive Methodist meeting recorded in the Meon valley was that at Meonstoke – others were unofficial and unregistered. The record of the Census provides an example of the tetchy relations between the Church of England and dissenting bodies. The Primitive Methodist return for Meonstoke claimed that the building could accommodate 60 people and a further 20 standing. Three services were held that day: 28 attended in the morning, 61 in the afternoon and 84 in the evening. The rector of Meonstoke Charles John Hume felt that these figures gave a false impression of the strength of dissent in his parish: 'I think it just and necessary to add …' he wrote ' – that the Place of Meeting herein certified is simply a room, in a dwelling house occupied by Two separate Families. The room … measuring 13 feet square and about 7½ feet high, cannot possibly contain free sittings for 60 persons and standing room for 20. Moreover the average number reported does not represent the estimate of Dissent in this village. A meeting room being opened here they come from surrounding places and on the day of the Census extraordinary pains were taken to get up large numbers.' The Primitive Methodist entry signed by Charles Reeves, Manager admitted: 'We have not regular service on Sunday Mornings but on Sunday March 30th Special Meetings were held'.[14]

There was a spate of chapel building in the Meon valley in the 1860s. Meonstoke chapel was opened in 1865 and cost £180, Warnford opened in 1872 at a cost of £200. Camp meetings remained a feature of chapel life. At Meonstoke there was a Camp Meeting on 1st May 1881 and revival meetings at Warnford on 17th and 24th April in the same year. By 1884 the membership at Warnford was 26, at Meonstoke it had dwindled to six. Droxford appeared on the Circuit Plan for the first time with six members meeting in a private house.

The chapels in the Meon valley formed part of what was called the 'Hambledon Branch' of the Winchester Circuit. At Warnford services were held on Sundays at 2.30 and 6pm and at Meonstoke at 10.45 and 6pm. They were taken occasionally by the minister John Jopling who was stationed in the circuit from 1880–83 but more often by a local preacher. In addition there was at each chapel a weeknight service with another sermon: at Warnford on Monday and at Meonstoke on Tuesday at which John Jopling would often officiate.[15]

'The Hambledon Branch' (of the Winchester Circuit) became the Droxford Circuit in 1892. The circuit minister lived at Holly Cottage, Droxford, a sign perhaps of great hopes for Primitive Methodism in the village where a chapel had been opened in 1886: 'the purches (*sic*) of property at Droxford for the Primitive Methodist connexion bought of Mrs Pook, three cottages, a shop and a garden, price £300.' The chapel cost a further £221 to build. But these were years of agricultural depression when many people emigrated. In 1888 there were 20 empty houses in Warnford. In 1892 William Fidoe, then minister wrote in his annual report : 'Spiritually, financially and numerically the station cannot be called prosperous. It is with difficulty we are able to hold our own owing to the decreasing population of several villages.'[16]

In the later part of the nineteenth century Protestant dissenters had three grievances against the privileges of the Church of England. The abolition of compulsory church rate in 1868 removed the first. The Burial Laws Amendment Act 1880 which allowed the burial in the parish churchyard of dissenters by a minister of their own choice using whatever form of service he chose remedied the second. The first such burial at Meonstoke was conducted by Urban Gale on 19th October 1880. The third grievance and the one which roused most opposition resulted from Balfour's Education Act of 1902 which placed voluntary schools, most of them Anglican, on the rates. Two successive Primitive Methodist ministers in the Droxford Circuit persisted in their opposition and went to prison at Winchester briefly for withholding the portion of the rate devoted to education.[17]

The early years of the twentieth century saw the Primitive Methodist chapels surviving, but not much more. In 1915 there was a new society at West Meon but it was really a replacement for Warnford which closed four years later.[18] At the end of the First World War there was still a debt of £35 on the chapel at Meonstoke.

The First World War brought the churches closer together and the inter-war years saw better relations with the Church of England. The Methodist minister was often invited to take part in services held to consecrate village war memorials and to mark Armistice Day. At Droxford Leonard Etheridge (rector 1926–46) enjoyed particularly cordial relations with the ministers of the Droxford Circuit. Percy Hassam (minister 1924–30) preached in Droxford Parish Church and Leonard Etheridge took services in the Methodist chapels.

In 1932 the Primitive Methodist church united with the Wesleyan Methodist and United Methodist churches to form the Methodist Church but it made little difference to the Droxford Circuit. The only addition to the existing circuit was the United Methodist chapel at Soberton. The original building was a bakehouse converted into a chapel about 1849. It was registered as a chapel and is listed in the 1851 Census with James Gale of Soberton Mill as Elder. On 30th March 1851 it held two services with 18 attending in the morning and 40 at night. The chapel was built in 1868 and rebuilt in 1902.[19]

The puritan and protestant emphasis of the Droxford Circuit continued. Members were urged to practise total abstinence from alcohol. They disapproved of gambling in any form as well as the Sunday opening of cinemas. They would not participate in any united Remembrance service in which prayers for the dead were said since this implied acceptance of an unbiblical belief in purgatory. The circuit continued its practice of lay administration of the Lord's Supper though now permission of the Methodist Conference was needed. The Circuit deplored the Methodist Sacramental Fellowship founded in the 1930s to encourage liturgical worship and increased observance of Holy Communion and called on ministerial members to leave either the ministry or the Sacramental Fellowship.[20]

By the 1960s union between the Methodist Church and the Church of England seemed a possibility. The Droxford Circuit voted against union fearing dilution of the protestant witness in the larger body but in any case the Church of England failed to muster the necessary 75% majority in 1969 and again in 1972. The Circuit voted against the ordination of women to the Methodist ministry on scriptural grounds.

All the free churches experienced decline from the 1960s as the older generation which had been the mainstay of the chapels was not replaced by their children and grandchildren. The chapels of the Meon valley were badly hit. Meonstoke closed in 1964. It was described between the wars as a 'quaint box like structure … measuring 38 feet by 22 feet with no surrounding land', so small in fact that permission of the neighbours had to be sought to clean the windows. Ten years later West Meon closed and the building became a private house. Droxford chapel had never flourished and closed in 1978 when one of the two remaining members died and the other left the district. Ironically the Droxford Circuit so named in 1892 was renamed in 2001 the Meon Valley Circuit at a time when there were no longer any chapels in the valley. The first years of the twenty first century saw the closure of the chapel at Soberton. The only free church in the Meon valley was at Titchfield; all the others had closed.

12

The Garniers of Wickham

❦

THE GARNIER FAMILY and subsequently the Carpenter-Garniers have lived in Wickham for three centuries and members of the family, though now with a different surname, are still living in the village in the early years of the twenty first century. The last Carpenter-Garnier died in 1993 three hundred years after the first Garnier to live in Wickham moved to the village.[1]

The family traces its ancestry to Guillaume Garnier who was living about 1530 in the village of Vitry le Francois, a small town on the river Marne east of Paris. At some time during the sixteenth century the Garniers became Huguenots, followers of John Calvin. Isaac Garnier born in 1631 was the first member of the family to come to England. He left France on 21st January 1685 in anticipation of the Revocation of the Edict of Nantes by Louis XIV 'preferring his conscience to his country', as the family chronicler writes. The revocation ended the toleration which had been accorded to Huguenots a century earlier and led many to leave France and to settle in England and other neighbouring countries bringing with them skills much valued in their adopted country.

Isaac, married to Marguerite Bechefer, was an apothecary who, while living in France, treated poor patients free and was known as 'the Charitable Apothecary', though denied a medical diploma on account of his religious faith. His skill was appreciated in England and within five years of his arrival he was appointed Apothecary General to Chelsea Hospital. There was a large and comfortable house and garden with the job so Isaac and Marguerite settled down in Chelsea. When Isaac died in 1712 he was buried in the grounds of the hospital and was succeeded as Apothecary General by his son, also Isaac and in turn by his grandson.

It was Paul, the fourth son of Isaac and Marguerite, who established the family in Hampshire, becoming the tenant of Rokeby a house in the grounds of what later became Rookesbury Park in Wickham, probably in 1692. Paul married Elenor Wynne the daughter of Charles Wynne the owner of Rokeby and a number of other copyholds in the parish of Wickham. It was at Rokeby that Paul and Elenor raised their family. Paul was a friend of Lord Chesterfield and knew many of the leading literary figures of the early eighteenth century including David Hume, Charles Churchill, William Hogarth, Edward Gibbon and David Garrick, all of whom were entertained at Rokeby. On the death of Elenor's father in 1722 she and Paul inherited the estate at Wickham. They died within a few days of each other in 1735 and were buried on the same day, 11th October 1735.

32. George Garnier 1703–63.

33. George Charles Garnier (1739–1819).

Paul's son, George born in 1703, who now occupied the Wickham property, married Frances Soper, another rich heiress in 1736 and continued the entertainment of prominent literary figures. Only three years later, a few days after the birth of their son, Frances died and George never remarried. Soon after the death of his father in 1763 George Charles was able to buy Wickham Manor which included 3300 acres of land and trees to the value of £20,000 from Jonathan Rashleigh. He thus became Lord of the Manor of Wickham though the advowson (right to present to the living) of St Nicholas' church remained in the hands of the Rashleigh family.[2] George Charles now owned a substantial estate some of it inherited from his mother and grandmother. He married Margaret Miller of Froyle Place and in due course they had six sons and three daughters.

Two of their sons, William and Thomas, were ordained in the Church of England, in the last generation when pluralism was taken for granted by many including Brownlow North, Bishop of Winchester (see page 110). William, the elder son, went to New College, Oxford of which he became a fellow and in 1797 married Lady Harriet North the daughter of his bishop. He was made a prebend of Winchester cathedral at the age of 29, entitling him to a house in The Close at Winchester. William Garnier as a new prebend in 1800 lived at No.10 which he occupied until 1802 when he moved to No.2 and from 1807 until his resignation in 1831 he lived for part of the year at No.3 The Close.[3]

In the meantime the bishop presented William Garnier to the living of Upham with Durley, a post he held until 1814 when he was succeeded by John Haygarth, another relation of Bishop North. In 1801 William became also rector of Droxford succeeding Dr James Chelsum (1782–1801). Droxford Rectory is a handsome Georgian residence built in the early years of the eighteenth century probably by Dr Lewis Stephens (1722–46) described by Leonard Etheridge, a twentieth century successor, as 'a man of some large private means and a cultured man of literary tastes'.[4] At Droxford William Garnier's memorials include the village school which was erected in 1835, and the beech walk which he planted in order to enjoy a shady perambulation between his parsonage and Meonstoke House where his friend Edmund Poulter, yet another relation of the bishop and rector of Meonstoke, lived. William was responsible too for laying out the rectory garden where he planted a tulip tree, a species recently introduced to England from South America, as well as the yew and box hedges. To Lady Harriet is attributed the wide sweep of gravel in front of the house needed by her four-in- hand, which as Leonard Etheridge commented, 'has been found so useful in the days of motors'.[5]

Like many another well-to-do parson William Garnier did not attend personally to the chores of the parish; he employed curates to take services, baptise, marry and bury. In 1810 Edward Nott was curate of Droxford, paid £75 per year plus £15 towards accommodation whilst at Upham and Durley there were two curates. Timothy Davies lived in the parsonage house at Upham and received £55.[6] Joseph Essen lived at Exton on £42 per year.[7] In 1851 the living of Droxford was worth £1103 and Upham £415 so William Garnier made a substantial profit out of his livings quite apart from the capital he inherited from his father and income as Lord of the Manor. [8]

34. The Revd William Garnier (1772–1835) Rector of Droxford.

35. Lady Harriet Garnier wife of the Revd William Garnier and daughter of Bishop Brownlow North.

William Garnier succeeded his father as Lord of the Manor of Wickham in 1819 and in 1824 demolished the old house called Rokeby which lay closer to the then Southwick road. He employed the architect Charles Heathcote Tatham to design a new house in Portland stone to be named Rookesbury Park, at a cost of £40,000, built on the lofty site of Pye's Farm, with views on every side. The front featured Ionic pillars which still stand. It is described enthusiastically by David Lloyd: 'Some fine rooms; the former drawing room has an elliptical bay, the former dining room Corinthian pillars simulating granite. The library has similar pillars simulating marble and the original mahogany shelves ... Stables with cupola'.[9] Upstairs were two more cupolas lighting the semi-circular first floor bedrooms which had curved doors. There were substantial grounds, an orangery, walled garden, ample woodland walks and lakes and to the north a tower which was both a folly and a viewpoint offering a wide vista over the surrounding country.[10] There were lodges to the estate at the entrance from the Southwick road and from the then recently constructed turnpike up the Meon valley.

William died in 1835, Lady Harriet outlived her husband by 12 years and died at Tunbridge Wells in 1847. Both were buried at Wickham. The estate which he had created was completed by his successor another William. He demolished cottages at Wickham Corner which were little more than hovels, lived in by workers in woodland crafts – hurdle, faggot and hoop making – which were visible from the new house. He set aside Hundred Acres to rehouse the cottagers some distance from the Rookesbury though owned by him. Here he built 24 semi-detached flint and brick houses each with an acre of land attached for which the cottagers paid the spectacularly low rent of £5 per year. Many of the houses have been enlarged but the distinctive grey brick of which they were built can still be seen and some still carry the monograph 'WG 1845'. The road on which the cottages were built is still a private one and the Hundred Acres is a unique part of the parish. At first the villagers grew vegetables on the plots allocated to them but later the land proved ideal for growing strawberries. In 1851 William Garnier financed the building of Newtown church and parsonage to met the needs of the occupiers of the Hundred Acres employing John Colson as architect.[12]

Thomas, the younger brother of the William who had built Rookesbury Park was born at Rokeby in 1776 and educated at Winchester College and Worcester College Oxford where his tutor Dr Jacob introduced him to horticulture which became a life-long enthusiasm. As early as 1798 he published a paper on the rare flowers of Hampshire and was introduced by Sir Joseph Banks to membership of the Linnaean Society of which he eventually became the Father. He was briefly rector of Wickham and in 1807 moved from the rectory to Beverley a house to the east of Wickham church, often occupied by a member of the family, with Mary Parry the wife whom he had recently married who was the sister of Admiral Sir William Edward Parry, the Arctic explorer who in the course of exploring for the North West passage named 'Garnier Bay'.

In 1808 Thomas Garnier was appointed rector of Bishopstoke where he was to remain for 62 years. Here he exploited to the full his enthusiasm for plants. Since the

36. The Very Revd Thomas Garnier (1776–1873)
Dean of Winchester.

37. The return of William Garnier (1799–1863) to
Wickham with Countess Zelli his second wife 1854.

existing garden was not large enough to satisfy his ambitions he bought additional
land and created a garden to rival Kew. He attracted the interest of the Prince Consort
who visited the garden in 1851 and in the following year he was invited to dine at
Osborne House.[13]

Thomas was appointed a prebend of Winchester Cathedral in 1830. Ten years later,
already aged 64, he was appointed Dean of Winchester and was to remain in that post
for 29 years, a familiar and much loved figure in the Close and the city. When he had
been rector of Bishopstoke for 60 years 1500 people assembled to celebrate the occasion. He resigned the deanery in 1869 but not before he had entertained the new
bishop, Samuel Wilberforce. He died on 29th June 1873 at the age of almost 98 and was
buried at Bishopstoke. The Dean and his wife had eight children all but one of whom

38. Rookesbury House, Wickham built by
the Revd William Garnier c.1824.

39. Rookesbury Tower demolished 1971 as
a result of vandalism.

he outlived. His son Thomas (1809–63) was a member of the Oxford crew of the first
university Boat Race rowed at Henley on 10th June 1829.[14]

When William Garnier died at the age of 63 in 1835 he left his son an ample income
but during the American Civil War (1861–5) he bought federal bonds which he was
obliged to sell at a substantial loss and as a result Rookesbury Park was mortgaged.
Although William married twice, first Selina Thistlethwaite and after her death

Countess Zelli whom he met in Italy, there were no children of either marriage so the future of the estate was precarious. William left it to his young nephew, John Carpenter, the son of his sister Lucy, who had married John Carpenter of Mount Tavy in Devon, believing that his family was more likely to ensure its future than leaving it to a closer but less well-heeled relation. He made two provisos: that his nephew John should move from Devon and live at Rookesbury and that he should add the name Garnier to his own and so perpetuate a name which by now had a firm place in Wickham history.

John Carpenter-Garnier born in 1839 was an Oxford Cricket Blue and later in life Member of Parliament for South Devon (1873–84). He played a full part in the life of both Wickham and the county. He was High Sheriff of Hampshire in 1890, a member of the County Council when it was created in 1888, the first chairman of the Parish Council when that came into existence in 1894 and Justice of the Peace sitting on the Fareham bench. He was also a benefactor of the village, building the Coffee House and Tavern in the Square as a reading room and library. He was the last squire to live at Rookesbury Park and in 1898 moved to London.

The house was let to Arthur Lee (1868–1947). After an eventful career abroad he married Ruth Moore, a rich American and in 1900 became Conservative Member of Parliament for South Hampshire. The Lees bought 10 Chesterfield Place as their London home and rented Rookesbury Park as their country residence. Arthur Lee described it as 'a fine Georgian house in the constituency with a large park and shooting'. The Lees arrived in Wickham in their recently acquired Lanchester steered by a tiller rather than a steering wheel. Motoring was a novelty in the early years of the century and the Lanchester must have been one of the first motor cars to be seen in the valley. Arthur Lee enjoyed driving it himself and only later, when driving became more commonplace, employed a chauffeur. The people of Wickham do not seem to have warmed to the Lees perhaps because they did not become involved in village life and stayed for only a short time. In February 1909 Arthur and Ruth Lee held a farewell dinner, relinquished the lease and instead bought *Chequers*. Arthur Lee is best known for the presentation of *Chequers* to the nation as a residence for future Prime Ministers which took effect in 1921. In the following year he became a Viscount [15]

The First World War saw the death in action of the squire's eldest son John Trefusis (known as Jack) Carpenter-Garnier. Born in 1874 and educated at Harrow and Christ Church Oxford he entered the army and at the beginning of the First World War was a Major in the Scots Guards. He was killed at the battle of the Aisne in September 1914. When the squire died in 1926 he was therefore succeeded by his second son George William, born in 1877.

By now the world was changing and after the First World War many large houses were demolished or sold by their owners often to become institutions – hotels or schools, for example – for which their size fitted them. Rookesbury Park was too large for a world in which servants were hard to come by, families smaller and fuel increasingly expensive. At Wickham 1490 acres of the Garnier estate of 3500 acres, including the Hundred Acres, was sold in a three day sale held at the Victory Hall in Wickham on 18th, 19th and 20th July 1928 – farms, cottages and land – though about 1,500 acres was retained. The house was leased and became Rookesbury Park girls' school opened in May 1929 with Eileen Glenday as the first headmistress, a post she held until her death in April 1962. The squire built a new house off Mill Lane, Wickham named *Cutlers* after the copse which had occupied the site and it is here that the family still lives.

George William who became Lord of the Manor in 1926 had in earlier life studied horticulture and worked as a fruit farmer in Canada where he met and married Helen Gregory. She died giving birth to their son Leonard George in 1911 and George Carpenter-Garnier returned to England. He served in the First World War was gassed and invalided out of the army. Meantime he remarried – Cheston Isolda Prideaux-Brune. Their only son John Prideaux was a Lieutenant in the Scots Guards in the Second World War and like his uncle was killed, in his case at Salerno in Italy in 1942. When George died in 1960 his son George Carpenter-Garnier became squire, the last of the line and with his death in 1993 the male line of Carpenter-Garniers became extinct.

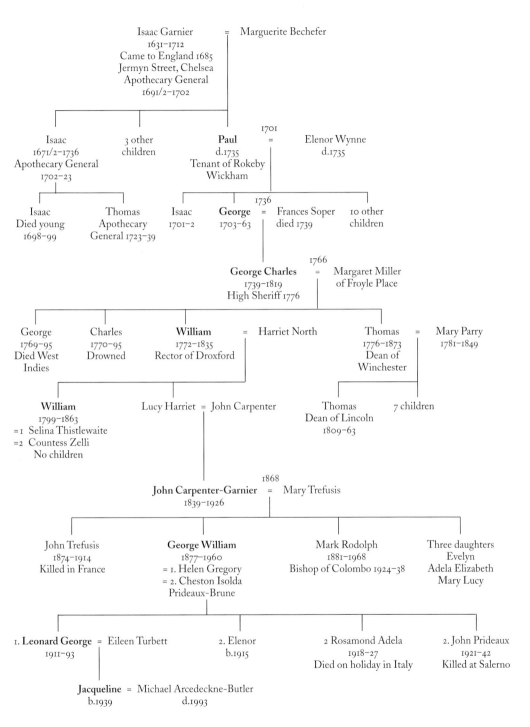

Isaac Garnier = Marguerite Bechefer
1631–1712
Came to England 1685
Jermyn Street, Chelsea
Apothecary General
1691/2–1702

Isaac
1671/2–1736
Apothecary General
1702–23

3 other
children

1701
Paul = Elenor Wynne
d.1735   d.1735
Tenant of Rokeby
Wickham

Isaac
Died young
1698–99

Thomas
Apothecary
General 1723–39

Isaac
1701–2

1736
George = Frances Soper
1703–63   died 1739

10 other
children

1766
George Charles = Margaret Miller
1739–1819   of Froyle Place
High Sheriff 1776

George
1769–95
Died West
Indies

Charles
1770–95
Drowned

William
1772–1835
Rector of Droxford

= Harriet North

Thomas
1776–1873
Dean of
Winchester

= Mary Parry
1781–1849

William
1799–1863
=1 Selina Thistlewaite
=2 Countess Zelli
No children

Lucy Harriet = John Carpenter

Thomas
Dean of Lincoln
1809–63

7 children

1868
John Carpenter-Garnier = Mary Trefusis
1839–1926

John Trefusis
1874–1914
Killed in France

George William
1877–1960
= 1. Helen Gregory
= 2. Cheston Isolda
Prideaux-Brune

Mark Rodolph
1881–1968
Bishop of Colombo 1924–38

Three daughters
Evelyn
Adela Elizabeth
Mary Lucy

1. Leonard George = Eileen Turbett
1911–93

2. Elenor
b.1915

2 Rosamond Adela
1918–27
Died on holiday in Italy

2. John Prideaux
1921–42
Killed at Salerno

Jacqueline = Michael Arcedeckne-Butler
b.1939   d.1993

The Garnier and Carpenter-Garnier family of Wickham

13

The Village School

❧

T HE EARLIEST SCHOOLS in many villages were dame schools where a small number of children were taught the rudiments of reading and writing in the home of those who ran the school. Schools for the labouring poor were the creation of the first half of the nineteenth century. The National Society for Promoting the Education of the Poor in the Principles of the Established Church – a cumbrous title for a society usually referred to as the National Society – was founded in 1811 and gave grants for the building and running of schools which provided religious and moral education, basic literacy and as a spin off would keep the village children out of the clutches of nonconformity, thought by many to be subversive.

Enthusiasm for the founding of a school was not shared by all. In his early years as rector of Meonstoke Charles John Hume (rector 1832–93) hired a room and maintained a school at his own expense. But a school building was needed and he canvassed financial contributions from better-off parishioners. He met with a mixed response: 'There is very little disposition on the part of the farmers', he wrote, 'to aid with money the objects I have in view and one of them is hostile altogether to the education of the common people.' Some farmers thought they might be deprived of useful child labour at haymaking, potato picking or harvest time. Schooling might in addition give children ideas above their station. The rector persevered and aided by £25 from the National Society and £45 from the Committee of Council on Education the school was built. It opened in 1842.[1] Asked if the National Society could provide a teacher he received a discouraging answer from the secretary: 'The salary you offer although raised with difficulty in a country place is less than that which teachers trained in this establishment usually expect'.[2]

The Trust Deed often specified that the managers, as well as the master or mistress should be members of the Church of England. Droxford school built in 1835 is an example: management, premises, finance and staff were vested in a committee consisting of the rector, the curate and four other local people. Members of the committee, including 'a committee of Ladies to assist management and visitation of girls and infant schools', as well as the master or mistress must be members of the Church of England. As countless school logs make clear the parson was in all schools a frequent, sometimes daily, visitor and either provided or inspected the religious instruction. The school was intended for 'children of the labouring class, manufacturing and other poorer classes in the parish of Droxford'.[3]

40. 'The Schools', Church Hill East Meon opened 1845.

The first school for the labouring poor in the Meon valley was probably that at East Meon where Charles Walters, master of the grammar school at Bishop's Waltham and curate of the parish church there, noted in 1816 that there were both Sunday School and day schools meeting in the north transept of the church. He had been gratified to see 160 children attend on a Sunday – how such a number could be accommodated in such a small space beggars belief. William Vinn is named as the first schoolmaster and was also parish clerk.[4]

A narrow strip of waste together with an even narrower strip of Church Hill Field was given by the Bishop of Winchester in 1844 at the east of the village on the road from East Meon to Petersfield where in the following year a school was built. It was a substantial building faced with knapped flints with separate entrances for boys and girls and a house for the master and mistress. The building is still a prominent land-mark, now privately owned and named Park Hill House.[5] It remained the only school for village children until 1947 when pupils over the age of 11 were transferred to Petersfield Secondary Modern School. It then remained a primary school until it was rebuilt on a more suitable site in 1964. By 1864 it, like other local schools, was offering evening classes to those who had left school – often after only a brief period of educa-tion – and were now in employment.[8] At Titchfield the National Society built a school in West Street at a cost of £400 in 1830. It was enlarged in 1855 and again in 1871 to cater for the large number of children in the village. Until 1891 children brought 'School Pence' to school on Monday morning and parents with several children and who could not afford to educate all of them at once would send them to school in rotation.[7]

41. Meonstoke School opened 1842.

The small school opened by Charles John Hume at Meonstoke in 1842 had a gallery occupied by the infants. Many of the 50 children whose names are to be found on the register walked to school from a considerable distance in all weathers. There was one teacher who was assisted by the rector who heard the children recite their catechism and by ladies of the parish who taught needlework and heard the children read. Like many rural schools continuity of staff was a major problem. There was no school house, salaries were small, teaching all ages was demanding and older boys often swore and were rude or disobedient. On many Mondays children were punished for bad behaviour in church on the previous day. It is not surprising that there was constant staff instability. Not until the arrival of Miss Frayling in 1883 was the problem solved. She stayed for no less than 24 years retiring in 1907.[8] Droxford National School was built in 1835 on glebe land belonging to the rector and overlooked the village green sited between the rectory and the manor house. It consisted of one classroom with a gallery.[9]

At Warnford the school was built in 1846 by Edward Tunno, the owner of Warnford Park, with additional accommodation added 30 years later by Henry Woods the new owner of the Park so that it could take the 70 children who now wished to attend. At West Meon a new school was built and opened in 1852 using dressed flints left over from the church completed in 1846. It cost £1393 mostly given by Mary Touchet, the sister-in-law of the former rector Henry Vincent Bailey, founder of the church. A second school in the same parish was opened at Privett in 1867. Exton was the last village to acquire its own school when in 1871 a school was built close to the church to serve the neighbouring villages of Exton and Corhampton.

At the beginning of the nineteenth century few children of the labouring class were literate, by the end of the century all were in school and literacy was almost universal. The village schools were for the children of working people. You would not expect to find there the son of parson or squire. By the 1870s they invariably sent their sons to board at one of the increasing number of public boarding schools while girls of the same social class were kept at home and educated by a resident tutor or governess or perhaps at a private school in the village. At West Meon in 1867 Miss Bridgen 'received young ladies' at Ivy Cottage [10] Only in the second half of the twentieth century did education for girls come to be regarded as important as it was for boys.

Schools for the labouring poor were built on the cheap and run on a shoe string. Accommodation was cramped, infants were often taught in an ill lit gallery. Heating was inadequate and insulation poor. In the winter pupils were frequently cold. The winter of 1890–91 was particularly severe and on 15th December the ink froze in ink wells at Corhampton & Exton School (Log 15.12.1890). When school resumed after Christmas it was even colder and the following day 'Cocoa was sent from the Rectory for 'Dinner Boys' (sic) on account of the cold'. On 1st January 'A gallon of good broth was sent from the Grove by General Snow' (Log 1.1.1891). It could of course also be stiflingly hot in summer. The 'offices', a Victorian euphemism for lavatories, were notoriously noisome well into the twentieth century.

Such features could be illustrated from most of the schools in the Meon valley. At West Meon, for example, the Inspectors commented in the 1870s: 'A Gallery is much needed in the Infants' room'(Log 1.3.1873), 'The Infants' room is unfortunately darkened

42. Pupils at Warnford School 1913.

43. Pupils at Droxford School c.1900.

by neighbouring trees'(Log 21.1.1876), 'The drainage requires immediate attention by the Managers as the smell in the Infant room is most offensive. I think fires should have begun – a thermometer is missing'. (Log 2.11.1876).

Despite deficiences parishes were inordinately proud of their school. From 1870 the alternative was a School Board which would levy a compulsory education rate. In the countryside at least this was to be avoided at all costs. At Hook with Warsash, in the old parish of Titchfield, it was claimed that a church school was better value than a board school. The cost per pupil drawn from official statistics was £5.7.0 per child per year in a voluntary school compared with £12.7.8 in a board school. 'It is a wanton waste of public money', concluded the writer (probably the vicar). in an article entitled *Voluntary Schools versus School Boards*.[12] The truth was that board schools were already beginning to provide better facilities than church schools dependent on a National Society grant and voluntary contributions could do. In 1887 the accounts of the school at Hook with Warsash showed a government grant of £84, school pence £29 and voluntary contributions from better off parishioners £55. There was a balance of £44 from the previous year. Salaries of teachers came to £140, assistants £40 and a pupil teacher £7.10.0 which alone more than accounted for the income. There was little left for books and stationery (£10), fuel and lighting (£10), repairs and cleaning (£3.6.7).[13]

Staffing remained inadequate for many years. For the smaller schools one certificated teacher assisted by one or more pupil teachers was the norm. Pupil teachers were young people between the ages of 13 and 18 learning on the job and hoping to qualify for a place at a Diocesan Training College. The system formed a limited career ladder for working class children to move to lower middle class white collar respectability. In some schools there were also monitors, pupils on the lowest rung of the ladder which led to certificated teacher status. Teachers faced a dauntingly large number of children covering a huge range of ages and ability. Usually there was a school house in which lived the schoolmaster and his wife both likely to be employed in the school and often expected also to run the Sunday School.

*   *   *

West Meon was a large and sparsely populated parish which included the distant hamlets of Woodlands and Privett. Many pupils came from outlying farms, and were members of large families where children were needed to assist a labouring father on the farm or a harassed mother looking after younger children. The present West Meon school was built in 1852 though there was a National School in the village earlier in the century. Next door is the School House also built in 1852 constructed from the same squared flints, where the schoolmaster and his wife lived and which belonged to the school until the 1960s. West Meon has a set of *Log Books* running from 1862, when log books were first required to be kept by schools receiving government grant, as well as Admission Registers from 1893. The *Log Books* contain a remarkable day-to-day picture of one rural school over 150 years of its life.[14] The first *Log Book* was brought by the rector William Bradford and the first entry reads: 'I, R.W. Fencott, schoolmaster make this first entry'. The staff in those far off days appears to have been one schoolmaster and one or possibly more pupil teachers: 'Very difficult to manage without the Pupil Teacher' (Log 4.7.1865).

Before the new school was built the rector recorded that in 1851 there were 51 boys and 98 girls on the books. The much larger number of girls probably indicates the greater usefulness of boys on the farms whereas girls could more readily be spared to attend school.[15] In 1862 the annual feast held in October and the Christmas party held before the school broke up on Christmas Eve were both attended by 160 children. The average daily attendance was recorded as 103 – just 60% of those who attended the party which probably represented the number on roll.

Attendance fluctuated wildly and depended among other things on the exigencies of family life and the weather which particularly affected small children some of whom had to walk miles along narrow country lanes from outlying farms in the remote parts of the parish. Until at least 1870 most children attended school irregularly and for only a few short years. Henry Vincent Bayley who was to become rector of West Meon had written many years before (1825) when he was in the Lincoln diocese:

> As soon as a child is capable of earning anything, he is that moment removed from school, never afterwards to attend with regularity and certainty – perhaps a quarter during the winter season. In the spring they are employed in frightening the birds from new sown lands, in dropping beans or planting potatoes. In the autumn they glean corn, and in October a child of 12 or 13 can earn 1/- a day gathering potatoes.[16]

44. West Meon School built 1852.

Bayley's strictures are reflected in the Log Books of West Meon 40 years and more later. 'Fred Dawe left to work with his father in the stables' (Log 19.5.1863); 'First class girls left some for service, others to take the place of elder sisters who have gone to places' (Log 17.7.1863). 'Several boys left to work in the fields – some of them only 7 or 8 years old' (Log 9.4.1866). You can sense the regret felt by the teacher at the loss of a promising pupil in this entry: 'W.Harris left for service. He leaves with an excellent character for attendance, conduct and attention to his studies' (Log 19.9.1863). The small income generated by the children as servants in the big houses was needed by their families.

Then there were those who attended when they could be spared from more urgent tasks – 'This being the season for haymaking the attendance has not been good this week.(Log 12.6.1874),'The harvest has begun in some places, many scholars away' (Log 27.7.1863). The harvest did not wait for term to end so fewer attended each day until finally the harvest holiday began. 'The harvest having become general many children away'(Log 1.8.1863). Nor did harvest necessarily end when school resumed: 'Gleaning not quite over' (Log 12.9.1863). Pupils were slow to come back after a holiday and it was usually the second week of term before the malingerers returned: 'The attendance this week very small. Gleaning not over' (Log 11.9.1874). Some anticipated the end of the week: 'Usually a thin school on Fridays'.

Epidemics led to a closure since infection could easily spread throughout the school and might have disastrous effects. In January 1877 there was scarlet fever in the parish and the managers closed the school for a fortnight and when it reopened attendance was very poor (Log 12.1 & 2.2.1877). In March 1890 the school closed for a week on account of influenza. In May of the same year ' Whooping cough has broken out among the scholars, the infants especially suffering' (Log 30.5.1890). The Log notes outbreaks of diphtheria, scarlet fever and chicken pox.

The death of pupils was by no means unusual: 'I have to record this day the death of James Hasted of consumption. The poor boy suffered much but seemed happy with the thought of going to his Saviour' (Log 15.7.1863). In March 1864 Fred Bone a boy aged 4 died of 'fever'. In February 1869 a former pupil and Sunday School teacher died at the age of 20. In 1895 three pupils died. The first on the 28th January was Ethel Lucas 'one of our best and brightest scholars [she] will always be remembered with affection by us all'. In April Willie Davis died after a short illness and in November Jessie Smith aged 7 died (Log 28.1, 5.4 & 12.11.1895).

Then there were frequent holidays some of them for traditional country celebrations. The 1st of May was 'Garland Day' long before it became Labour Day. National events were celebrated too. On 10th March 1863 the Prince of Wales (later Edward VII) was married and the school closed. The anniversary of the Queen Victoria's Coronation was an annual holiday. In October each year there was a School Feast when there were tea and buns on the rectory lawn followed by prize giving when pupils were rewarded for attendance, punctuality and school work. The school was not unaware of events far away. In 1862 during the American Civil War there was great hardship in the north of England caused by a shortage of raw cotton. The children of West Meon contributed 5/- 'to distress in the north'.

The Admissions Books at West Meon School records arrivals (with date of birth) and departures. Leavers include an 11-year old 'Gone to the workhouse', and a 12-year old who had 'Left for Alton Cripples Home'. Most leavers are aged 12 or 13 and the reason is often for girls 'Mothers help' or 'Gone to service' and for boys 'Gone to work'. A few remain to the age of 14 and the reason for leaving is simply 'Age limit'.

In its early years the school at West Meon was largely financed from two sources. In 1851 'school pence' amounted to £24.14.11 ½ whilst donations from richer parishioners, solicited by the rector, amounted to £40.17.01 ½ . Of the donations £15 was contributed by the rector and his wife and a further £10.0.0 by Mrs Touchet. Salaries, building repairs and other expenses amounted to just short of the amount collected.[17]

* * *

Forster's Education Act of 1870 did not as is often claimed make education compulsory. It nonetheless represented an important landmark, laying down for the first time the principle that there should be sufficient places for all children to attend school. Where voluntary – usually church – provision was inadequate School Boards might be formed to build and run schools. There were no School Boards in the Meon valley.

Further changes took place in the last years of the nineteenth century. By a series of acts of parliament passed between 1876 and 1891 elementary education became free and compulsory. The Droxford Log for 21st September 1891 reads 'School reopened as a 'Free School', 53 present in the morning, 54 in the afternoon'. School Attendance officers were appointed to chase miscreants and delinquent parents were taken to court at Droxford and fined. The law was complicated. You could leave school at 12 provided you had attained standard five and had passed 'the Labour Examination'. There are frequent references in the West Meon Log Books to pupils entering for the Labour Examination. At the age of 13 you could leave provided your attainment at school was satisfactory but if not you had to stay until you were 14.

Since its invention by Robert Lowe and promulgation in the Revised Code of 1862 schools were tied to 'payment by results' – the grant was dependent on the results of tests conducted by Her Majesty's Inspectors each year. The result was rote learning of material likely to be included in the test. It was a system reviled by the teachers. At long last in 1895 the Code substituted HMI 'visits without notice' though in practice the date was notified well in advance. Schools were now free to determine their own curriculum.

The school remained dependent on pupil teachers until the system was abolished in the Fisher Act of 1918. In 1893 the pupil teacher at West Meon was Augustus Trodd. Three years later he failed his final examination but remained at West Meon School until 1900. When he left this euphoric note appeared in the Log 'Mr Augustus Trodd left today after seven years faithful service. By his upright conduct and genial manner he has made himself beloved by all the village. I can speak in the highest terms as to his ability as a teacher and of the excellence of the work he has done for the school' (Log 19.10.1900).

* * *

The Balfour Education Act of 1902 placed all schools whether Voluntary (church) or Board schools under the local authority and so Hampshire County Council assumed responsibility for the schools in the Meon valley. In voluntary schools there were now four foundation managers appointed by the church and four representing the local authorities. The managers could recommend appointments of staff but ratification was the responsibility of the Hampshire Education Committee.

The Managers of West Meon School held their first meeting on 19th October 1903 and elected the rector Robert Herbert Fair chairman. George Springer had been head since 1892 and the managers would like to have raised his salary to £115 but the County Education Committee would not agree. There was an assistant mistress who taught the infants, as well as needlework to the older girls. Ralph Treble was pupil teacher and his sister Grace was monitor. Mrs Taylor was caretaker paid 4/- per week which the managers would like to have raised to 5/-, but again the County Education Committee demurred.

Conditions were spartan. Water came from a well but does not appear to have been drinkable since those from a distance who brought their lunch were obliged to ask a neighbour to provide drinking water. Inspectors commented that the old gallery should be removed, the infant room should 'be better warmed', the cloakroom was inadequate, the boys 'offices' 'not good', whilst girls and infants 'shared three seats in one closet'.

In the summer of 1906 the new head F.D. Allen got married and the managers in a fit of generosity awarded the school a week's extra holiday to mark the occasion. Meanwhile Ralph Treble had completed his training and returned as an assistant teacher at a salary of £65.

To read the Log Books of West Meon School for the years before, during and after the First World War is to realise the odds against which the school was labouring in order to offer its pupils an adequate education. The children are described as 'dull, surly and uncooperative', parents 'hostile and reluctant' to send their children to school regularly or to support the school in matters of discipline. Teachers faced large classes consisting of pupils with a wide age range and variety of both ability and attainment. His Majesty's Inspectors (HMI) were critical, the local authority sympathetic but powerless. Staff turnover was a major problem. In May 1913 the teacher wrote in the Log Book, 'The neighbourhood is far from being even moderately intellectual' and she adds a list running to three pages of children with serious problems. She reckoned that 30% of the children were bad material to work on 'in addition to parents who loathe the name of the school'. HMI had already commented on 'irregularity of attendance … general passivity of children' who are often given 'formal teaching and mechanical exercises'.

West Meon may have been an isolated village but world events were nonetheless noted. The sinking of the *Titanic* merited reference in the Log: 'More definite news of fearful catastrophe on *Titanic*. Spoke impressively about it to class. Some of their compositions showed that they had been reading the accounts' (Log 18.4.1912).

Arthur Elson became head of West Meon School on 31st May 1915. Within six months he felt obliged to enlist, joined the Portsmouth Battalion of the Hampshire Regiment and left the school in December. He was severely wounded in France and his wife was given permission to visit him in St Thomas's Hospital in London. He recovered but was unable to return to work until March 1919. He remained at West Meon until 1932 when he moved to Waterlooville.

On 11th November 1918 'School has been abandoned this afternoon on receiving news of the Signing of Armistice'. (Log). The world was changing. On 13th January 1919 a Handley Page aircraft made a forced landing nearby: 'The children were marched to the place and after the pilot had given them a brief explanation of the machine they were marched back to school'. Five years later there was a school excursion by train to London: 'Most of the children had only ridden a few miles in a railway train before. The greatest astonishment was expressed at the sight of the roofs of houses (outer London)'(Log 19.7.1924).

From the 1920s schools were increasingly required to adhere to local authority or

45. Titchfield School – boys 1916.

46. Titchfield School – boys' Geography class 1913.

national policy. There were in future a specified number of days schooling each year with occasional days at the discretion of the managers. The Burnham Scale fixed teachers' salaries and there are no further references to pupil teachers or monitors. The local authority issued a circular entitled 'Choice of Employment' the beginning perhaps of careers advice. At West Meon the Touchet charity was used to provide scholarships for pupils who passed into secondary school.[18]

Empire Day was celebrated each year. On 24th May 1928 'Lady Penrhyn broke the Jack on the flag staff in the playing field after which Patriotic Songs were sung and a drill display was given by the older children' (Log 24.5.1928). Four years later 'Mr Tulley having kindly lent a wireless set the children listened to Lady Jellicoe, who deputised for her husband giving an Empire talk. After this I gave a talk on Empire and the morning session closed with the singing of 'empire' and national songs and hymns'(Log 24 .5.1932). On 21st January 1936 the head recorded in the school log the death of George V and added – without irony: 'King Edward VIII succeeds him. May he prove as wise and good as his father'.

* * *

From 1918 the school leaving age was 14; exceptions were ended by the Fisher Act and most pupils spent the whole of their school life in one school, though the first vestiges of secondary education reached the Meon valley. Pupils could now go, with county junior scholarships at the age of 14 or sometimes 11, to selective grammar schools, boys to Churcher's Grammar School at Petersfield and even fewer girls to Eggar's School at Alton. But the number was always small – one or two a year. In the south of the Meon valley provision was better; there were grammar schools in Fareham, Eastleigh and Winchester though few from the village schools went to them and until the arrival of buses in the 1920s these schools were difficult to reach. But bigger changes were now envisaged.

In 1926 the government set up the Hadow Committee which recommended that education should in future be divided at the age of 11 into primary and secondary and each should take place in separate buildings. In order to provide four years of secondary education for all, the school leaving age should as soon as practicable be raised to 15. Hadow's recommendations provided a huge challenge to local authorities not unlike that provided 40 years later by the introduction of comprehensive education. In both cases the problem was to provide buildings for the new schools.

Hampshire County Council had a large number of rural schools whose buildings could not be adapted to become secondary schools. New buildings were needed and money was tight. This was certainly true of the Meon valley. At Titchfield Hadow Reorganisation, as it was called, was achieved in 1933 when pupils over the age of eleven went to Sarisbury Senior School (now Brookfield School) and a new primary school was built. But in the rest of the Meon valley little progress had been made by 1939 though a site for a secondary school at Swanmore had been purchased. The onset of war meant that plans were put on hold. The best that could be achieved was a degree of rationalisation made possible by the urgent need to provide a new building at Droxford. From 1904 HMI reports regularly deplored the state of Droxford School. The managers were fighting a losing battle against a building which could never be more than barely adequate however hard they tried. At long last the Board of Education wrote in 1924 to the Hampshire Education Authority:

The Board of Education note that it is not within the power of the Managers to

provide satisfactory accommodation… Having regard to the serious nature of the
defects in the existing premises I am to inform the Local Education Authority
and the Managers that the Board of Education has decided to remove the School
from the List of Public Elementary Schools as from 31st March 1926.[19]

A two-year reprieve was obtained but on 21st December 1928 the Church of England
School closed for the Christmas holiday and for good. The Log reads: 'The Reverend
L.S.Etheridge (Rector) gave an outline of the school's existence … After prayers and
the saying of the doxology the old school closed and the children dismissed'. On 7th
January 1929 the new council school opened without ceremony. The new Droxford
School was 'almost idyllic by comparison with the old'. There was a large playing field,
earth closets across the playground and a separate practical instruction room. It was
commodious, safe and well equipped.[20]

The authority was able to close two other schools whose buildings were unsatisfac-
tory. Pupils from the church schools at Exton and Soberton were transferred to
Droxford when the new school opened. In 1936 pupils over the age of 11 came from
Meonstoke to Droxford. It was not until after the Second World War that further
rationalisation was achieved. In 1953 secondary age pupils from Droxford were transferred to Cowplain, Meonstoke became an infant school and its pupils over the age of
8 were transferred to Droxford.

At the northern end of the valley East Meon became a junior school in 1947 when
pupils over the age of 11 transferred to Petersfield Secondary Modern School leaving
only 72 primary age children. Not until the opening of Swanmore Secondary Modern
School in 1961 (now renamed the Swanmore College of Technology) were the Hadow
proposals implemented in the central part of the Meon valley. Hadow reorganisation
had taken more than 40 years to achieve and the Meon valley was one of the last places
in the country where there were all-age schools. There is and never will be a secondary
school in the central part of the valley. The next reorganisation was already on the
horizon. Swanmore Secondary Modern School had a life of only 13 years before it
became a comprehensive school in 1974. It grew rapidly and a school built for 200 now
accommodates 1200 and in 2002 it became Swanmore College of Technology.

Schools serving the Meon valley since 1800

Village	National School	Major changes	Modern rebuilding	Present status
Titchfield	1830	1855, 1871	1933[1]	CP
Wickham	(1827)[2]	1869[3]	1968 1876[4]	VC
Droxford	1835[5]		1929	CP
Meonstoke	1842	1936 11+ to Droxford 1953 8+ to Droxford	1961[6]	VCI
Soberton	1851[7]	1875[8] Closed 1928. Pupils 5–11 to Meonstoke 11–14 to Droxford	—	
Corhampton	1816	Endowed 1669 became National School 1816. Closed, new school at Exton 1871	—	
Exton	1871[9]	Closed 1928 pupils to Droxford	—	
Warnford	1846	Rebuilt 1876 Closed 1931 pupils to West Meon	—	—
West Meon	c.1830[10]	New building opened 1852 1947 14+ to Alton 1951 11+ to Petersfield	—	VC
East Meon	(1816)[11]	1845[12]	1964	VC

1 Hadow reorganisation. Titchfield became a primary school in a new building, 11+ pupils went to Sarisbury Senior School (now Brookfield School)
2 Provided by William Garnier
3 Source White's Gazetteer
4 Infant School enlarged
5 Condemned by HMI, closed 1928; new school provided by LEA
6 Additional classroom, cloakroom, kitchen, grass playground, head's room, waiting room etc.
7 On the Bank in High Street.
8 School rebuilt in Upper Street now School Hill.
9 New school built and named Corhampton & Exton Endowed School
10 There was a National School before the new building of 1852
11 School in north aisle of parish church
12 National School on new site in Church Hill Fields

CP County Primary School
VC Voluntary Controlled Church of England School
VCI Voluntary Controlled Church of England Infant School

14

The Church of England in the Long Nineteenth Century 1780–1914

THE YEARS FROM 1870 to 1914 were a golden age for the Church of England. It had recovered from the torpor of the early years of the nineteenth century. Pluralism and non-residence had been eradicated, its buildings had been restored and parsonages built or rebuilt. There was now a resident priest in each parish and often a curate as well. Theological colleges had helped in the creation of a clerical profession differentiated from mere gentry. Bishops gave a spiritual lead, confirmed in the parishes and ordained in their cathedrals. Each parish had a National School in which the parson took a close interest. How then had such a transformation been achieved? It was of course a complex process begun perhaps by the evangelical revival in the eighteenth century which led to a different sort of bishop. The state took a hand through the creation of the Ecclesiastical Commission by Peel's short-lived government of 1834. The purpose of this chapter is to describe aspects of this transformation as it took place in the parishes of the Meon valley.

*   *   *

The bishop of Winchester from 1781 to 1820 was Brownlow North, brother of Lord North, First Lord of the Treasury (Prime Minister) from 1770 to 1782. Bishop North not only accepted pluralism and non-residence as part of the natural order but practised the most blatant patronage appointing his kith and kin to some of the richest livings in his gift. Amongst North's relations none benefited more spectacularly from his patronage than Edmund Poulter (1756–1832). Born Edmund Sayer, after attending Harrow School and Trinity College, Cambridge he moved to Lincoln's Inn, was called to the bar in 1780 and assumed the name Poulter. He married the new bishop of Winchester's sister-in-law and concluded, wisely, that ordination was likely to be more rewarding than the bar. He was made deacon by Bishop North in June 1782 and priest five weeks later. He became rector of Crawley (1788–90), Meonstoke (1791–1831), Bishop's Waltham (1794–7), Buriton with Petersfield (1796–1813), and Alton with Selborne, Binsted and Kingsley (1816–32). He was also a prebendary of Winchester cathedral with a house in the Close.[1]

Edmund Poulter was a magistrate and examining chaplain to the bishop. He lived for part of the year in his rectory at Meonstoke House and was a close friend of William Garnier, rector of Droxford. He was not a popular rector and his long absences from the parish were accepted willingly.[2] His successor was Charles John Hume, rector for a record period of 61 years dying in harness on 29th July 1893 shortly after his 95th birthday. He was buried just outside the church door. The funeral was conducted, like that of Hume's wife, by their son Francis Glynne Hume also an Anglican priest. In 102 years there had been two rectors of Meonstoke. Eighteen months later Henry Wooldridge aged 96 died. *The Hampshire Chronicle* pointed out that he had been churchwarden for 61 years and had been warden when Charles Hume was instituted and was still warden when his successor was appointed 61 years later.[3]

*   *   *

In 1810 the Archbishop of Canterbury Charles Manners-Sutton (1805–28), prompted by parliament, asked for information about the churches in the Winchester diocese. As a result of the French Revolution and the war with France, parliament wanted to know whether the parish system of the Church of England was an adequate bulwark against the spread of revolutionary ideas. Bishop North was not pleased to be asked at all and certainly not to be required to furnish information promptly. He nonetheless complied and the replies provide a picture of the parishes in the Meon valley in 1810.[4] The richest living was Droxford, worth £799 and the poorest Corhampton valued at a mere £39; it was however the exception. Both were in the hands of pluralists. At Corhampton the rector was William Richards who lived in his rectory at Little Cheverill in Wiltshire whilst the curate was Charles Walters who was also curate at Soberton and headmaster of the Grammar School at Bishop's Waltham where he lived.

Value of livings in the Meon Valley 1829–31

Titchfield & Crofton	£266
Wickham	£578
Droxford	£799
Corhampton	£39
Meonstoke & Soberton	£568
Exton	£331
Warnford	£502
West Meon & Privett chapel	£602
East Meon, Froxfield & Steep	£903

Extracted from Smith 2004 Appendix 3. The richest parishes in mainland Hampshire were Alverstoke £1257 & Buriton & Petersfield £1194 and probably Old & New Alresford & Medstead for which there is no return. In 1835 the Bishopric of Winchester was worth £10,000.

*   *   *

When the Rashleigh family sold the Wickham estate to the Garniers in 1765 they kept the right to appoint the rector. At the beginning of the nineteenth century the patron of the living was Philip Rashleigh of Menabilly near Fowey in Cornwall. When John Andrew Thomas rector of Wickham since 1800 died on 23rd October 1804 at the early age of 36 (already a prebendary of Lichfield cathedral) he was buried in the chancel of Wickham church.[5] Jonathan Stackhouse Rashleigh (born 1782) was probably already intended for the family living but he was still in his third year at Wadham College, Oxford. Immediately on taking his degree in 1805 he was ordained deacon by the bishop of Winchester and became curate of Martyr Worthy. A year later he was ordained priest this time by the bishop of Exeter and at the tender age of 24 was presented to the family living of Wickham which he held for 57 years until his death in 1863. In the intervening year 1805–6 Thomas Garnier was rector of Wickham, presumably on the understanding that he would resign as soon as Jonathan Rashleigh was ordained priest and so became eligible to be presented to the living.[6]

*   *   *

After 50 years as rector of West Meon John Dampier was succeeded by Henry Vincent Bayley whose name is recalled by present day inhabitants of West Meon if only because he was the rector who built the new church about which even today feelings are ambivalent. Henry Bayley was born in Manchester in 1777 and was ordained by the bishop of Chester. Soon afterwards he became tutor to the son of George Pretyman, bishop of Lincoln. George Pretyman (he added the name Tomline on inheriting an estate in 1803) had become bishop of Lincoln as well as Dean of St Paul's in 1787 at the age of 37. His rise in the ecclesiastical firmament was the result of being tutor at Pembroke College Cambridge to William Pitt the Younger (Prime Minister from 1783). In 1805 Pitt tried to appoint him Archbishop of Canterbury but was outwitted by the king.[7] So he had to wait for preferment until 1820 when Pretyman-Tomline was appointed to the prestigious and financially advantageous post of bishop of Winchester. Like his predecessor he suffered no qualms about pluralism. Henry Bayley spent 21 years in the Lincoln diocese during which he collected an impressive number of appointments in the gift of the bishop including the sub-deanery of Lincoln cathedral (1805–28) and the Archdeaconry of Stow (1823–44). In the 1830s he was not surprisingly a strong opponent of the Ecclesiastical Commission which sought to end such pluralism.[8]

In 1826 the bishop of Winchester presented his friend Henry Bayley to the living of West Meon. He was to be the last pluralist in the Meon valley, retaining the archdeaconry of Stow and at least one of his Lincolnshire parishes. He took the degree of Doctor of Divinity at Cambridge in 1824 and in 1828 exchanged the sub-deanery of Stow for a canonry of Westminster Abbey. In that capacity he had to keep one month's residence in London each year. He attended the coronation of Queen Victoria. 'He was', says a twentieth century successor, 'one of the last of the grand gentlemen in Holy Orders'[9]

47. West Meon church built by Henry Vincent Bayley, consecrated 1844.

The wealth he obtained from his many offices enabled him to spend a substantial amount of money in West Meon. When he arrived the rectory was the present *Red Lion* public house. He bought West Meon House, added to it and it remained the rectory until 1917. The chimneys facing north still contain his initials and coat of arms. He laid out the gardens so that they grew into 'a little paradise'. He repaired the old church at Privett and supported schools at both Privett and West Meon. Henry Bayley appointed and no doubt paid a pittance to curates who did most of the work of the parish. A record of their names can be gleaned from the book kept by the rector recording the banns of marriage called in the parish. No less than eight curates signed the banns book during his incumbency.[10]

He suffered from poor health by the 1820s, which perhaps explains why such a vigorous parish priest should have rejected suggestions made on two occasions that he should allow his name to go forward for the Regius Chair of Divinity at Cambridge. He did not trust himself even to preach unless a curate, who could if necessary take over, was present. By 1839 he suffered from gangrene first in one and later in both feet. His eyesight was poor, he had cataracts in both eyes and in his last years was blind. After 1842 he walked little and rode not at all. His wife whom he had married in 1807, the daughter of James Touchet of Manchester, was also an invalid and died in 1839.[11]

When he could no longer read Henry Bayley employed a boy of 12, son of the local postmaster to look up words in his lexicon. After a mere six months the boy could translate the gospels and epistles in Greek and Bayley then taught him Latin. He is not named in the anonymous *Memoir* of Bayley. His name was William Benham. Did he write the *Memoir*? He was only 15 but always precocious so it is not impossible. After Henry Bayley's death, helped by the Bayley family, he became a teacher and was ordained. He was a remarkable character, in later life a large man with bushy side-whiskers, who went about with an enormous stick. His *Who's Who* entry gives his recreation as 'riding on the tops of omnibuses'.[12] He must by any standard be one of the most colourful characters produced by West Meon.

The project closest to Henry Bayley's heart was the replacement of the old church at West Meon with a new one. 'The old edifice, though by no means an elegant or stately building was to all appearances a solid one but on careful examination it was found to be in a state of decay which rendered an effectual restoration hopeless'- a carefully worded justification for Bayley's rebuilding perhaps.[13] The villagers were opposed to its replacement and Bayley had been at West Meon for 17 years before he was able to achieve his objective. The villagers' opposition was no doubt softened by the rector's gift of £10,000 of the £11,000 cost of the new church leaving only £1000 to be raised from a church rate. The stone laying at which Bayley was present took place on 9th August 1843 and was 'the most intensely gratifying of his clerical life'.

Archdeacon Bayley, by now blind, did not live to see the completion of the project which had meant so much to him. He died on 12th August 1844. The new church, designed by George Gilbert Scott (1811–78) the famous Victorian architect responsible among other buildings for St Pancras station and hotel in London, was consecrated on 5th May 1846. *The Hampshire Chronicle* gave the event full coverage. There was a congregation of 1300. The paper was impressed by: 'The particularly clean and happy appearance of the labouring population together with their orderly demeanour.'[14] At the service the children of the National School were part of the choir which sang the anthem, psalms and hymns. Afterwards two hundred people 'adjourned to the rectory'; the children of the parish schools were given 'tea, bread and butter and buns' whilst 100 workmen were 'supplied with an abundant dinner' in a temporary building in a field near the church which had been given by Archdeacon Bayley as a playground for the schoolchildren and parish of West Meon'.[15]

The new church is one of the few faced with knapped flints, knapped by women of the village in what became known as Knapps Yard, for which they were paid ¼d per flint.[16] The roundels of stained glass in the windows must rank amongst the most unusual in any parish church in England. They include the arms of Queen Victoria, the Duke of Wellington, the Archbishop of Canterbury, the Bishops of Winchester, London and Lincoln and the Dean of Winchester. In other windows Bayley immortalised no less than 27 friends from Eton and Cambridge. He himself and his sister-in-law Mary Touchet also figure in the windows. Seats in the new church were allocated by rank – in the front pew sat the Honourable Piers Legh, the choir sat towards the back of the nave and the children were allocated seats at the rear of the church – where they were unlikely to see or hear. The old church was pulled down and the walls round the church-yard built. Surplus knapped flints were used later to build the new school.[17]

The final entry in the book of Thanksgivings which Henry Bayley kept, on a page by itself reads: ' June 9th 1844 Henry Vincent Bayley Rector of this Parish desires the prayers of the congreg.' (*sic*) Underneath appear the words 'Died on Monday August 12th 1844 at ½ past 11 o'clock P.M'.[18]

*   *   *

One of the most curious monumental inscriptions in any churchyard is to be found at Droxford and dates from the middle of the nineteenth century. It was presumably composed by the Revd Thomas Penny White. It reads:

> In memory of the The Revd Thomas P. White
> who was born in sin September 19 AD MDLXXVIII [1778] born again MDCCI [1801]
> Senior Wrangler 1st Smith's Prizeman and Fellow of
> Queens' College Cambridge AD MDCCCII [1802].
> Ordained minister of the Gospel AD MDXII [1812]
> Resident in college till his marriage December MDCCCXII [1812].
> Curate of Soberton, Droxford and the neighbouring parishes
> March MDCCCXII [1812} to March MDCCCXXXVIII [1838]
> Minister of St John's Chapel, Winton
> March MDCCCXXXVIII [1838] to March MDCCCXLLIIII [1844]
> Fell asleep in Jesus July 24th MDCCCXLIIII [1844]

> 'He hath made with me an everlasting covenant ordered in all things and sure: for this is all my salvation, and all my desire'. 2 Samuel 23.5

> It may be added that preferment in the Diocese
> was three times offered to me and declined.

Thomas's widow Charlotte Eliza *nee* Channing rates little more than the dates of her birth and death, January 1791 and January 1861, which will be found on the reverse of her husband's tomb.

*   *   *

The reawakening of church life in the early nineteenth century led to the building of chapels of ease in large parishes. Droxford's first two nineteenth century rectors were responsible for the provision of chapels of ease at Shidfield (as the district was then spelt) in 1829 and at Swanmore in 1845. Both were originally modest buildings to meet the needs of villagers whilst the aristocrats of the parish continued to drive to the mother church at Droxford. Later both were enhanced.

At Shedfield the chapel of ease was dismantled in the 1870s leaving only the tower. It was replaced by an impressive building designed by John Colson whose father lived

48. Droxford Rectory (now the Old Rectory) c.1880.

at Hall Court in the village. Frederick Townsend contributed £1000 on condition that the church should have a brick interior. David Lloyd describes the interior: 'Spacious, well proportioned, almost entirely in brick – light red brick, deep red brick, yellow brick, even patches of black and blue brick… A much more interesting and original piece then most of Colson's work'. [19] It was consecrated in 1880. Later a tower was added paid for by Annie Franklyn of Shedfield Lodge. It was also she who early in the twentieth century gave the distinguished marble pavement for the church.

At Swanmore the original chapel of ease was embellished with a tower, peal of bells and chancel by Walter Medlicott who became vicar in 1871. Both Shedfield and Swanmore became ecclesiastical parishes in the 1840s when it became possible to create new parishes. In the parish of Soberton a church, paid for by William Garnier and also designed by John Colson was built at Newtown and opened in 1851.

The large parish of Titchfield was first divided in 1837 when Sarisbury was formed. Not until 1871 was there further division when Crofton became a parish and a new church at Hook-with-Warsash was consecrated by Samuel Wilberforce (bishop 1869 –1874). Later still in 1893 Locks Heath and Lee on the Solent were separated from the mother parish.[20] At the other end of the valley George Waddington of Langrish House paid for the building of a church at Langrish which was opened in 1870 and Langrish was separated from East Meon.

Privett was separated from West Meon in 1873 and provided with a remarkable church built in 1876–8 and paid for by the gin millionaire William Nicholson (1824–1909) who had bought Basing Park following the death of Joseph Martineau in 1863. The old church was demolished and a temporary building was used until the new one was ready. The architect was Sir Arthur Blomfield. (1829–99) later the architect of St Mary's Portsea. The church at Privett cost £22,000 (over £1 million in today's currency) which was borne entirely by Nicolson.[21] No expense was spared. The red stone round the lower walls came from Dumfries, the off-white stone from Bath, yellow stone from Ham Hill in Somerset, the steps from Yorkshire, and the floor mosaics from Italy. The church has a four bay nave, with aisles and clerestory, transepts and a sumptuously appointed chancel with mosaic floor.

Fittings, including pulpit, lectern, pews and font, were contemporary and of high quality. The church's most remarkable feature is the west tower with a broach spire, 160 feet high, standing on the edge of high ground and visible for miles around. It is impressive as a monument to the man who inspired and paid for it and to the architect who designed it and anybody viewing it today can only agree with the architectural historian Nikolaus Pevsner, when he describes it as 'exceptionally good'.[22] But Privett church can never have been appropriate for the worship of the villagers for whom it was presumably intended. After a century of existence it was closed and in 1980 passed to the Churches Conservation Trust.[23] By then the fine organ and the pews had been dispersed and the congregation had retreated to the south transept.

*   *   *

The Pluralities Act of 1838 required clergy to have only one parish and to live there, and at long last was effective in eliminating pluralism and non-residence largely because new style bishops enforced its provisions.[24] The rights of incumbents already in post were respected so the act was not fully operational until the 1870s but from 1838 the number of non-resident incumbents steadily diminished. In the Meon valley parishes there were no longer curates in charge and non-resident rectors. Whereas in 1810 five parishes were served by curates by mid-century there were none. Instead smaller and more manageable parishes had been created, churches built and resident clergy appointed though the stipend of these new parishes was much smaller than that of the more prestigious, older parishes. Curates were now young men serving an apprenticeship in a parish before being appointed to a parish of their own.

Charles Sumner was bishop of Winchester from 1827 until the passing of the Bishops' Resignation Act in 1869.[25] He represented a half-way house between eighteenth and nineteenth centuries. He opposed the Ecclesiastical Commission and refused to appoint honorary canons. He was one of the first evangelicals to reach the episcopal bench and appointments in his gift went only to like minded evangelicals. He began the practice of three yearly visitations of his diocese, was the first bishop for 300 years to be enthroned in person in his cathedral and revived the use of rural deans.[26] The huge medieval deanery of Droxford was divided in 1856 and 24 deaneries created. Most of the parishes of the Meon valley were in the deanery of Droxford North West. As a result of a further reorganisation in 1872 the deanery of Bishop's Waltham was created covering the parishes of the Meon valley from Wickham to Exton.[27] Titchfield was now in the deanery of Alverstoke (later renamed Gosport) whilst the deanery of Petersfield included the Meon valley parishes of Warnford, West Meon and East Meon.

By the mid-nineteenth century there was a new spirit of earnestness about the clergy. In the deanery of Droxford North West a Clerical Society was formed whose object was 'to promote friendly meetings of the Clergy, for the purpose of studying the Holy Scriptures together, and conversing on subjects useful to themselves and their Parishes'. Meetings were held every six weeks at the houses of members ' in the alphabetical order of their parishes'. They began at 12 Noon with prayer led by the president for the day. A portion of the Greek Testament was read and 'examined' until 1.30pm. The second half of the meeting consisted of discussion of a pre-arranged topic until 3pm when the meeting closed with prayer. Dinner followed and was to be 'of the simplest character'.[28] (See page 121)

*   *   *

The only national religious census which has ever taken place was held at the same time as the decennial census in March 1851.[29] Both the fact of the census and the results were controversial and ensured that there would not be another one. The figures collected are hard to interpret since they were not always consistent, for example some clergy counted children separately some did not, some people attended church more than once but who could tell? The figures nonetheless provide a valuable means of estimating church attendance when it was close to its Victorian zenith. At almost all churches there were two services, held usually in the morning and afternoon. Only at Titchfield was there also an evening service. Not all clergy believed that estimating or counting their congregation was a seemly activity. Titchfield for example seems to have been without a resident rector. The curate, William Cosser, after estimating his congregation wrote 'I cannot count my congregation myself and do not feel justified in so occupying any other person during Divine service'.[30]

A useful addition to the Religious Census of 1851 is provided by the notebook kept by William Bradford who followed Henry Bayley as rector of West Meon in 1844.[31] The book issued by the SPCK from 1820 onwards is itself evidence of the new spirit of earnestness to be found amongst the clergy. The book's title is given in Greek, Latin and English – in Latin *Speculum Gregis* ('A View of the Flock') and in English *Parochial Minister's Assistant*. The incumbent or curate is urged to list every family in the parish and to indicate for each name, occupation, age, 'general health', whether they attended church and sacrament, whether they possessed a Bible and Prayer Book and whether they could read or write or were at school. The book was intended to provide an aid to parish visiting.

Church attendance in the Meon valley parishes of the Church of England on 30ˢᵗ March 1851.

Parish/chapelry	Population		Attendance		
	1801	1851	morning	afternoon	evening
Titchfield	2949	3956	490	290	300
Crofton			150	140	–
Sarisbury			212	276	-
Droxford	1199	2005	163	185	–
Shedfield			253	253	–
Swanmore			191	220	–
Droxford Union			–	62	–
Wickham	901	1049	No return		
Meonstoke	289	431	120	130	–
Soberton	672	1147	149	111	–
Newtown			144	140	
Corhampton	120	225	75	52	–
Exton	224	283	96	93	–
Warnford	272	414	121	137	–
West Meon	536	901	365	360	–
Privett	185	281	123	155	–
East Meon	1061	1543	297	396	–
Froxfield	437	729	125	130	–
Steep	414	581	200	300	–

Source: Vickers ed.1993

ΚΆΤΟΠΤΡΟΝ ΤΗ͂Σ ΠΟΊΜΝΗΣ,

SPECULUM GREGIS;

OR,

PAROCHIAL MINISTER'S ASSISTANT.

BY THE REV. R. B. EXTON.

" He understands but little of the nature and obligations of the priestly office, who thinks he has discharged it by performing the public appointments."—BISHOP BURNET.
" The readiest way of finding access to a man's heart, is to go into his house."—CHALMERS'S CHRISTIAN AND CIVIC ECONOMY.

FIFTH EDITION.

LONDON:
PRINTED FOR J. G. & F. RIVINGTON,
ST. PAUL'S CHURCH YARD,
AND WATERLOO PLACE, PALL MALL.

1839.

49. *The Parochial Minister's Assistant* published 1820.

House. No.	Names of Inhabitants.	Occupation.	When Born.	General Health.	Attends Church and Sacrament.	Uses Family Devotion, has a Bible or Prayer-Book.	Attends other Service.	Reads, Writes, or goes to School.	OBSERVATIONS
81	Th.* Simpson	Labourer	34	good	yes	B & P	yes	yes	wife & 6 children
82	W Kill	do	30	good	yes	B & P		yes	wife 4 children
83	J.* Harris	Poulter	41	good	never			no	wife & 3 children
84	J. Paice	Labourer	53	good	yes	B & P		yes	wife 4 children
85	Jph.* Paice	do	41	good	irregular	B & P	sometimes	yes	wife 4 children
86	Widow Phillips	Baker Shop	57	good	yes	B & P	yes	yes	a daughter 11 son ..
87	W.m Phillips	Labourer	40	good	yes wife	B & P	wife	yes	wife
88	W.m Jarrett	Farm	51	good	dissenter				wife 1 daughter
89	G Ford	Labourer	41	good	irregular	B & P	.	yes	wife 3 children
90	H Tutt	Carpenter	44	good	wife	B & P	wife	yes	wife & 5 children

50. Extract from the record of his parish kept by the Revd William Bradford Rector of West Meon 1844–72.

William Bradford's record for West Meon in the year 1851 has survived though its usefulness is reduced because he lists only heads of families with brief notes about wives and children. The book contains the names of 183 heads of families probably all the houses in the parish. Regular attenders at church appear to be about 52% of all those listed. Somewhere about 20% did not attend, one of them described as 'Infidel'. A further 20% were regarded by the rector as occasional attenders – listed as 'irregular', 'sometimes' or 'seldom'. There were 12 dissenters (about 7% of the total families) one of whom is described as a 'Ranter' – probably a Primitive Methodist. At the beginning of the book William Bradford provides totals for the year 1851: the average attendance on each Sunday was 437 and at the 14 celebrations of Holy Communion (monthly, Christmas and Easter) – the average was 48. The rector could only guess how many of his parishioners could read and write. In just under half he answers 'Yes' indicating that the head of the household was literate, only eleven were known not to be literate. In some cases he felt unable to enquire – it must have been a sensitive question.

The villages were self-contained communities. The banns book of West Meon from 1828 to 1864 records 181 marriages. In 60% of these marriages both partners came from West Meon and almost all the remainder lived in neighbouring villages, most in East Meon (10), Warnford (7), Privett (7) and Droxford (5). Only five came from outside Hampshire – two from the Isle of Wight and one each from Dorset, Surrey and Sussex.[32]

* * *

In the nineteenth century not only were new churches provided but most existing churches were enlarged, embellished or even rebuilt often with money provided by the incumbent or by one or more leading parishioners. Alterations were sometimes under-taken with more enthusiasm than discrimination; buildings were erected which we now find hard to maintain. One alteration never regretted was the demolition of

RULES OF THE CLERICAL SOCIETY

FOR THE   *n d*

RURAL DEANERY OF DROXFORD, N.W.

I.—The object of the Society is to promote friendly meetings of the Clergy, for the purpose of studying the Holy Scriptures together, and conversing on subjects useful to themselves and their Parishes.

II.—All Clergymen residing within the N. W. Division of the Deanery of Droxford, and any others who, though beyond its limits, are yet within a reasonable distance, may become Members of the Society, upon the recommendation of one Member, and the approval of the majority.

III.—Any Member, once elected, may be excluded by the unanimous vote of the rest.

IV.—The meetings shall be held every six weeks at the houses of those Members to whom it may be convenient, in the alphabetical order of their parishes. The Member at whose house the meeting is held being president for the day.

V.—Every Member shall consider himself bound to attend the meetings, unless prevented by illness, or some unavoidable engagement. Any Member neglecting to give notice to the President of his intended presence or absence previously to a meeting shall be fined half-a-crown.

VI.—The meetings shall commence punctually at *twelve* o'clock, and shall be opened with Prayer by the President. After which a portion of the Greek Testament shall be read and examined until half-past one : from which time a subject previously chosen by the President shall be discussed until *three* o'clock, when the meeting shall be closed with Prayer.

VII.—The President shall open the Discussion, after which he shall call upon the Members to speak, in rotation. The President shall preserve order, and may call upon any Member speaking to address him.

VIII.—There shall be a permanent Secretary, whose duty it shall be to give a fortnight's notice to every Member of the time and place of the next meeting, of the portion of Holy Scripture to be read, and of the subject to be discussed. He shall also take Minutes of the Society's proceedings and notes of the Discussions, and shall enter them in a book, which shall be brought to each meeting, when the Minutes of the previous meeting shall be read. The Secretary shall also keep the accounts of the Society, calling upon the Members for Subscriptions as often as is necessary.

IX.—The Dinners, which are to take place at *three* o'clock, shall be of the simplest character.

X.—Every Member is earnestly requested, previous to each meeting, to pray for all the Members, that the grace of the Holy Spirit may be abundantly vouchsafed to them at the next meeting, and also that it may rest continually upon themselves, their Congregation, and Parishes at large.

51. Rules of the Clerical Society of the Rural Deanery of Droxford North West c.1860.

galleries. Built in the eighteenth century they were no longer needed. The 'singers', renamed the choir and by the end of the century often robed, were on the cathedral model, placed in the chancel. Galleries provided for extra accommodation were no longer needed as pew rents were phased out and congregations declined. Box pews fitted with cushions, carpets and fireplaces disappeared when the church was repewed uniformly, though leading families occupied seats near the front of the nave. Lighting was at first by candles, later gas and by the mid-1930s many had installed electric light.

All these features are to be found in the Meon valley churches. Wickham church is described by David Lloyd as 'a most unfortunate building'. There were heavy restorations in 1862 and again in 1872–7 when 'it lost all medieval interest without gaining any positive Victorian character'.[33] At Titchfield the galleries were removed. but the Norman south aisle was also demolished in the restoration of 1866–7 and rebuilt in the fourteenth century style at the expense of Louisa and Emily Baring of the rich banking family. Exton was largely rebuilt in 1847 when it was closed for a year. The chancel, vestry and buttresses at the east end are all new and the gallery at the west end was removed. At Meonstoke a gallery built in 1737 was demolished about 1870. A letter from Bishop Wilberforce (1869–74) to the rector Charles Hume describes the gallery as 'intolerable' and makes trenchant criticisms of the renovation then proposed[34] At Corhampton the east end and the north wall of the chancel were undermined in 1842 by road widening and collapsed. The rebuilding in red brick in 1855 seems insensitive and was done 'poorly and clumsily'.[35]

*   *   *

In the last years of the nineteenth century two new parish documents become available – the parish magazine and the service register. Copies of the former, often in yearly bound volumes, are sometimes found when attics are cleared. Parish magazines began to appear from the late 1870s the result of increased literacy, cheaper paper and the desire to provide suitable reading for Sundays when novels were thought by many to be too 'worldly'. By 1885 many churches had a magazine.[36] The church and village component is usually a single sheet but, taken over a period, much can be gleaned not only church and parish news but attitudes to contemporary events because writers did not have an eye to posterity. The magazine of St Peter's Titchfield was started in April 1888 as a result of an invitation from the former daughter parishes of St Paul's, Sarisbury and St Mary's, Hook with Warsash which had begun a magazine in March 1885. Each parish was allocated a single page and the whole was published at 1d a copy with a 12 page syndicated magazine entitled *The Dawn of the Day*.

Early numbers reported the closure of the National School on account of an epidemic the nature of which was not revealed but lasted five months. The school reopened in August 1888 by which time the 'late sickness had abated'. The opportunity had been taken to make structural alterations, to redecorate the school and the school house and to attend to 'sanitary conditions' for all for which donations were invited – £130 –£150 was needed. Failure to raise the money might lead to a School Board which would involve a compulsory rate as well as forfeiting its Church of England status.

The vicar Reginald White spent his holiday in Zermatt and contributed articles to the August and September issues of the magazine. He promised a magic lantern show on his return. The choir men – no women as yet – had an outing to Chichester leaving from *The Bugle* at 7am, visiting the cathedral and Goodwood where they had lunch and then attended a flower show in the grounds of the Bishop's Palace. At 5 pm they dined at *The Dolphin* before beginning the return journey by horse drawn brake which took three hours. They arrived in Titchfield at 10pm. The vicar of Titchfield was concerned at the empty places at the morning service: women might reasonably be preparing Sunday lunch but where were the men? There are signs that men were not assiduous churchgoers and the vicar decided to institute a monthly 'men only' service[37]

At West Meon it was the recently appointed rector Robert Herbert Fair (rector 1899–1917) who began the magazine in January 1900, soon after he arrived in the parish. 'It will be a kind of monthly history of the parish' he wrote in the first number. At the parish church there were services at 8am, 11 and 6.30, a childrens' service at 2.45. At Woodlands mission church there was a monthly communion at 9.30, weekly even-song at 3pm and there were both choir and Sunday School. Later in the year there was a confirmation at Privett to which 15 candidates were taken in three carriages lent by well heeled parishioners. Like many parishes West Meon had a team of district visitors who in addition to paying 'friendly visits to the residents', collected subscriptions for a variety of good causes which included the National School, the Sunday School, missionary societies and a soup kitchen. The parish ran coal and clothing clubs which enabled poor parishioners to buy 30/- worth of goods for 24/-.

The rector of West Meon was a keen supporter of British troops in the Second Boer War then raging and in each month's editorial provided a running commentary on its progress. When Ladysmith was relieved the rector described the celebrations in the parish:

> The sturdy blacksmith, Mr Burrow, and his merry men exploded detonating charges during the day, the ringers sent forth peal after peal … flags were flying and streamers waving. The children after a lesson given up to South African geography … rejoiced in a half holiday . The West Meon band went from point to point discoursing patriotic melodies to a late hour. There was dancing in the streets and a huge bonfire.[38]

The June issue reported similar celebrations when Mafeking was relieved by a force commanded by Robert Baden-Powell who it was noted had been at school at nearby Charterhouse.[39]

Later in the year progress in building the Meon Valley Railway was reported. It was possible to see the 'steam navvy' at work 'like some living piece of machinery'. Watching it the rector looked into the boundless future. 'The day is not far off ', he wrote, 'when many of our field operations like digging, harvesting, ricking and perhaps the building of houses will be done for the most part by machinery either by steam or by electricity'. [40]

*   *   *

Changes in church services took place slowly in the nineteenth century particularly in country churches which were little affected by the Oxford Movement. From 1820 hymns were no longer illegal and spread slowly until the publication of *Hymns Ancient and Modern* in 1861. At Hook the opportunity was taken to replace worn out hymn books with *Hymns Ancient and Modern* in 1885 and copies were made available to members of the congregation at the reduced rate of 6d and 3d.[41]

At long last from the 1870s the morning service of Morning Prayer, Litany, Ante Communion and sermon could legally be divided into its component parts and became shorter though many clergy were slow to embrace change. Until 1888 the morning service at Titchfield remained undivided, advertised in the Parish Magazine as 'Morning Prayer, Litany, the AnteCommunion Service and Sermon'. The new vicar Reginald White seems at once to have shortened the morning service. Holy Communion was still celebrated after the morning service in many churches but the practice of an early service at 8am at first once a month but soon weekly became the practice in most churches by the end of the century. All magazines contain exhortations to parishioners to attend 'this most important service' regularly but the old practice of taking Holy Communion only at the major festivals and particularly at Easter died hard.[42]

In their late teens most of the youth of the parish were confirmed. In two confirmations held in consecutive months for parishes in the Alverstoke deanery 210 candidates were confirmed. Harvest Festival was not yet a regular Sunday event but might be marked by a week night gathering and service.

Until the state began to provide welfare early in the twentieth century it was the church which met the needs of those who could not provide for themselves. Soup kitchens, coal and clothing clubs, district visitors, parish reading rooms and libraries were organised. At Sarisbury there was a lending library which you could join for 1d per month and you could change your book at 3.45 pm after Sunday School.[43] At Hook the lending library had 460 books from which to choose.

Each parish was intent on keeping people out of the clutches of the pubs and there were a variety of temperance organisations. At Hook the reading room was open every evening except Sunday from 6–10pm and provided a variety of games – bagatelle, draughts, dominoes, solitaire – as well as local and daily papers, all providing what the magazine described as 'rational enjoyment'. The Church of England Temperance Society had a branch in every parish and the Band of Hope was its junior branch. At Hook a Temperance Society was formed in February 1885 when Mr Glover ' the well known Temperance orator' gave his 'heart-stirring' address drawing on his experience 'in the colonies' and 34 children joined at once. 'We must all feel the great need … for vigorous Temperance work throughout the land'.[44]

Few ordinary people could afford a holiday and the variety of outings organised by the church were an accepted substitute. Twice each year in the summer and at Christmas every organisation had its outing, treat or party at which games were played and to the cost of which the better off parishioners contributed. The church was outward looking. Every parish supported 'foreign' missions. When the Fareham to Southampton railway line was being built in 1886 the Sarisbury Parish Magazine reported that there would be 800–900 men working on the line and supported the work of the Navvy Mission Society.[45] May Day was celebrated and a flower festival held to which children were asked to bring flowers which were then conveyed to sick children in London hospitals. The parish of Hook with Warsash was aware that many still found it difficult to reach the church and school and in 1886 built a mission room on Titchfield Common which was dedicated on Friday 25th March 1887. The day school there was soon accommodating 50 children. At the end of 1888 the Fleet End mission was established.

In the years before the First World War the Rector of Droxford was John Vaughan (1902–09), described by Kenneth Ward as 'the most notable of a long line of Droxford rectors. Great churchman, botanist and naturalist, author [and] humanitarian'. He was responsible for a major programme of restoration which resulted in the discovery at Droxford of many features of the pre-Refomation church which had been lost. In 1909 he was appointed a residentiary canon of Winchester Cathedral where he made a major contribution to the history and topography of the cathedral. He wrote *The Memorials and Monuments of Winchester Cathedral* and partly as a result of the finding of the Wainscot Book in an oak settle in the south transept of the cathedral he wrote *Winchester Cathedral Close: its History and Library*. He also published three anthologies: *The Wild Flowers of Selborne, Lighter Studies of a Country Parson* and *The Music of Wild Flowers*. He died suddenly in 1922 and his funeral was attended by huge crowds. He is commemorated in a memorial tablet on the south wall of the nave of Winchester Cathedral.[46]

15

Mills and Water Meadows

FOR 1500 YEARS the mills of the river Meon were amongst the most prominent features of the villages and in many cases constituted their life-blood. From the sixteenth century to the twentieth water meadows also featured among the most important landmarks on the river. Neither is any longer in operation but their history is nonetheless fascinating.

There were once as many as 300 mills on rivers in Hampshire; by 1900 there were under 100 working mills left and by 1939 only 34. A survey carried out in 1968 listed 13 mills on the river Meon of which parts survived but only one of them was still in use as a mill. Maintenance of the mills was costly, weed had to be removed and worn parts renewed. Left unused, mills quickly became derelict and were often demolished; for example the mill at Exton which once stood close to the river opposite to the present site of *The Shoe*. Other mills have been converted to new uses. The mill at Corhampton is now a private house with the mill-race still flowing beneath the house. At Soberton the mill was in 1968 a store and the erstwhile millstones were flagstones. Several were private houses – Frogmore Mill and Drayton Mill both at East Meon as well as Droxford Mill.[1]

The large parish of Titchfield had in the middle ages no less than five corn mills all mentioned in the Domesday book. The most northerly was Great Funtley Mill occupied in the twentieth century by members of the Tappenden family who were also millers at Wickham. Little Funtley Mill became a fulling mill by the fourteenth century but by 1610 was no longer used and by the nineteenth century its buildings had disappeared. Segensworth Mill too was in disrepair by 1350 and its site can no longer be found, perhaps obliterated when the branch line from Eastleigh to Gosport via Fareham was built in the early 1840s. Titchfield Mill was the village corn mill, in existence before the Norman Conquest. The present building dates from 1830 and incorporates stones from Place House by then partly demolished. It continued to be used for milling until the 1950s and is now a hotel. Finally south of Titchfield was Hubbard's Mill at Crofton but by the nineteenth century this too had disappeared.[2]

Although most mills were used for corn there were in the Meon valley two iron mills one of which was of seminal importance not only in Hampshire but countrywide. The first was north of Wickham where the 3rd Earl of Southampton owned and leased to Sir William Uvedale a plate mill, even the site of which can no longer be seen since in the late twentieth century it was flooded to form a fishing lake.

52. The Old Mill at Exton now demolished.

53. Corhampton Mill, now a private house.

54. Droxford Mill 1973 (rebuilt).

The most important iron mill in the Meon valley was at Funtley. It too owes its origin to the 3rd Earl of Southampton but its importance is due to Henry Cort (1740–1800) who was a naval contractor who in 1783 and 1784 took out patents for purifying iron by 'puddling' – stirring molten iron to remove carbon and other impurities. This revolutionised the production of wrought iron and instead of being an importer Britain became an exporter of wrought iron. In 1788 Britain produced 68,000 tons of pig iron, by 1804 250,000 tons. There are few remains to be seen of Cort's mill at Funtley as many of the buildings were destroyed by fire in the late nineteenth century. Henry Cort himself was ruined by bankruptcy and the suicide of one of his main creditors and was unable to protect his patent when it lapsed in 1789.[3]

The one corn mill still in use in 1968 was the last to be rebuilt as a mill as well as the largest and most imposing – Chesapeake Mill at Wickham. Still then used to grind cattle food, it owed its name to the source of the beams employed in its reconstruction. Milling had gone on at Wickham at least since Domesday recorded two mills in the village. At the end of the eighteenth century the mill was owned by the Prior family. During the war of 1812–14 between the United States and Britain – an offshoot of the Napoleonic Wars – the American frigate *Chesapeake* was captured off Boston by *HMS Shannon* and for a time was incorporated into the British navy. In 1819 it was broken up and timbers from the ship were advertised in local papers and bought by John Prior who was about to rebuild Wickham Mill. He demolished the old mill and used the

55. Paper Mill Cottage, Warnford built 1618.

56. Paper Mill, Warnford before the storm of 1953 which destroyed it.

57. Chesapeake Mill Wickham.

deck timbers from the *Chesapeake* almost unaltered. The provenance of the timbers has been authenticated by the National Maritime Museum at Greenwich; some of the beams bear marks of grapeshot from *HMS Shannon*.

The rebuilt mill changed hands several times in the next century or so. The last miller, who lived in the adjoining miller's house, was Bruce Tappenden, the historian of Wickham and a blue plaque on the house commemorates both aspects of his life. It remained a working mill until 1991. Since then it has been bought by Hampshire County Council and leased by them to Chesapeake Mill Limited which has opened it to the public as a retail outlet including a small museum organised by the Wickham History Society.[3]

Why then had the mills, once so prominent a feature of the economy and the landscape, ceased to operate so suddenly? The wheat imported from the United States from the late nineteenth century onwards produced whiter flour, more attractive to users than the courser flour available earlier. It needed however to be ground by roller mills which were soon installed at ports of entry. In an attempt to compete the Hurley family who had bought Droxford mill in 1885 installed in 1898 a two-sack roller plant driven by water and steam power and employing a coal fired boiler. The cost of structural alterations to the building, machinery and installation, the running costs and overcapacity was prohibitive and by 1905 the mill was in debt and the mortgagee of the Hurley family foreclosed. The mill was bought by Richard Westbrook farmer of Northend, Droxford who worked it until 1925 but never profitably. In 1927 'the Droxford Flour Mill' was sold at *The Station Hotel* (now *The Hurdles*) and bought by Howard Rogers who pulled down the old building and used the timbers in houses which he was then building. The remains of the Mill were bought by Tom Hulbert who had moved into Fir Hill in 1927 on returning from India.[5] He built a generator house and put in a water-turbine which provided electricity for the house and for the church. The mill building left empty rapidly became dilapidated.

During the Second World War Droxford Mill was a salvage store and a training centre for the Red Cross. After the war John Hulbert who had inherited Fir Hill on the death of his father in 1938 left Fir Hill in 1954, reconstructed the Mill and converted it into the attractive private house it has since become, a well-known landmark by the river at Droxford. He lived there until 1976. The recent fortunes of Droxford Mill are typical of many of the mills on the Meon.[6]

*   *   *

Water meadows were a feature of the fields which lay beside the river Meon from source to the sea. The chalk streams of Hampshire were ideally suited to water meadows and the county contains almost half of all the water meadows in England. Oliver Rackham found the earliest reference to water meadows as early as 1523.[7] John Worlidge of Petersfield, the well known Hampshire agriculturalist, described water meadows in 1669 as 'one of the most universal and advantageous improvements in England within these few years'. [8] Water was moved on to the meadow through a system of feeders from the main river. Water meadows were constructed on the rivers of southern England and in Hampshire they were found on the Avon, Itchen and Test as well as on the Meon on which there were 41 systems.

Early nineteenth century minutes kept by the clerk of the Droxford Vestry include a long running saga of non-payment for water used 'for the Benefit of the Meadows called Kings Meades at Mislingford'. The rent was 10/- per year which the Vestry intended to raise to £5.0.0 per year but not even the 10/- had been paid recently. Three years later the minutes record that rent had not been paid since 1806 so the Vestry instructed their clerk Thomas Holland to inform the lessee that 'in the name of the Parish they have determined to pull down and destroy the Hatches or water stops'. It was 17 years since the rent had been paid so the lessee owed the overseers the sum of £8.10.0 not counting any increase in rent. Sadly the outcome of this threat is not recorded.[9] There was trouble at Droxford once more in 1824: this time the lessee of land in Midlington Lane had led the water over the public highway The Vestry declared that 'nobody should direct or turn a water course to bring it across a Public Highway'. It was 'a nuisance which ought to be abated'.[10]

After about 1850 no new water meadow systems were established since the cost was high. But in the early years of the twentieth century there were still as many as

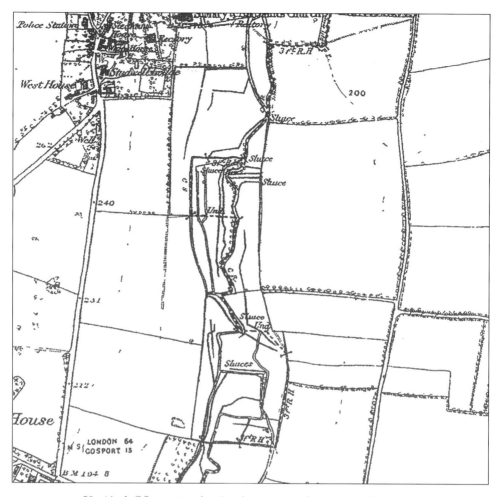

58. 6 inch OS map 1874 showing the water meadows south of Droxford.

23 functioning water meadows in the Meon valley. Few however lasted much beyond the Second World War. John Hurst who came to West Meon as rector in 1950 states that the water meadows of the parish were repaired in the 1940s by Italian prisoners of war but dropped out of use soon afterwards.[11] Den Marriner who worked in the late 1940s at Exton Manor Farm recalls that one of his jobs was to help maintain the water meadows fed by a channel under the A32 as well as the meadows on the south-west of the Grinch, by digging out in early spring the drainage ditches which had been trampled by the cattle. But by the early 1950s the introduction of silage to feed cattle meant that early grass, the result of flooding the meadows, was no longer needed and in any case maintenance of the water meadows was not cost effective and they gradually decayed. In some cases they were ploughed out; others were neglected and decayed.[12]

Writing in *The Hampshire Magazine* in September 1969 Norman Goodland recorded the great reduction in the number of water meadows which had taken place in the previous five years. By the late 60s he claimed that few farmers were actively irrigating. He attributed decline to the rarity of 'drowners', men who controlled the system, understood the river and repaired hatches and weirs. At times of danger – storm, high water or frost – they needed to be available at once to open or close the hatches. Water meadows were labour intensive and ceased to be used and in some cases were destroyed by neglect, as a result of mechanisation of farming and the spread of chemicals. By 1997 only two systems in the Meon valley were well preserved and a further two 'partially preserved'.[13]

The best preserved water meadows in the Meon valley are those south of the paper mill in Meonstoke. The carrier leaves the river at the south end of Warnford Park and runs east of and close to the A32 for half a mile. Overflow water can be emptied into the Meon by an iron sluice which survives. The remains of three brick culverts which could be opened to allow minor carriers to feed 'furrows' transferring water on to the fields at 20 feet intervals survive too. The feeder turns east and there are further culverts. The whole system stretches as far as the river Meon at the Grinch at Exton. It was a complex and sophisticated piece of engineering and even though it has long been disused the bright green, healthy grass in the early Spring still bears witness to the effectiveness of the system.[14]

The remains of channels and brick sluices which facilitated the winter flooding of the meadows can also be seen in fields opposite *The Bucks Head* at Meonstoke and are

59. Remains of a sluice in the water meadows south of the Paper Mill, Warnford.

60. The Bays at Meonstoke used to open the sluice to the water meadows
opposite *The Bucks Head.*

visible from the A32. The feeder channel left the Meon at a sluice on the east side of
the A32, and went under the road. Droxford too has several systems. The 6" ordnance
map of 1874 shows at least six sluices which were used to flood the fields. Vestiges
survive: remains of brick culverts as well as fields with ridge and furrow and channels
for the water to run.[15] At Wickham until the Second World War cattle were led to
natural water meadows where the Meon flooded each winter. To mark the Millennium
the parish has laid out the former meadows as an attractive open space (see pages
238–9).

At Titchfield Haven five acres of water meadow created in the seventeenth century
and not used since the First World War have been repaired and reconstructed. The
New River is the high level carrier to the west and there is a fall of three metres to the
river Meon to the east.[16]

16

Four Big Houses

❦

T HE NINETEENTH CENTURY and up to 1914 were the halcyon years of the big
houses. Living-in servants were easy to obtain, taxes were low, death duties were
not levied until the 1890s, huge disparities of income were accepted as part of the
natural order and a hierarchical society in which the leading families were deferred to
was taken for granted. The village aristocracy, the male members of which provided
members of parliament, Justices of the Peace, and after 1888 county councillors as well
as churchwardens, were the leaders of social and cultural life.

Preshaw House is at the centre of a large country estate. Until well into the twentieth
century it consisted of 2500 acres and still today covers 1290 acres. It is entered by the
north drive which runs from the road from Warnford to Winchester flanked by an
entrance lodge. The drive, which was realigned and the north lodge built, between 1870
and 1895, winds for a mile or so through an avenue of mature beech trees, planted when
the road was made, before opening out to a magnificent viewpoint over house and hamlet.

There was a manor house at Preshaw in the middle ages. *Presshawe* and *Richard de
Preysagh* are names which occur in deeds which can probably be dated to the thirteenth
century. Like Lomer it belonged to Hyde Abbey.[1] In 1538 John Croppe who probably
lived at the manor made a will which included the traditional catholic preamble
'I biquith my soule to almyghti God to o'lady and to all the companye of hevyn'.[2] An
inventory of the goods of John Loremer made in 1578, the year in which he died, gives
us an idea of the contents of his house. It included a hall, kitchen and parlour, a
chamber over the parlour and five other chambers, a study, buttery, larder, milk house,
wool loft, well-house, stables, cellar and outbuildings. His furniture, if not luxurious,
suggested a comfortable life style including cushions, carpets and hangings. His agricultural assets included 13 horses and geldings, 16 kine and a bull, 448 wether 'shepe',
313 ewe 'shepe' and 182 teggs. His total assets came to £532-13-4 which constituted a
considerable estate.[3]

The heart of the present house of three bays was built about 1634 and then occupied
by John and Cary Stewkely. It is thought by some to be where General Waller spent
the night before his victory at the battle of Cheriton in March 1644 during the Civil
War.[4]It must have been a substantial house since in 1665 John Stewkely paid Hearth
Tax on 17 hearths.[5] An estate map of 1684 drawn by Moses Neave, in the possession of
Sir Richard Pelly, includes the house as well as outbuildings, courtyard and gardens
and there are also between four and six cottages to the north of the house.[6]

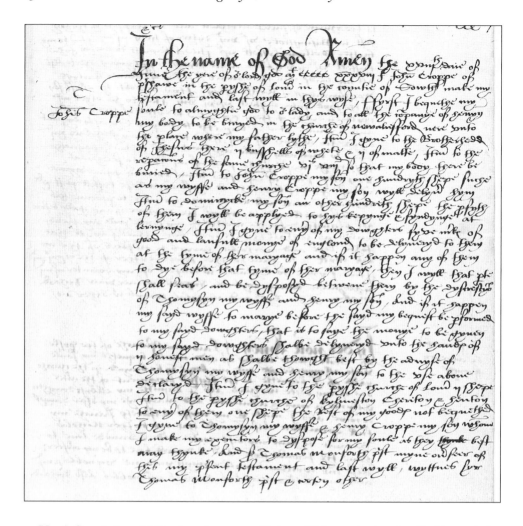

Hugh Stewkely sold Preshaw in 1707 to Robert Kirby and when he died in 1728 the estate was bought by John Long. The Longs lived at Preshaw for 170 years and were responsible during that time for two major extensions to the house. Some time after 1770 three bays were added on the east and in the early nineteenth century the architect John Nash was commissioned to build further rooms on the south side doubling its thickness and giving the house the massive appearance which it still bears. At the same time the interior was decorated with plaster cornices and ceilings. The Ordnance Survey map of 1870 shows an ice-house in woodland to the south, a small gas works next to the house and an engine house on the north side connected with the supply of water.[7] The chapel was added in 1864.[8] Pelly family memorials have been installed in the chapel brought from the crypt of a West Ham church when it was demolished.

The Longs were a Wiltshire family who bought the estate for £7,600. Many Long family memorials are to be found in Corhampton church though the family vault was

61. (*left*) Will of John
Croppe of Preshaw 1538.
(*right*) Transcription
Borthwick & Chandler
Vol. 2.

In the name of God Amen, the 18ᵗʰ daie of June the yere of o 'Lord God 1538 I John Croppe of Preshawe in the paryshe of Lom' in the countie of South't make my testament and last wyll in thys wyse. First I biquithe my soule to almyghti' God to o' lady and to all the companye of hevyn, my body to be buryed in the churche of newalsifford nere unto the place where my father lythe,

- *Item I gyve to the Brotherhedd of Jhesus there 2 busshills of whete and 2 of malte.*

- *Item to the reparacions of the same churche 6s 8 d so that my body there be buried.*

- *Item to John Croppe my son one hundryth shepe such as my wyffe and Henry Croppe my son wyll delyv 'hym.*

- *Item to Dominyck my son another hundreth shepe the profyth of them I wyll be applied to hys kepynge and fyndinge at lernynge.*

- *Item I gyve to every of my dowghters five m'ke of good and lawfull money of England to be delyveryd to them at the tyme of ther maryage and if it happen any of them to dye before that tyme of ther maryage then I wyll that parte shall seas and be dysposyd betwen them by the dyscrestyon of Thomysyn my wyffe and Henry my son. And if yt happen my sayd wyffe to marye before the sayd my bequest be performed to my sayd daughters that is to saye the money to be gyven to my sayd daughters shalbe delivered unto the hands of 2 honest men as shalbe thowght best by the advyse of Thomysyn my wyffe and Henry my son to the use above declaryd.*

- *Item I gyve to the paryshe churche of Lom' 2 shepe.*

- *Item to the paryshe churches of Kylmeston Cheriton and Henton to every of them one shepe.*

The rest of my goods not bequethed I gyve to Thomysyn my wyffe and Henry Croppe my son whom I make my executors to dispose for my soule as they best may thynke. And Syr Thomas Monforth priest myne overseer of this present testament and last wyll wytnis Syr Thomas Monforth priest and certen other.

The Will of John Croppe of Preshaw 1538 Transcribed from HRO WR/3 p.193

at Upham church. The Longs were keen huntsmen and Preshaw became a well-known hunting venue. For a third of the nineteenth century a member of the family was Master of the Hambledon Hunt.[9] A younger son William Long (1817–86) was a noted antiquary and wrote an early account of Avebury.[10]

The wedding in June 1895 of Katherine Theresa Long and Robert Eden Richardson of nearby Morestead House provided a fitting pastoral swansong to the Longs occupancy. The guests drove to the wedding over the Hampshire Downs, 'from the breezy summits of which were to be seen scores of miles of green country with undulating valleys and woodland glens and glimpses of fresh scenery in every direction…. Soon after noon carriages … arrived in rapid succession and discharged their occupants opposite the main entrance where they were received by Mrs Long … in a manner indicative of a family brimful of human kindness.'[11]

In 1898 three years after the wedding Walter Long left Preshaw and the estate was

62. Preshaw House by G. F. Prosser, 1755.

63. Preshaw House now divided into four apartments.

sold to Baron De Bush. He did not stay long and it was sold again in 1901, this time to Reginald Cholmondeley who in 1911 added a further nine bedrooms on the south side of the house. He was a kinsman of Frederick Raymond Pelly (1869–1940) who bought the estate at the end of the First World War.

The Pellys were originally a Dorset family drawn to the east end of London in the early eighteenth century. They settled in the 1730s at Upton – better known by the name Upton Park now home of West Ham Football Club – and though not them-selves Quakers were associated with a number of Quaker families who were both philanthropists and successful merchants and bankers – the Frys, Buxtons and Gurneys for example. John Henry Pelly (1777–1852) was governor of the Hudson Bay company and responsible for sending out parties which mapped the coastline of North America and attempted to discover the north-west passage. It was for these exploits that he was made a baronet in 1840. In the North West Territories of Canada, north and west of Hudson Bay are to be found Pelly Bay and Pelly Lake reminders of the key part which John Pelly had played in the opening up of the region. The title of the baronetcy 'of Upton' commemorates the link with east London. John Pelly was also a director of the Bank of England and Deputy Master of Trinity House.[12]

The Pellys who bought Preshaw in 1919 were an affluent family with a town house in St James's Place, a prestigious part of London, close to St James's Palace, as well as their country seat at Preshaw in Hampshire. There was a substantial staff at both houses. In London the staff included butler, footman, cook, ladies maid, kitchen maid and three housemaids. The domestic quarters where staff worked were in the semi-basement and their bedrooms, often shared, were on the third floor. Uniform was worn by all servants – blue dress, white apron (blue one for washing up) and black shoes for junior staff. The upper servants – butler, footman and cook – ate apart from the remaining servants and were themselves waited on by junior staff – early morning tea, meals served, beds made and room cleaned. The cook, whether married or not, was accorded the courtesy title of 'Mrs'. Staff meals were taken before or after the family – staff lunch was at 12 Noon, family lunch at 1pm; family dinner at 8pm, servants' supper at 9pm. Pay began at £27 per year and increased on promotion.[13]

Weekends were often spent in the country. On Friday cook, ladies maid and footman would travel by Rolls Royce to Hampshire – with a stop at a pub on the Hog's Back – to supplement the permanent staff at Preshaw which included another butler, four housemaids and a kitchen maid. At Preshaw there were also three chauffeurs, three laundry maids, three gamekeepers and no less than 18 gardeners. Preshaw was a large house with its own servants' hall and housekeeper's room. It was a chauffeur's job to fetch the papers from Basingstoke whilst the postman called at 8am and was given breakfast and returned with the second post at 4pm and was given tea.

Preshaw was a shooting estate and when there were visiting parties the ladies' maids and gun loaders had their meals in the housekeeper's room. The shooting party would leave with food for the day – a lunch hamper including chicken pie, Irish stew, cheeses, cold ham and jacket potatoes. The loaders and beaters would need similar fare and beer to accompany it. At the house lunch was served for the ladies who had not accom-panied the shoot.

Every other year the Pellys went to Scotland for the grouse shooting. Staff shared a sleeper and had breakfast on the train, arriving at Moffat or Drumnadrochit the following day. Life was hard but lightened by outings to Fort William, Loch Ness or even Glasgow or Edinburgh. At Preshaw there would be dances in the surrounding villages often lasting until 3 or 4am but the servants would still have to be up at 6am[14].

On the death in 1940 of Frederick Pelly the estate and house were left to a relation Sir Alwyne Pelly the 5th baronet and in 1981 he was followed by his son Sir John Pelly the 6th baronet (1918–97). By now the house was far too big for a single family and perhaps in any case deserved Pevsner's laconic description 'a strange house'.[15] In 1986 Sir John sold the house but retained the estate.[16] A developer converted the house into four self-contained dwellings and built Preshaw hamlet round the church, adapting farm buildings no longer in use – laundry, dovecote, shippons, stable, carpenter's shop and calf sheds for example. Sir John built The Manor House on the site of the former Gardener's Cottage. Since 1991 Sir John's nephew has farmed the estate and on his uncle's death in 1993 became the 7th baronet.[17]

* * *

On the east side of the A32 just short of the village of Warnford (going north) lies Warnford Park, not easily visible from the road since the erection of an earth bank separating the estate from the road, built to reduce the noise of traffic on the A32. Only on Sundays may vehicles enter the park, to attend services at the parish church first built in Saxon times. On Sunday afternoons in February the present owner allows the gates to be opened so that visitors may enjoy and marvel at the profusion of snowdrops which have been growing among the trees of the estate for longer than anybody can remember.

The Warnford estate has a complex story: every blade of grass contains layers of history. Since the thirteenth century there have been three successive houses in the park. The first usually called St John's House but sometimes, erroneously, King John's House is now a picturesque ruin east of the church. The second stood from the end of the sixteenth century north of the church parallel with the river and was constantly enlarged and altered until its demolition began in 1956. The third was built by the present owners Andrew and Carolyn Sellick and was completed in 2005 on a site to the south of the church. In addition there is an eighteenth century dower house described by Nikolaus Pevsner as 'a summer house' but looking much more like the folly regarded as an essential adjunct to a fashionable estate in the eighteenth century.[18]

The Norman hall house was built by either Adam de Port, a member of the family who had come over with William the Conqueror and become one of his tenants in chief, or by his son William, about 1240. William took the name St John when he married the heir of the St John family and the old house still goes by that name.

Some 300 years later in 1577 the manor was bought by William Neale, Auditor of the Exchequer to Queen Elizabeth I who had until that time lived at The Cloisters, part of the church of St Bartholomew the Great in Smithfield. He set about building a new house at Warnford probably using material from the original St John house which until then had been habitable. The house, built on a new site to the north of the church, was called Place House, the usual name for the leading house of a locality. [19]

64. 'King John's House', Warnford.

65. Warnford Park by G. F. Prosser, 1755.

Charles Millen, rector of Warnford from 1946–1963, who wrote a brief history of the house, believed that about 1635 the old house was re-roofed and subsequently used as a barn. Although the new house was extended by Sir Thomas Neale, son of William, it was not lived in after 1646 and in 1678 the Neales sold it.[20]

It was William Neale who was responsible in 1618 for building, just south of the estate, one of the first paper mills in Hampshire together with the timber framed miller's cottage. It was a small concern, probably making brown paper and employing not more than six men. Three families dominated the making of paper at Warnford. The Filers (Martin who died in 1668 and his grandson Francis who died in 1742), were succeeded by the Bignells until the 1780s when the Haynes took over. Paper was made at Warnford until about the end of the eighteenth century after which the mill gradually became derelict. In 1953 the wooden superstructure was destroyed in a storm leaving only stone foundations. The present owner has erected a replica of the wooden superstructure.[21]

During the eighteenth century the Warnford estate changed hands several times.[22] By about the middle of the century the Clanricardes, an Irish family from Portumna in County Mayo, were first tenants and from 1754 owners of the estate. Their tenure lasted through three generations until 1826, though the thirteenth and fourteenth earls chose to be buried in Ireland and there are no Clanricarde monuments in the church.[23]

The Clanricardes made a number of changes to the Warnford estate. In 1773 there was correspondence with Capability Brown, consulting him about the lay out of the park. The resulting survey was undertaken by J.Spyers, one of Brown's employees who subsequently married his daughter. Though the survey has not been traced the influence of Capability Brown is evident in changes made by the Clanricardes. They renamed the house: in future it would be called 'Belmont' to accord with contemporary views and the park was named 'Senfoy'. The St John house, unroofed once more, became a 'romantick ruin' such as owners of eighteenth century estates liked to have close by. The Dower House built in Strawberry Hill Gothic was part of the same transformation. They added the lake, the Memento Mori bridge by the artificial canal on the side away from the lake. All the new buildings were flint faced and of Gothic design like the work done elsewhere by Capability Brown

The newly arrived Clanricardes took advantage of the turnpike, approved by act of parliament in 1758 though not built until the 1770s, to remodel the estate, enclosing the open fields by agreement, moving the cottages clustered close to the church and creating the ornamental park. The turnpike trustees meanwhile planned and built a fenced new road outside the park. *Hampshire Treasures* says that the foundations of the medieval village are still found when graves are dug along the south wall of the churchyard.[24] Michael Hughes describes Warnford as 'an example of a settlement shift caused by the laying out of a landscaped park'.[25]

The 14th Earl of Clanricarde who had inherited when he was only five in 1808 married the daughter of George Canning (Prime Minister briefly in 1827) and was later ambassador to St Petersburg. He sold Warnford Park in 1826 to William Abbot

66. The Dower House, Warnford Park.

who in turn sold it 20 years later to Edward Rose Tunno, a wealthy India tea merchant, who added further to the house and in 1846 founded the village school.

He died in 1862 and two years later the estate was bought by Henry Woods, Member of Parliament for Wigan where he had substantial mining interests. The name 'Belmont' was dropped and the house and estate became 'Warnford Park'. The house bought by Henry Woods was described by Charles Millen as 'a conglomeration of shapes and styles' so Woods encased the whole in a symmetrical façade. He built lodges at the north and west entrances, of which only the north lodge survives.

Woods was a benefactor to the village and in 1876 added to Tunno's school to enable it to accommodate 70 children. The Woods' tenure lasted for three generations – Henry, William (died 1932) and Henry Charles who died just before the outbreak of the Second World War. The contents of the house were then sold at a three day auction when the furniture of 'about 20 bedrooms', five reception rooms and a substantial amount of silver, much of it early Victorian, were auctioned.[26]

The estate, though not the house, had been bought in 1936 by Reginald Chester. He set up what by 1939 was the biggest pig breeding unit in Europe on what he described as '1000 derelict acres'. He improved the cottages in the village owned by the estate. In the first year some 20,000 rabbits were caught and netting installed to prevent further depradations. By the end of 1938 close on 6,000 pigs were being raised mostly Large Whites and Saddlebacks whilst pig manure was used to enrich the land with humus. Controversially the pigs were raised on concrete where it had been assumed that they would flourish only on mud.[27] The pigs however provided much needed employment. At West Meon school the head noted the rising numbers – 117 on the books – 'chiefly due to the developments taking place in Warnford where pig breeding and bacon curing is about to be developed on a large scale'.(West Meon School Log 5th April 1937).

Reginald Chester meantime lived at Wheely Down House. Wartime conditions, particularly the difficulty of obtaining sufficient food, meant that the pig business could not be maintained. The house in Warnford Park was by now scarcely habitable. During the Second World War when the Park was requisitioned and used for training by troops of the Lancashire Fusiliers it sustained further damage. It was used too to accommodate Italian prisoners of war. After the war the house was demolished. Reginald Chester died in 1969 and his son, Rex, took over the estate. By now the Chesters owned most of the village. Rex Chester had run the estate of 1500 acres with no less than 42 employees from an estate office in the village of Warnford. Properties were gradually leased and the number of people employed by the estate dropped. In 1995 Rex Chester sold the estate and it was bought by Andrew Sellick who in 2005 built a new house, this time south of the church.

The part of the estate lying to the west of the A 32 was sold to Malcolm Isaac who had for many years lived at Abbey House built as the Warnford rectory in the early nineteenth century by Richard Hume Lancaster. Malcolm Isaac had since 1955 grown watercress, first at Alresford on the river Itchen, then at St Mary Bourne near Andover

67. Demolition of the old house in Warnford Park 1956.

and in Dorset and later in Portugal. He also imported cress from Florida and else-where. Watercress was a traditional industry in the Meon valley suited to the chalk streams. At Warnford there are abundant springs as well as the river. The original beds were hand dug and the cress cultivated using artesian wells and water from the river. By the late twentieth century Health and Safety legislation required changes. The industry was now closely controlled, the cress had to be grown on gravel and the water tested for purity. Malcolm Isaac had by now diversified and pioneered new ways of growing other salad crops and Hampshire Watercress became Vitacress Salads. The business was sold early in the 21st century to a Portuguese buyer for between £40 and £50 million.

* * *

The village of West Meon contains three substantial houses: West Meon House in the centre of the village, Hall Place on the road to East Meon and Westbury House on the eastern boundary of the parish. Westbury House became a boys' preparatory school after the First World War and subsequently a nursing home.[28] Families continue to live in the other two houses.

West Meon House is partly Tudor and partly Jacobean with east and west walls built of an attractive mixture of weathered stone, flint and brick. The house is included in a survey of glebe belonging to the diocese of Winchester in 1759. Mary Touchet may have owned the house briefly in the 1820s and added to it. About 1830 the recently appointed rector Henry Vincent Bayley, brother-in-law of Mary Touchet, thought the then rectory – now *The Red Lion* – fronting on to the main road was not a suitable residence for a gentleman and so moved to the altogether grander West Meon House. It was already a substantial house with extensive grounds and gardens which Bayley proceeded to extend. The chimney on the north side bears his initials and coat of arms. On the front of the house was a substantial porch which was removed by a late twen-tieth century owner.

West Meon House ceased to be the rectory in 1917 and was empty for two years until it was bought by Cecil and Enid Waudby. The house had been neglected and the garden was a wilderness. Cecil Waudby, a professional soldier, had served as a major in the 18th Hussars during the First World War and was invalided out of the army. In a very short time he became the leading citizen of West Meon and a pillar of the church, the founder for example of the West Meon Players who often performed outdoors in his garden. The Waudbys restored the grounds to their former glory. In the years between the wars vestiges of the old life were still possible particularly in villages like those of the Meon valley. At West Meon House there were tennis parties, dinner parties and after church drinks each Sunday.

Servants were needed to run such a house and the gardens too required labour. At West Meon House Ruby Clay and her sister Ivy, housemaid and parlour maid, were among the substantial indoor staff. There was a butler – the last named 'Brewer' – until

68. The Rectory Donkey Cart & the Porter's Donkey Cart outside West Meon Rectory c.1900 (now West Meon House).

69. Group outside West Meon Rectory c.1900 (now West Meon House).

he was called up in 1942. The servants' hall and the back stairs which had led to the servants' bedrooms lasted until after the Second World War. In the servants quarters behind baize doors were bells connected to each bedroom and one of the maids' duties was to carry up hot water night and morning. The house generated its own electricity and water was pumped from a well in the stable yard, drinking water came from a spring in the garden and hot water was heated in a huge boiler in the scullery. There was – and is – no mains sewerage and no gas at West Meon. The telephone arrived between the wars and there was a manual exchange in the village: the telephone number was West Meon 36.

The head gardener for the whole time the Waudbys were at West Meon House was 'Phillips' who lived at Pansy Cottage. (His Christian name was Bert but like all male servants he was known to all by his surname.) There were two further gardeners and Phillips was also assisted by his two sons who joined him on leaving school and stayed until they were called up for war service. In addition the Waudbys were themselves keen gardeners and until the war the gardens were immaculate with glasshouses, extensive lawns and huge kitchen garden as well as two grass tennis courts. During the war the gardens were hard to maintain but many village events were still held there though performances by the West Meon Players were suspended.

During the Second World War life was austere. Parts of the house were closed and the Red Cross used the drawing room as its depot. Servants were no longer available – gardeners joined the army and girls the women's services – and the servants' hall became a dining room. The last living-in servants left in 1943. The house was cold since central heating consumed scarce fuel and wood fires were ineffective in such a large house. Motor cars were laid up as there was no petrol to run them. The Waudbys sold West Meon House in 1946.[29]

*   *   *

In 1545 West Meon was surrendered by the Dean and Chapter of Winchester Cathedral and granted by Henry VIII to Thomas Wriothesley, Lord Chancellor and soon to be Earl of Southampton, already a substantial landowner in Hampshire. At the end of the century the estate was occupied (though not owned) by Nicholas Sutton who lived at Hall Place, died there is 1635 and was buried in the old church at West Meon.[30] On the death of the 4th Earl of Southampton West Meon was sold to Thomas Neale who already owned Warnford Park. He sold West Meon in 1677 to Isaac Foxcroft a member of a family of rich clothiers in the town of Batley in the West Riding of Yorkshire.[31]

It was Isaac Foxcroft who, about 1680, built the present house, typical of the period of Charles II. It is red brick with a colour wash of yellow ochre on the front, now attractively weathered, with a tiled and steeply hipped roof. The house has three storeys, the top storey originally divided into cubicles for the large number of living-in servants which such a house employed. Isaac Foxcroft made amusing use of foxes'

70. Hall Place West Meon – front built by Isaac Foxcroft c.1680.

masks in the keystones of all the windows of the ground floor on the north side whilst the front door contains his and his wife's cipher. The carving may have been done by a Winchester carver familiar with the work of Grinling Gibbons in the chapel of Winchester College.

Isaac's son Henry enlarged the house somewhere about 1730, more than doubling it in size, adding bays on both sides of the main doorway and an imposing west front. Inside the house the impression is one of light from the many windows looking out over long vistas. The Foxcrofts owned the house for close on a 100 years and lived there until 1773 when it was sold to Charles Rennett. By 1839 the Rennetts had gone and the house changed hands several more times in the nineteenth century.

In the twentieth century it was to be on the periphery of events played out in high society. In 1920 Sonia Keppel (born 1900) married Roland Cubitt in the Guards Chapel in London and they established their country residence at Hall Place. Sonia was the daughter of Alice Keppel (born 1869) who from 1898 until his death in 1910 was the mistress of Edward VII and universally known as 'La Favorita'. Sonia wrote a memoir in which she records that when Edward VII died she was not deemed old enough to have explained to her why her mother should have been distraught. She was simply told 'Kingy was such a wonderful man'.[32]

Alice Keppel was a frequent visitor to Hall Place in the years between the two world wars and when she and her husband George Keppel had to leave Italy during the

71. Hall Place – cipher & one of the
fox head keystones placed above the
front door and lower windows by Isaac
Foxcroft.

Second World War they came to live at Hall Place.[33] Roland Cubitt ('Rolie') was, as a result of the death of his three elder brothers in the First World War, the heir to the 2nd Baron Anscombe, of the fabulously rich family who had built much of Belgravia, Pimlico and Eaton Square in the late nineteenth century. Sonia and Roland had three children – Rosalind (born 1921), Henry (born 1924 later 4th Baron Anscombe) and Jeremy (born 1927) – all of whom spent their childhood partly at Hall Place and partly in London. The marriage of Sonia and Roland was not a close one and as early as 1931 Roland gave his sole address as Hyde Park Gardens.[34]

The final act was played out after the Second World War. Alice Keppel died in September 1947 and was buried in Florence. In 1947 Sonia and Roland were divorced and the following year Roland remarried and succeeded to the title becoming the 3rd Baron Anscombe. In 1946 meanwhile Rosalind had married Bruce Shand at St Paul's Knightsbridge and no longer lived at Hall Place. Their eldest child was Camilla (born 1947 and now Duchess of Cornwall) who frequently visited Hall Place where her grandmother lived. It was here that she was accustomed to meet Prince Charles when he was in the navy and serving at *HMS Mercury*. At an early meeting Camilla is reputed to have said to Prince Charles 'Do you know that my great-grandmother was the mistress of your great-great-grandfather?' – Alice Keppel and Edward VII.

In the 1950s Sonia employed Lanning Roper to design the gardens though by the time she died in 1986 both gardens and house had inevitably deteriorated. Although she was born into the highest level of Edwardian society Sonia Cubitt nevertheless took part in West Meon society and employed West Meon staff including at the end of her life Derek and Olga Groombridge who were her butler and cook and were with her when she died in 1986. The following year the estate was sold.[35]

The present owners of Hall Place are Dru and Minnie Montagu who bought the 250 acre estate and moved to West Meon from Hungerford in Berkshire in 1987. They have restored the garden and added a number of features. They have replanted the rose gardens and rejuvenated the walled vegetable garden. Both Dru and Minnie restored the house and estate and to mark the millennium they created a habitat for rare chalkland butterflies. The superbly landscaped garden and paddock total over 20 acres. In front of the house is a lawn leading down to a newly constructed bridge over a branch of the river Meon which flows through the estate. At the side of the house are rose, vegetable and soft fruit gardens all contained within weathered walls.[36]

17

Roads, Bridges, Flood and Fire

Tʜᴇ ᴏʟᴅᴇsᴛ ʀᴏᴜᴛᴇ in the Meon valley is the South Hampshire Ridgeway, part of the track from Beachy Head to Salisbury Plain which can be traced between Butser Hill and Winchester. One branch came down Hayden Lane to Warnford where it crossed the ford and headed for Beacon Hill. An alternative route came south of Old Winchester Hill, along Harvestgate Lane, over the Meon by the ford where the bridge at Exton is now, up White Way, over Beacon Hill to Lomer Farm and rejoined the Ridgeway at Wind Farm. Part of the route is now followed by the South Downs Way.

A route in the south of the Meon valley was much later pioneered by the Romans and went through what became the parish of Wickham. The name Wickham first found in 826AD means 'small Roman town or villa complex'.[1] Both the Ridgeway and the Roman road predate the Saxon settlement of the Meon valley by several centuries.

*   *   *

In the middle ages long distance routes were needed chiefly by the king and his courtiers and by the bishop and his entourage who usually travelled by packhorse. Tradesmen sometimes travelled considerable distances to reach for example the market at Titchfield.[2] For peasants local paths and trackways which connected strips in the open fields sufficed and some still form paths and rights of way in the parishes of the Meon valley. There was no direct road from West Meon to Warnford nor from Meonstoke to Droxford until the turnpike (the present A 32) was built in the 1770s.

John Hurst traced the ancient route down the Meon valley before the building of the turnpike.[3] Coming south from the (much later) *Pig and Whistle* (now *The Lawns Hotel*) the old road branched left round Filmore Hill then straight across what is now the A32 and went down Horse Shoes Hill to the *Three Horse Shoes* which was then a pub, where it turned left down Budds Lane to what is now *West Meon Hut* but was earlier a coaching inn named *The George Inn*. From there the road followed the hedge at the back of Hut Cottage, passed Stoneydene and Marlands Farm – still in the mid-twentieth century described as 'the Old Road'. At Wolverton the old road turned into West Meon and then right on the north side of the Cross, past West Meon church to Lippen Wood where it followed what is now a green lane through the wood to emerge on to Lippen Lane which leads down to Warnford.

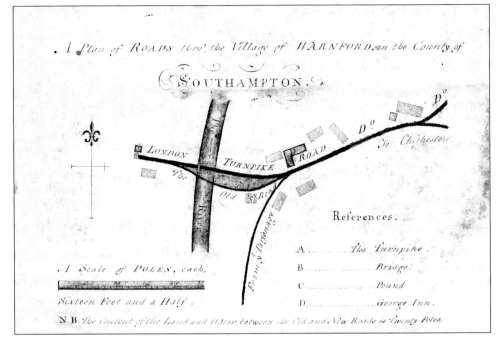

72. Plan of the roads through Warnford c.1776.

Here the road turned left, crossed the bridge over the Meon and then right to enter Warnford Park. It then went to the west of the lake in Warnford Park though there had probably been a medieval route on the east of the river and closer to the house. This view is corroborated by a plan in the Hampshire Record Office which shows the old road on the west side of the river and the new turnpike from Warnford village to the paper mill outside the Park.[4] The pre-turnpike road emerged from the Park at the paper mill and from there followed the same route as the later turnpike as far as Exton where it again crossed the river by a ford at the Grinch. John Hurst thought that the road then went through the yard of Smith's Farm into what is now called Rectory Lane, down the village street of Meonstoke, past the school and emerged on to the present road at the gate of Meonstoke House which was until the 1890s Meonstoke rectory. The road, he believed, followed what is now a pathway through woods to the west of the present road and emerged at Brockbridge. From there it followed what is now a pedestrian lane as far as the river which it forded and which led to Droxford Mill. He traced the original road as far as Mill Lane where it entered Droxford village.

Here John Hurst left the pre-turnpike route down the valley. The route from Droxford to Wickham followed what is now a green lane which went up to the brow of the hill above the river Meon, then through land belonging to Holywell House, a track which was extinguished when Droxford was enclosed in 1855. The road followed Frith Lane to enter Wickham at Mill Lane.

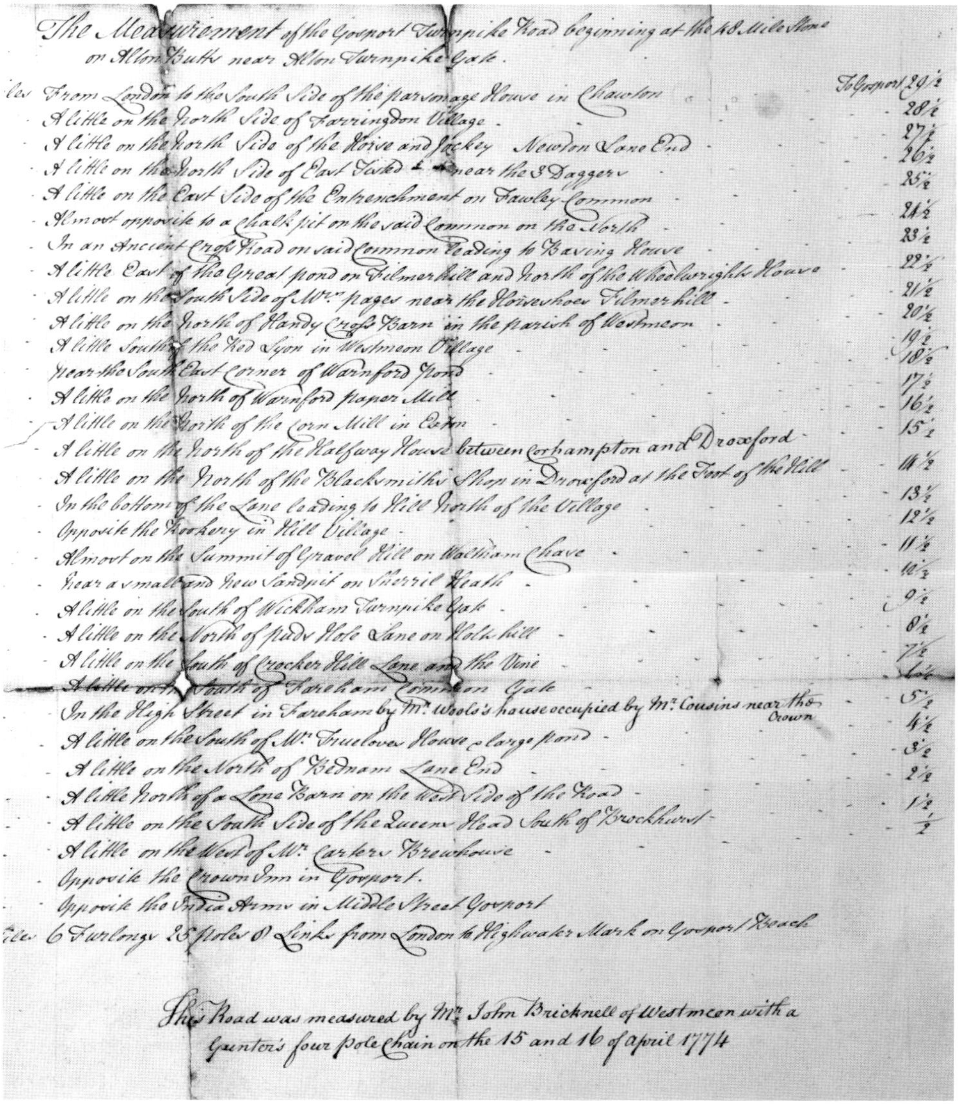

The Measurement of the Gosport Turnpike Road beginning at the 48 Mile Stone on Alton Butts near Alton Turnpike Gate.
Miles From London to the South Side of the Parsonage House in Chawton — To Gosport 29½
A little on the North Side of Farringdon Village — 28½
A little on the North Side of the Horse and Jockey Newton Lane End — 27½
A little on the North Side of East Tisted near the 3 Daggers — 26½
A little on the East Side of the Entrenchment on Fawley Common — 25½
Almost opposite to a chalk pit on the said Common on the North — 24½
In an Ancient Cross Road on said Common leading to Basing House — 23½
A little East of the Great pond on Filmerhill and North of the Wheelwrights House — 22½
A little on the South Side of Mr. Pages near the Horseshoe Filmerhill — 21½
A little on the North of Handy Cross Barn in the parish of Westmeon — 20½
A little South of the Red Lyon in Westmeon Village — 19½
Near the South East Corner of Warnford Pond — 18½
A little on the North of Warnford Paper Mill — 17½
A little on the North of the Corn Mill in Exton — 16½
A little on the North of the Halfway House between Corhampton and Droxford — 15½
A little on the North of the Blacksmiths Shop in Droxford at the Foot of the Hill — 14½
In the bottom of the Lane leading to Hill North of the Village — 13½
Opposite the Rookery in Hill Village — 12½
Almost on the Summit of Gravel Hill on Waltham Chase — 11½
Near a small and New Sandpit on Sherril Heath — 10½
A little on the South of Wickham Turnpike Gate — 9½
A little on the North of Pads Hole Lane on Holt hill — 8½
A little on the South of Crocker Hill Lane and the Vine — 7½
A little on the South of Fareham Common Gate — 6½
In the High Street in Fareham by Mr. Wools's house occupied by Mr. Cousins near the Crown — 5½
A little on the South of Mr. Truelove's House & large pond — 4½
A little on the North of Bednam Lane End — 3½
A little North of a Lone Barn on the West Side of the Road — 2½
A little on the South Side of the Queens Head South of Brockhurst — 1½
A little on the West of Mr. Carter's Brewhouse — ½
Opposite the Crown Inn in Gosport.
Opposite the India Arms in Middle Street Gosport
Miles 6 Furlongs 25 Poles 8 Links from London to Highwater Mark on Gosport Beach
This Road was measured by Mr. John Bricknell of Westmeon with a Gunter's four Pole Chain on the 15 and 16 of April 1774

73. Measurement of the turnpike from Chawton Pond to Gosport Beach April 1774.

There were other old roads for example Titchfield Lane which is almost certainly the route north from Titchfield to Wickham and beyond. It crossed the later Gosport to Chawton turnpike and followed Blind Lane to link up with the pre-turnpike road to Droxford via Frith Lane.

* * *

74. Milestone at Corhampton on the Gosport Beach to Chawton Pond turnpike.

75. The Old Toll House at the corner of Lippen Lane Warnford with milestone, early 20th century.

Complaints about the state of the roads begin about 1660 when packhorses were being replaced by wheeled traffic. From 1555 roads were the responsibility of the parish. There were to be two unpaid Surveyors of the Highways whose job it was to supervise obligatory statute labour at first for four days each year later six. The task was often neglected and in any case inconsistent and uncoordinated from parish to parish.

Though the state of the roads was not always as bad as is sometimes claimed there were well publicised examples of coaches bogged down in mud in winter and axles broken by driving over hard, rut-riven surfaces in summer. Drastic measures were needed and turnpikes were the answer. The authorisation of trusts and building of turnpike roads took off in what has been described as the period of 'turnpike mania'. Between 1752 and 1770 no less than 351 acts authorising their building were passed by parliament.[5] They laid the foundation of the modern road system. There was a local explosion of enthusiasm for turnpike road schemes in south Hampshire in 1758: between 25th January and 14th March no fewer than 10 petitions were presented to parliament seeking the improvement of the roads between Alton, Portsmouth and Stockbridge and all were referred to the same House of Commons Committee.

All the villages of the Meon valley, except East Meon, were in due course affected by the turnpikes. They were not necessarily new roads. They might be old ones widened and repaired; or partly new roads joining up old tracks with new stretches. The trustees were empowered to close up lanes which might otherwise facilitate the avoidance of tolls and sometimes incurred the wrath of drovers. Turnpike cottages were sited so as to reduce the opportunity to avoid paying tolls.

The new road up the Meon valley formed a section of the Gosport to Chawton turnpike authorised by Act of Parliament in 1758 (31 George II c.73) The title of the act of Parliament renewing the road in 1780, 21 years after its authorisation, provides a more accurate description of the road as it was eventually built: 'An Act for repairing and widening the Roads from Gosport in the County of Southampton through Fareham and Wickham to the town of Bishop's Waltham and from Wickham afore-said through Droxford, Exton, Warnford, West Meon, Ramsdean Bottom to Chawton Pond in the parish of Chawton' – where it joined the Basingstoke, Farnham and Winchester Turnpike. The Gosport to Chawton Pond road became the A32 after the First World War when roads were first numbered.[6] The trustees are listed in the front of the second minute book. Eighteen men had subscribed a total of £3,650. John Pooke by then treasurer subscribed £600 and George Garnier invested £400 – both sizeable sums. The total half yearly interest was £91.5.0.

There are two puzzles connected with the building of the turnpike up the Meon valley: when was it built and what was the original route? The first reference to the turnpike which I have located is in a letter written by John Mulso, newly appointed rector of Meonstoke, to his friend Gilbert White, the well known naturalist, on coming to live at Meonstoke House in 1771. He describes the outlook at the back of his house 'this Front is view'd from the Gosport (Turnpike) at about 17 miles from Alton'. But over two years later in April 1774 John Bricknell of West Meon took two days to measure the 29½ miles of the proposed road 'with a Gunter's four pole chain'. In 1776 land was purchased at Warnford to include the route of the new road. Meantime the first Minute book of the Trustees begins. From all of which I conclude that this section of road was built in stages beginning at the southern end about 1770 and took several years to complete.

Now to the route. Bricknell's survey of the route suggests that the road in a southerly direction was not originally intended to come directly down the hill to *The West Meon Hut* but instead followed the old road past *The Three Horseshoes.* (SU651271)[7] It also seems to have come through Exton rather than bypassing it.[8] Perhaps both changes of route happened early in the life of the new road.

The first Trustees' Account Book contains entries for the years from 1775–1796. By then the road was in use. There were five toll gates – at Brockhurst, Fareham, Cold Harbour, Waltham and Warnford – each with a toll house occupied by a 'collector' whose salary was £1.12.0 per quarter.[9] The first treasurer was James Bedford paid a salary of £42 per year in two half yearly instalments.[10]

Coming from Gosport the road divided north of Wickham. One branch went to Bishop's Waltham with a toll house at the end of Paradise Lane and the other through Shirrell Heath to Hill, where *The Rising Sun* was a coaching inn, and so to Droxford down South Hill. From there it kept to the west of the valley on a new stretch of road, through or past Exton and reached Warnford (outside and to the west of Warnford Park) where there was a toll house on the west of the road just before the village sited so that vehicles from Winchester as well as those coming up the Meon valley would have to pay tolls.

The turnpike then involved a new section of road from Warnford to West Meon, villages for the first time linked by a direct road. The new road cut through West Meon and followed a new route over the hill to West Meon Hut. The original route seems to have followed the old road past *The Three Horseshoes,* turned right over Filmore Hill and then left to rejoin the present A32. The direct section of the A32 bypassing Filmore Hill is not shown on the first edition of the Ordnance Survey map dated about 1810 and was probably built about 1830.[11] In 1780 a new toll house was built at Rotherfield and at the same time money was spent on bridges at Corhampton, Exton, and West Meon and the boards containing a list of tolls were relettered. The Cold Harbour gate, north of Wickham, does not seem to have been profitable and in 1793 the house was let at a monthly rental of £19.5.0 to the former collector William Hillier and from then on is named 'Wickham'.

The turnpike flourished and in the 1820s the trustees placed a bill before parliament called the Gosport Road Bill to reroute the section from Wickham to Droxford so that after descending Hoads Hill, it passed directly in front of Wickham church and along the valley of the Meon bypassing Wickham village. It would, the trustees argued, reduce the journey by ¾ mile but more important it would cut out three steep hills. Since 1¼ miles of road already existed it would mean only moderate additional expense. What is more 'The vast consumption of Timber in the neighbouring Dockyard of Portsmouth would be the more commodiously effected.'[12]

But not everybody shared the enthusiasm of the trustees. A letter dated 26th March 1827 was sent by 30 Wickham tradesmen to William Garnier, through whose land the new road would pass. They were concerned that the proposed road would leave 'the Village of Wickham entirely out of the Line of the Road' and 'would be extremely injurious and most probably ruinous to us as Tradesmen and Inhabitants of Wickham'.[13] Their intervention does not seem to have deterred the trustees and the bill received the royal assent in May 1828. The new road split the village in two with church and rectory on one side and the rest of the village on the other a split made more serious when the railway was built at the beginning of the twentieth century. A newspaper advertisement dated 1829 invited tenders for 'Cutting and Forming the New Line of Turnpike Road from Droxford to Wickham, viz from the North end of the Crown Enclosure near Mislingford, in the parish of Soberton, to the south end of the village of Droxford.' A toll house was built on the new stretch of road to the north of where the west lodge to Rookesbury Park now stands.[14]

A second turnpike affecting the Meon valley was authorised by Act of Parliament in 1801 (41 George III c.8) and ran from Curdridge Common through Bishop's Waltham to Corhampton (with a branch to Corhampton Down) where it joined the Gosport to Chawton turnpike (the present B3035.)

If the roads in the centre of the Meon valley were chiefly north-south, around Titchfield it was the east-west routes which carried most traffic. Until the Hamble was bridged the road from Portsmouth to Southampton went through Botley. The Cosham to Titchfield turnpike was authorised by Act of Parliament in 1810 and built soon afterwards (50 George III c.14 & c.22). Until the building of this road there had been no direct road from Fareham to Titchfield; the route was through Catisfield, down Fishers Hill to Stony Bridge and into Titchfield along Mill Lane. The new turnpike came directly from Catisfield fork down Titchfield Hill and into East Street. It involved the demolition of a house which stood in the way of direct entry to the village and the building of a bridge over the Meon which opened on 1st June 1811.

The road from Titchfield to Southampton was not a turnpike but a proprietary road with a board of directors in place of trustees and it is for this reason that tolls continued to be charged on this stretch of road until well after the First World War although the turnpike network had been wound up long before. The toll bridge across the Hamble at Bursledon built in 1799 had a stimulating effect on trade in Titchfield: trafffic which had previously avoided the village now came through Titchfield.[15]

To the north of the Meon valley itself but running through the large parishes of West and East Meon was the Winchester to Petersfield turnpike via Bramdean and Hinton Ampner authorised by act of parliament in 1825 with a turnpike cottage at Bramdean – ('An Act for making and maintaining a Turnpike Road from the City of Winchester to the Town of Petersfield, in the County of Southampton'). It replaced an earlier turnpike established in 1772 which climbed Stonor Hill (Little Switzerland) and passed *The Trooper* on its way to Ropley Dean.[16] It became the A272 after the First World War.

Turnpikes were unpopular with local people who did not see why they should pay to use roads which had hitherto been free and they often tried to avoid tolls by following lanes or drove roads which circumvented them and which the trustees were empowered to close. The realisation gradually dawned that trusts controlled lengths of road without accountability other than to their shareholders. The turnpike era lasted until the railways began to replace coaches in the 1840s. Abolition was piecemeal beginning locally in 1860. The Gosport to Chawton road was the last local turnpike and ended on 1st November 1878. Roads were now to be the responsibility of District Highways Boards which came into existence in 1877. Toll gates were removed and broken up while toll houses were sold and sometimes survive as private houses though their proximity to the road has often made them the victims of road widening, Wickham toll house (earlier Cold Harbour) was sold in November 1878, became a private house and was demolished in the late 1930s.[17] There are no toll houses left in the Meon valley.

The General Enclosure Act of 1766 required trustees to erect milestones at intervals along the roads but these too have often fallen victim to road widening or removal during the Second World War. The Gosport to Chawton turnpike, now the A32, is well supplied with milestones marked on the Ordnance Survey Map though few still have the metal plate which originally indicated miles to London and Gosport. Inns on the turnpike route are described as 'coaching inn' as a sign of their antiquity. They can often be identified by the wide and high entrance large enough to take coach and horses. *The Bugle* and *The Queens Head* at Titchfield, *The King's Head* at Wickham, *The Hunters Inn* at Swanmore and *The George* at Warnford (now *The George and Falcon*) were coaching inns.

The last meeting of the trustees of the Gosport to Chawton turnpike trust took place at *The Red Lion* Fareham on 1st December 1878. After the sale of the turnpike cottages and the settlement of outstanding claims the trustees declared a surplus of £111.12.9 and a final dividend of 2½%.[18]

It was the spread of car ownership and the beginning of regular bus services after the First World War which required better roads and in particular roads which bypassed the main towns. In 1933 Titchfield became one of the first villages in Hampshire to acquire a by-pass when the A27 was rerouted. Mill Lane was cut in two and the former Abbey, the historic barn and the mill lay on one side of the main road, the rest of the village on the other. After the Second World War a second by-pass of Titchfield was needed, this time to the east of the village so that traffic for Stubbington and Gosport no longer needed to enter the village. Instead travellers from Fareham could leave the A27 before reaching Titchfield.[19]

*   *   *

The earliest river crossings were fords, though in the middle ages the river was wider, deeper and faster flowing than it is today. Wickham, where there was a strand of gravel, was probably the lowest point at which the river could be forded and this may have accounted for the settlement there even before the arrival of the Saxons. There were also fords at Mislingford, Droxford and Meonstoke. At Warnford the suffix makes clear that a ford preceded the bridge. John Hurst pointed out that if you stand at the east end of the road which leads to ford and bridge the alignment of the

Turnpike and by-pass roads affecting the Meon Valley.

Act	Date	From – To	Present road
31 George II c.73	1758	Chawton Pond to Gosport Beach	A32
		Built c.1770 via Shirrell Heath & Swanmore	
41 George III c.8	1801	Curdridge Common to Corhampton	B3035
50 George IIIc.14	1810	Cosham to Titchfield	A27
50 George III c.22	1810	Titchfield to Twyford	A3051 & 4
6 George IV c.14	1825	Winchester to Petersfield	A272
Gosport Road Act	1828	Wickham to Droxford	A32
		replaced Shirrell Heath & Swanmore	
Titchfield By-pass	1927		A27
Titchfield northern By-pass	1978		B3334

road makes clear that it originally led not to the bridge but to the ford.[20]

Bridges came later, the first probably at Titchfield. The Warebridge (Weirbridge) taking travellers out of Titchfield to the east was probably in existence by Domesday and prevented the tide from reaching beyond this point. John Leland crossed the Warebridge in 1542 but earlier still it was mentioned in a fourteenth century document. It was built south of the village at the point to which the Meon was tidal and carried the road to Hollam and Crofton.

Stony Bridge also in Titchfield, close to the medieval abbey, is better known. It carried the pre-turnpike road from Fareham. Like the abbey it appears on Ordnance Survey maps as a site of antiquity. Probably the abbey and the bridge were built at the same time (1232). It appears in the late fourteenth century as Kettelbridge when it was made of wood with stone piers. It too was crossed by John Leland in 1542. The name Anjou Bridge appears later taking its name from Margaret of Anjou wife of Henry VI who used it in travelling from Southwick Priory to Titchfield Abbey after their marriage in 1445.[21]

Later centuries saw the Meon bridged many times. At Wickham for example the bridge opposite the church was, according to a stone set into the parapet, built by subscription in 1793. The river here was broad and fast flowing and a four arch brick bridge was needed; the road leading to it inevitably became Bridge Street.[22] At Exton the bridge was also rebuilt by subscription, in 1805, and at the same time the road leading to the turnpike was straightened.[23]

* * *

The Meon like all rivers was liable to flood particularly in the winter months when heavy and prolonged snow melted or there was exceptionally heavy rainfall. Flooding had serious consequences where the river ran through the village as at East Meon or Exton, where it was level with the village street and often overflowed its banks. *The Shoe* at Exton was rebuilt in the 1930s on the other side of the road to avoid frequent floods. Parts of other villages were affected – for example the eastern and southern parts of the village of West Meon and the church and *The Bucks Head* at Meonstoke. At East Meon the school log has many references to the effect of flooding on school attendance. On 2nd December 1863 ' the lower districts were inundated and children from a distance were sent home at noon'. On 28th October 1903 '…roads are impassable'. On 7th January 1921 floods kept the children away from afternoon school – 'Only 50 out of 150 on roll were present 6 of those 50 were fetched home in a cart at 1.45'. On 13th November 1935 'Owing to many roads being flooded the attendance was low'. On 8th December 1954 'Afternoon session cancelled and the children sent home on account of severe flooding in the village'[24].

These were not the only occasions when parts of East Meon were flooded and adults as well as children greatly inconvenienced. Yet despite frequent debates in the Parish Council amelioration was all that was attempted until the 1950s. A major scheme would involve heavy expenditure which would fall on the rates. A drastic solution was planned but postponed. In November 1953 it was reckoned that flooding was the worst for 40 years and at last a major scheme was implemented. By 1955 work had begun. The course of the river through the village was widened and deepened, six bridges were rebuilt to allow a greater volume of water to flow freely and a new straight course at the west end of the village by-passed and shortened the former route. Since 1955 there has been no serious flooding in East Meon.[25]

Flooding was not confined to East Meon. A photograph shows the flood in the main street and *The Shoe* at Exton in February 1937.[26] Schooling was affected at West Meon. On 16th February 1900 the head reported: 'East end of the village flooded. Many children away. Rain falling in torrents. Roads flooded again'. On 12th October 1903 'Village flooded' and on 28th October 1903 it was not only East Meon where the weather merited comment: 'The East End of the village flooded. Sent 18 children home with wet feet.'

Floods were not the only hazard which the weather could provide. Drought was a summer risk. The river might still flow but during a prolonged drought the wells upon which households depended before the arrival of piped water would dry up. The summer of 1911 was exceptionally dry and women relied on the river to provide water for washing. In the autumn of 1934 village wells at Droxford once more dried up. For several weeks the Fire Brigade pumped water from the river to a trough in the square where inhabitants queued for water which they were then obliged to boil before use. The wells it appeared had been dug only just below the level of the normal water table and so could not withstand a drought. Westbrooks, the Droxford building firm, embarked on a profitable well deepening programme.[27]

At West Meon school the recently appointed head, Robert Russell, had come from Farnborough and was able to compare facilities there with those in the village where he now worked. On 8th June 1934 there had been heavy rain for the first time for many weeks. He wrote: 'So ended the long spell of drought. How much a real piped water supply is needed cannot be imagined …the fear of drought and the regular epidemics would both disappear. The regularity of the latter in these country areas is due solely to the present archaic system … which appears a deep disgrace in this year and age of progress.' Six weeks later on 16th July he wrote: 'The County Analyst called and reported that the supply taken from the Cross …is polluted. There is no supply in the village unpolluted so we must carry on and chance it. When will the state carry out essential duties that the local authorities fail miserably in doing?'.

But the effects of the drought were not over for many months. In November the head of West Meon school felt constrained to write once more in the Log: 'The wells are filling …personally I have had no water in my house [School House next to the school] since the first week in July …the villagers have suffered very greatly… there is a water scheme under discussion now with the project of a deep bore and the village will then have its own – but it is really a disgusting and deplorable condition – the sanitation and water in our villages – to be in this year of Grace … we in the villages are denied the essential of life – water.' (Log 18th November 1934).

*   *   *

Until the Fire Brigades Act of 1938 the parish vestry and later the parish council was responsible for ensuring that protection against fire was available but only the larger parishes had their own brigade. Others relied on and paid for fire protection when they needed it. Better off citizens depended on private enterprise and fire insurance companies attached plaques to the buildings whose owners had paid their premium; some can still be seen on old buildings. Each parish kept a long handled fork which

76. The first Droxford Fire Brigade 1904.

could be used to remove fire threatened thatch. In the Meon valley there was no fire brigade until the twentieth century. Villages in the north of the valley called out the brigade at Petersfield. Bishop's Waltham set up a volunteer fire brigade in 1891 and was prepared to help smaller villages.[28] Even where there was a brigade it could not hope to be effective if the fire was far away. With no telephone and no motor transport it was difficult to summon the brigade or to reach the scene of the fire in time to prevent disaster. Firemen were summoned by bugle or bell, the pump was pulled by horses and water supply was uncertain. Many buildings were built of wood with a mixture of wattle and daub, all constituting a fire hazard.

The most spectacular fire in the Meon valley broke out in High Street Meonstoke in 1719 and destroyed 23 houses before it was brought under control. Sadly no Samuel Pepys was present to record where it began, how it spread, by what means it was extinguished, nor how rebuilding was achieved. Frances Collins speculates that it may have started at Little Stocks Farm and, fanned by a north wind, swept southwards along the High Street. Most of the buildings in the High Street were rebuilt and so are of eighteenth century date.[29]

In the early years of the twentieth century there were three major fires in the valley, at Droxford, East Meon and West Meon. In the early morning of 2nd February 1902, a wild morning of sleet and driving rain, a fire broke out at Midlington House just south of Droxford. The nearest fire brigade, at Bishop's Waltham four miles away, was summoned, presumably by horse or bicycle since there was neither motor car nor telephone. The fire quickly got hold and despite heroic attempts to rescue them two servants died in the blaze. By the time the fire brigade arrived the situation was hopeless. The only water was in a well inside the burning house. The roof was now well alight and molten lead poured from the roof. When the roof fell in people miles away saw the spurt of flame and sparks as from a volcano erupting. It was this fire at Midlington House which led Dr Edgar Pern, the village doctor, to set about forming a volunteer fire brigade for the village. In the meantime the house was rebuilt and the garden landscaped by F.H.Christian, a retired tea planter.[30]

Less than two years later on a freezing November night in 1904 a fire destroyed much of the Palladian mansion of Westbury House owned since the late nineteenth century by Colonel Le Roy Lewis. The fire alarm was raised by the French governess and Colonel Lewis himself set about rescuing family and servants from the burning building. By the time the Petersfield brigade arrived they could do little to save the house which included Grinling Gibbons carvings, as well as library and pictures. There was only one fatal casualty, the 69 year old housekeeper who died of smoke inhalation and fright. After the fire Colonel Lewis resolved to rebuild the house which he accomplished remarkably quickly.[31]

Only a few years after the Westbury fire, this time on a hot summer morning, 20th June 1910 six Tudor thatched cottages on the south side of the High Street in East Meon were burnt. The conflagration arose from a fire lit to heat the copper on washing day. It spread first to the chimney and then to the thatch of the cottage where it started and fanned by a light breeze spread rapidly. Hay and tanks of petrol provided fuel for the fire and periodic explosions sent smoke and flames over the whole area. The Petersfield Fire Brigade was summoned by telegram at 9am. The voluntary firemen rushed from their workplaces, harnessed the horses and set out on the six-mile journey along narrow and hilly roads to East Meon arriving an hour later. In the meantime all hands had been recruited including the schoolmaster and the recently formed Boy Scout troop who passed buckets of water from the nearby river. By 11am the fire had been largely extinguished leaving the six cottages a smouldering heap of ruins with outer walls and chimneys alone standing. Furniture was salvaged by the owners and those rendered homeless by the fire were temporarily accommodated. Nobody who saw the fire ever forgot the experience.[32]

Under the Fire Engines Act of 1898 parish councils were empowered to acquire fire fighting equipment and the Droxford Council resolved to do so. The Merryweather manual pump and trailer pulled by two horses was an improvement on the earlier provision of a hand truck and ladder. The alarm was sounded by a constable on a bicycle ringing a hand bell. The horses might have to be brought in from the fields and had then to be harnessed.

Soon after the First World War motorised transport became available and represented a great improvement but at Droxford the parish could not afford its own lorry but was dependent on a charabanc loaned by Meringtons, then in Mill Lane, to tow the Merryweather pump. In 1935 the parish council prompted by John Hulbert, discussed the provision of its own motor driven trailer and the building of headquarters in which to house it. Still the problem was money. The cost of the scheme could be reduced by continuing to use Meringtons garage to provide a towing service when it was required. Eventually Corhampton, Meonstoke and Soberton agreed to join and it was decided to proceed though a parish meeting hoped that the cost would not exceed the product of a penny rate. It is ironic that only two years later the responsibility was taken from the parish and placed in the hands of the RDC who in due course bought the fire fighting equipment from the parish. In 1943 the council received £105-7-8 and was free to sell the tender.[33]

18

The Meon Valley Railway

༇

FEW RAILWAYS were built after the end of the nineteenth century: the Meon Valley line was an exception. There had been talk of a railway down the Meon valley since the opening of the Botley to Bishop's Waltham railway in 1863 but nothing had come of any of the projected routes. There are several mysteries about the origins and nature of the new railway. It was built by the London and South Western Railway Company to protect its revenues and territory from the Great Western Railway. It would run from Alton to Fareham, a distance of 22¼ miles, through country which was largely agricultural and sparsely populated, and on that account unlikely to generate either substantial passenger or freight revenue.[1]

Yet it was not built with a view to economy. The Basingstoke and Alton line which opened in 1901 under the Light Railways Act of 1896 was a typical Edwardian light railway. It had sharp curves, steep gradients and stations of corrugated iron, all to save money.[2] On the Meon Valley line, by contrast, no expense was spared. It has been suggested that the War Office secretly subsidised the building of the line. In the event of a French invasion, still thought to be a possibility before the *Entente Cordiale* in 1904, there would be need for an alternative route from Aldershot to the south coast for troops and supplies. There is however no evidence to support such a view. Although the Meon Valley railway was built as a single-track railway, with passing places at stations, sufficient land was bought to provide double track throughout if this were required later. Bridges, tunnels and the West Meon viaduct were made wide enough for a double track and the gradients and curves were laid out for running at speed. All these features as well as others represented superfluous luxury.

Military needs alone would not explain other aspects, though the availability of ready money may do. Platforms were 660 yards long, sufficient to accommodate ten carriages though the line was never used by trains of that length. Stations were handsome buildings, well designed and constructed of brick, faced with Portland stone and with lavish fixtures and fittings. Dr Edwin Course the historian of the railways of Southern England wrote of West Meon station 'the buildings were of red brick with stone surrounds to doors and windows; the fine gables had a Tudor air, and even the gentlemen's lavatories were far from merely functional: square detached buildings like Chinese pagodas'. He adds that the stations represented some of the most costly stations per head of population to be found anywhere'. The railway cost about £15,540 per mile compared with £5,360 per mile for the Basingstoke and Alton.[3] Expenditure

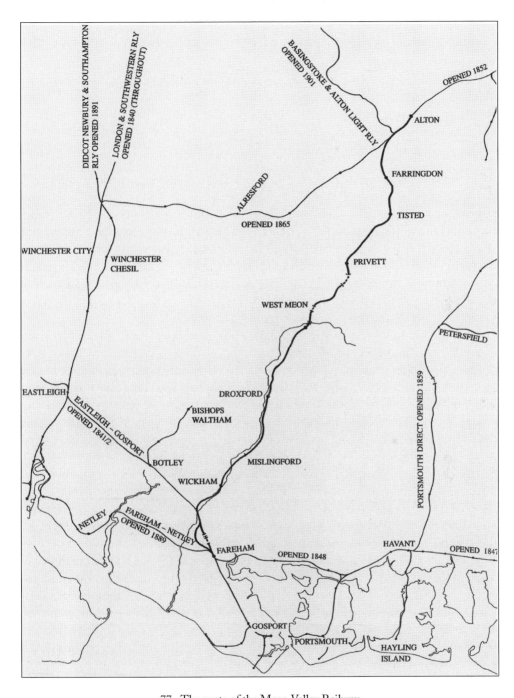

77. The route of the Meon Valley Railway.

on the railway overall was just under £400,000.[4] The five stations – Tisted, Privett, West Meon, Droxford and Wickham - were about four miles apart and in many cases some distance from the villages they were designed to serve.

Work began in 1898 close to Alton. Land was purchased from a number of owners including John Carpenter-Garnier of Rookesbury Park, Wickham, William Nicholson of Basing Park, Privett, who was also the local member of parliament and William Woods of Warnford Park. Nicholson insisted that the station closest to his residence should be named Privett though it was some distance from the village of that name, rather than West Tisted, the parish in which it was located, preferred by the company. He threatened that unless agreement were reached he would not release the land the company needed. There are other curiously named stations – 'Droxford for Hambledon' though the station was in the parish of Soberton and nowhere near Hambledon and 'Tisted for Selborne' though the distance to the advertised destination was considerable.

Work started at the north end of the line and until Droxford was reached the soil was chiefly chalk, easily workable but devoid of water so artesian wells were sunk at considerable expense. (Permission could not be obtained to draw water from the river Meon.) The northern section of the new railway was from an engineering point of view the most difficult and two tunnels were required. The first at Privett built on a curve, was 1056 feet in length and presented substantial difficulties for its builders. It was here in January 1899 that the first fatality occurred when part of the tunnel collapsed burying two navvies, only one of whom was rescued alive.[5] The second

78. West Meon viaduct looking towards West Meon.

79. Construction of the embankment near West Meon viaduct c.1899.

80. Group on the embankment near West Meon viaduct c.1899.

tunnel close to West Meon station was about half the length of the Privett tunnel and workmen digging from either end achieved a perfect junction which was marked by appropriate celebrations. Both tunnels produced large amounts of chalk, more than was needed to build the impressive embankments at a number of points on the line. The massive road tunnel to the east of West Meon Hut on the Petersfield to Winchester road (A272) provided a means of using some of the chalk spoil. Still *in situ* and likely to remain so for a long time, it is 167 feet long with an embankment 64 feet high and provides lasting evidence of the scale of the undertaking.

The most spectacular engineering feat was the building of the West Meon viaduct carrying the railway 62 feet above the river Meon close to West Meon village using 725 tons of steel and costing about £10,000. The original intention was to build an eight arch concrete viaduct. When building began it became clear that the soil on the south side would not bear the weight so the length was reduced, four arches were built with steel piers instead of concrete, supported by two massive concrete bases on either side of the road. Since each span was the same length the overall dimensions were reduced by half and the embankment was extended.[6]

After West Meon the going was easier though there was still need for deep cuttings and substantial embankments. When first built and until vegetation covered them photographs make clear that the chalk embankments stood out glaringly white against the green of summer or the black of winter. At Mislingford the railway ran into the unstable clay of the Reading beds which required the building of a concrete retaining wall. The line used 16 million bricks of which about 6 million came from local yards at Fareham.

The railway had a dramatic physical effect on at least one village on its route – Wickham. Three bridges were needed, one a huge structure to cross the river Meon and two, rather less spectacular, to cross Bridge Street and the Fareham to Bishop's Waltham road. Opposite the church the new bridge and embankment necessitated the demolition of two cottages on the south side of Bridge Street. On Fareham Road a row of cottages had to be removed and the line of Asylum Lane (later Mayles Lane) was altered. The village had been divided over 70 years earlier by the turnpike but this was now emphasised by the railway, which had a substantial effect on the topography of the village.[7] Between Wickham and Knowle junction the railway ran on level ground dispensing with the need for either cutting or embankment.

At the southern end of the railway before it crossed the main line into Fareham a halt was opened in May 1907 called until 1922 Knowle Asylum Halt, to serve the needs of visitors to the Mental Hospital. It was one of the first stations in the district to have electric light, provided by the hospital generators.

Irish labourers were recruited to build the railway and came to live for the duration close to their work. Local people were reluctant to accept Irish labourers as lodgers and so 27 cottages were rented and 41 huts built to accommodate them. At the height of construction no less than 600 navies were employed. Some lived at the camp established in a field close to what until recently was called *The West Meon Hut*, whilst others lodged, sometimes with wife and family in the villages. Some were accommodated in 'the Barracks' at Wickham.[8] Shops did good business selling beer, bread, cheese and pickles to the men and their families. The work was hard manual labour with pick and shovel and hours were long. The effect of the navvies was, in the words of John Hurst, who spoke to people who remembered them, to 'turn the life of the village upside down'.[9] The head of West Meon School noted the deleterious influence of the navvies on village life: 'Caned Ernest Knight for swearing. A very bad feeling is present in the school of late undoubtedly due to the bad influence of the railway. Bad language is frequently heard'.[10]

The 6d.per hour paid to the navvies was better than that paid by local farmers who could only keep their labour by threatening to eject from their tied cottages anybody defecting to the railway. William Martin recalled many years later that on leaving school he went to work as a stoker on the construction engine which ran up and down the line. His father was employed by W.G.Nicolson on the Basing Park estate so young William lodged with his aunt in West Meon in case his father's employer learnt that he was working on the railway and ejected the family from their cottage.[11]

81. Building the railway bridge over Bridge Street, Wickham.

There was an element of the wild west about the life style of the navvies. On Saturday nights in particular there were sometimes drunken fights at the pubs particularly *The West Meon Hut* and *The Horse Shoes* at Woodlands the two pubs nearest to the camp. Sometimes the police intervened sometimes they chose to turn a blind eye. In the village of West Meon the locals refused to drink with the navvies and at *The White Horse* which had opened as a pub in anticipation of the building of the railway a tin hut was provided in the front garden for the navvies who were considered too rowdy to be served inside.[12]

The new railway was opened on Whit Monday 1st June 1903 with no recorded celebration though William Woods held a luncheon party at Warnford Park with an afternoon ride on the new railway for his guests. There were at first six trains each weekday in each direction, the first however did not leave Alton until 8.57 and arrived at Fareham at 9.48 too late for boys travelling from the Meon valley villages to Price's Grammar School or for business men working in Fareham. Later this was rectified (see page 171). Trains were at first made up of four or six coaches. On Sundays there were two trains in each direction. Later the railway was served by two-carriage 'push-pull' trains.

All the stations were built to the same design, the houses intended to accommodate the station master and his family as well as waiting room and ticket office. Three of

82. Flier announcing the opening of the Meon Valley Railway 1903.

them are now family houses of character – East Tisted, Privett and Droxford each now occupied by devotees of the railway. Close to each station there were cottages for railway employees several of which can still be identified, for example the row of cottages on the A32 close to Privett station. Close by a hotel was also built in anticipation of trade generated by the railway and named *The Privett Bush*. It later became *The Pig and Whistle* and more recently still *The Lawns Hotel*.

Throughout its life freight was more important than passengers. The railway was within reach of the strawberry growing country of south Hampshire and in the season strawberries grown locally were loaded at Wickham or Mislingford for sale in London. Milk churns from local farms were sent by train bound for the Coop dairy at Fareham. Livestock travelled to and from Alton in cattle trucks. Each station had its coal siding to which coal was delivered and from which it was distributed. Alton market was a draw and on market day, Tuesday, a ticket from Fareham cost only 1/9d and from West Meon 1/4d. Cheap weekend tickets were also available from Meon Valley stations to London; from Droxford they cost 14/- first class, 8/9 second class and 7/- third class.

Villages on the route wanted a station. Before the railway opened the Swanmore

375 SOUTHERN–Western Section

LONDON, ALTON, DROXFORD, FAREHAM, EASTLEIGH, and SOUTHAMPTON

Down

		Week Days														Sundays					
Miles		a.m	a.m	a.m	a.m	a.m	a.m	p.m	p.m	p.m	p.m	p.m	p.m			a.m	a.m	a.m		p.m	p.m	p.m
	London (Waterloo) 390 dep	5 55	6 25	7 25	7 25	10 27	11 57	12 57	2 27	2 57	4 27	6 57	6 57			7 25	10 27			3 27	6 27	6 57
	Alton .... dep	7 36	..	..	9 5	..	1 30	..	..	4 35	..	8 30	..			8 23	..			..	..	8 28
48¼	Farringdon	7 43	..	..	9 12	..	1 37	..	..	4 42	..	8 37	..			8 30	..			..	..	8 35
52¼	Tisted	7 48	..	..	9 16	..	1 41	..	..	4 46	..	8 41	..			8 35	..			..	..	8 41
55¼	Privett	7 55	..	..	9 23	..	1 48	..	..	4 53	..	8 48	..			8 43	..			..	..	8 48
59¼	West Meon	8 3	..	..	9 31	..	1 56	..	..	5 1	..	8 56	..			8 51	..			..	..	8 56
63¼	Droxford B	8 11	..	..	9 38	..	2 3	..	..	5 9	..	9 3	..			9 0	..			..	..	9 4
68¼	Wickham	8 22	..	..	9 48	..	2 13	..	..	5 18	..	9 14	..			9 9	..			..	..	9 13
70¼	Knowle Halt	8 28	..	..	9 53	..	2 18	..	..	5 23	..	9 20	..			9 15	..			..	..	9 19
72¼	Fareham 37c, 380 .. arr	8 33	..	..	9 59	..	2 24	..	..	5 29	..	9 25	..			9 21	..			..	..	9 25
76¼	Fort Brockhurst	9 37	..	..	10 23	..	3 51	..	..	6 19	..	9 37	..			h	..			..	..	h
77	Gosport	9 41	..	..	10 27	..	3 55	..	..	6 23	..	9 41	..				..			..	..	
	Alton	..	7 53	9 0	..	12 0	..	2 30	4 10	..	6 0	..	8 35			9 0	12 5			5 0	8 15	..
51¼	Medstead & Four Marks ..	..	8 5	9 12	..	12 12	..	2 42	4 22	..	6 12	..	8 47			9 12	12 17			5 12	8 27	..
54¼	Ropley	..	8 11	9 18	..	12 18	..	2 48	4 28	..	6 18	..	8 53			9 17	12 23			5 17	8 33	..
57	Alresford	..	8 16	9 22	..	12 22	..	2 53	4 32	..	6 22	..	8 58			9 22	12 28			5 22	8 38	..
60¼	Itchen Abbas	..	8 24	9 29	..	12 28	..	3 2	4 41	..	6 28	..	9 4			9 30	12 35			5 28	8 46	..
66	Winchester C .. arr	..	8 35	9 40	..	12 40	..	3 15	4 54	..	6 39	..	9 15			9 41	12 48			5 39	8 57	..
69	Shawford D	..	8 42	9 47	..	12 46	..	3 22	5 0	..	7 14	..	9 22			9 47	12 54			5 45	9 4	..
72	Eastleigh F 376, 380 ..	..	8 50	9 55	..	12 54	..	3 30	5 8	..	7 18	..	9 35			9 55	1 2			5 53	9 12	..
75	Swaythling	..	9 2	10 55	..	1 28	..	3 44	5 26	..	7 29	..	9 50			10 39	1 28			5 59	9 19	..
76¼	St. Denys 376	..	9 13	10 39	..	1 32	..	3 48	5 30	..	7 33	..	9 54			10 43	1 32			6 3	9 23	..
77¼	Northam	..	9 17	10 43	..	1 36	..	3 52	5 33	..	7 37	..	9 58									
78	Southampton G	..	9 20	10 47	..	1 40	..	3 56	5 37	..	7 41	..	10 2			11 15	..			6 9	9 29	..
78	Southampton Cen	..	9 56	10 26	..	1 19	..	4 35	5 28	..	7 28	..	..			10 50	1 20			6 35	9 55	..

Up

		Week Days														Sundays					
Miles		a.m	a.m	a.m	a.m	a.m	p.m	p.m		p.m	p.m	p.m	p.m			a.m	a.m	a.m		p.m	p.m	p.m
	Southampton Cen. dep	..	6 47	..	9 54	..	12S20	12S055	1 49	..	..	6 48	..			..	..	..		..	..	6 40
	Southampton Ter ..	6 0	6 57	..	9 36	..	12S20	12S053	1 53	..	2 54	6 58	..			7 20	9 51	3 0		..	..	6 15
¾	Northam	6 3	7 0	..	9 39	..	12S24	12S056	1 53	..	2 57	7 1	..			7 29	10 0	3 9		..	..	..
2	St. Denys	6 7	7 7	..	10 2	..	12S28	1S0 2	2 2	..	3 1	7 5	..			7 29	10 34	3 30		..	..	6 51
3	Swaythling	6 11	7 11	..	9 47	..	12S32	1S0 6	2 5	..	6 5	7 8	..			7 45	10 46	3 42		..	..	6 58
5¼	Eastleigh F	6 35	7 40	..	10 29	..	..	1 15	..	2 15	3 59	7 15	..			7 50	10 53	3 49		..	..	7 8
9¼	Shawford D	6 42	7 47	..	10 36	..	..	1 22	..	2 22	4 6	7 22	..			7 59	11 0	3 56		..	..	7 21
12¼	Winchester C .. arr	6 50	7 55	..	10 44	..	..	1 29	..	2 29	4 14	7 31	..			8 11	11 12	4 8		..	..	7 32
17½	Itchen Abbas	7 2	8 8	..	10 56	..	..	1 41	..	2 41	4 26	7 44	..			8 18	11 19	4 15		..	..	7 39
21¼	Alresford	7 9	8 15	..	11 3	..	..	1 48	..	2 50	4 34	7 51	..			8 26	11 25	4 21		..	..	7 45
24	Ropley	7 15	8 22	..	11 10	..	..	1 54	..	2 59	4 41	7 59	..			8 36	11 35	4 31		..	..	7 53
27¼	Medstead & Four Marks ..	7 25	8 32	..	11 20	..	..	2 4	..	3 9	4 51	8 9	..			8 45	11 44	4 41		..	..	8 4
31¼	Alton A 392 .. arr	7 34	8 41	..	11 29	..	..	2 13	..	3 18	5 0	8 18	..									
—	Mls Gosport .... dep	..	..	7 40	..	11 3	..	..	..	..	5 30	..	7 54			..	..	..		..	..	..
—	¾ Fort Brockhurst ..	..	..	7 43	..	11 8	..	..	..	..	5 33	..	7 58			..	..	..		..	..	h
—	Mls Fareham .... dep	..	..	7 53	..	11 47	..	..	2 48	..	6 50	..	8 45			8 21	..	..		..	..	6 36
—	2 Knowle Halt	..	..	7 58	..	11 51	..	..	2 52	..	6 54	..	8 49			8 27	..	..		..	..	6 42
—	4¼ Wickham	..	..	8 3	..	11 57	..	..	2 58	..	7 0	..	8 55			8 33	..	..		..	..	6 48
—	9¼ Droxford B	..	..	8 12	..	12 7	..	..	3 8	..	7 10	..	9 4			8 43	..	..		..	..	6 58
—	13¼ West Meon	..	..	8 21	..	12 19	..	..	3 17	..	7 19	..	9 14			8 52	..	..		..	..	7 7
—	17¼ Privett	..	..	8 30	..	12 32	..	..	3 29	..	7 29	..	9 23			9 5	..	..		..	..	7 18
—	20¼ Tisted	..	..	8 36	..	12 38	..	..	3 36	..	7 36	..	9 29			9 13	..	..		..	..	7 25
—	22¼ Farringdon	..	..	8 41	..	12 42	..	..	3 40	..	7 40	..	9 33			9 19	..	..		..	..	7 30
—	25¼ Alton A 392 .. arr	..	..	8 49	..	12 49	..	..	3 47	..	7 48	..	9 41			9 27	..	..		..	..	7 38
78¼	London (Waterloo) 392 arr	8 57	9 55	10 16	11 16	2 16	..	3 46	4 46	5 16	4 89	9 16	9 46	11 16		10 16	1 16	6 16		9 21	9 46	

¶ Miles from Southampton Terminus   **A** Station for Selborne (4½ miles)   **B** Station for Hambledon (3½ miles).
B Arr. 10 16 a.m on Sats.   **C** 1 mile from Cheesehill Station.   **D** Sta. for Twyford.   **F** Sta. for Bishopstoke.
G Southampton Terminus (for Docks).   **h** Thro Train to or from Portsmouth and Southsea, see pages 378 and 382.
S0 Saturdays only   **SX** Saturdays excepted

LOCAL TRAINS between Winchester and Southampton, page 384—Knowle Halt and Fareham, 376—
Fareham and Gosport, 376

OTHER TRAINS between London & Southampton, 324

SOUTHAMPTON, TOTTON, and FAWLEY

83. Extract from the timetable of the Meon Valley Railway c.1930.

84. Station staff at Wickham c.1909.

85. The goods yard at Wickham 1908 – the stationmaster is wearing a peaked cap.

Parish Council supported by Shedfield and Bishop's Waltham asked for a halt at Mislingford. In 1922 Corhampton and Meonstoke parish meetings asked for a halt or siding to serve the needs of the parish and in particular local farmers but nothing came of either application. As late as 1946 a halt was again requested by Meonstoke and Soberton. By the 1920s motor cars, motor buses and charabancs were proving more versatile and attractive forms of transport and the railway never matched the optimistic expectations of its initiators. The 1920s saw the beginning of retrenchment. In 1926 footbridges at Tisted, Wickham and West Meon were replaced by foot crossings.

Christmas 1927 was often recalled. One of the worst snow storms which anybody could recall began on Christmas Day and continued, accompanied by a biting wind, for three further days. There were deep drifts at Farringdon, Privett and West Meon and trains were snowbound. The line was deeply rural, a fact illustrated by the story of the driver who set his rabbit snares near Droxford on the outward journey to Fareham and collected the trapped rabbits on his return.

The railway played a memorable part in the life of all who lived in the villages. Children used it to travel to and from secondary schools in Alton; dinner party hosts would order fish from Grimsby and collect it from the station the same afternoon.[13] Visitors used the railway to reach Treloar Hospital at Alton.

The railway's finest hour occurred during the Second World War. From Thurday 2nd June to the evening of the 5th June 1944, in the run-up to D Day, the War Cabinet including Winston Churchill as well as Commonwealth leaders and service chiefs were accommodated in a siding at Droxford station. Droxford was chosen rather than Wickham, which would have been nearer to Southwick House where General

Eisenhower had his headquarters, because it offered better concealment and made possible tighter security. Folklore has it that the decision to postpone D Day for one day on account of the atrocious weather was taken at a meeting at Droxford station. There are also numerous stories of unexpected encounters with the allied leaders taking an off duty walk in the lanes round Droxford station with minimal protection.

Anybody fortunate enough to travel on the railway will recall its extraordinary beauty particularly in the Spring. It figures in Louis MacNeice's poem *Autumn Journal* published in 1939. He had driven down to a country house weekend north of Lee-on-Solent and travelled back on the Meon Valley railway giving us the only poetic reference to the line.

> *And I am in the train now and summer is going*
> *South as I go north*
> *Bound for the dead leaves falling, the burning bonfire,*
> *The dying that brings forth*
> *The harder life, revealing the trees' girders,*
> *The frost that kills the germs of laissez-faire;*
> *West Meon, Tisted, Farnham, Woking, Weybridge,*
> *Then London's packed and stale and pregnant air.*[14]

Anthony Hulbert remembers as a boy travelling from Droxford station to London via Alton and noticing 'what a wonderfully beautiful journey up the Meon valley it was'.[15] It lives in particular in the memory of children who travelled on it. In the early 1930s Norah Blyth then a girl of 12 lived in the station house at Privett. Now almost 90 she recalls helping at the station – acting as porter, handling the signals and filling the slot machines – everything except issuing tickets. The railway provided a road to Basing Park where once a week a basket of line-caught salmon from the river Tay arrived at the station and had to be delivered to the big house for which Norah received a tip of 2/6, then a fortune.[16]

It was however one of those lines whose demise was inevitable in the years after the Second World War though little attempt seems to have been made to persuade passengers to use it and perhaps forestall closure. There was for example a cheap day return to Waterloo but in order to catch the last train from Alton you had to leave London at 6.57. In 1951 the number of trains per day in each direction was reduced from six to four and the last train from Alton now left at 4.30 which effectively ended the cheap day return. The Sunday service was also withdrawn in 1951. The location of stations remote from the villages they were supposed to serve remained a drawback throughout the life of the line.

Normal passenger services ended on Saturday 5th February 1955 and at the same time freight services were withdrawn from Tisted, Privett and West Meon. There were of course protest meetings and a public enquiry. The National Farmers Union wondered how members would market their sugar beet without the railway. But all to no avail. The die was cast. The last few weeks saw the photographers and souvenir hunters descend on the stations. On 5ᵗʰ February the *Hampshire Chronicle* reported that most of those travelling were people 'whose practice it is to attend the last rites of dying railways'.[16] One enthusiast had travelled all the way from York, others present remembered the opening of the railway over half a century earlier. On the following day the Railway Travel Society ran a train pulled by two engines from Waterloo to Pulborough, along the Midhurst to Petersfield line which closed on the same day, on to Havant and Fareham and finally up the Meon valley line back to Waterloo.[17]

For the next 13 years until August 1968 there was a goods service at either end of the line from Alton to Farringdon and from Fareham to Droxford carrying mostly sugar beet, at first daily and later three per week. Meanwhile demolition began on the middle section.[18] The most spectacular sight was the removal of the West Meon viaduct, sold for the not inconsiderable value of its scrap metal. Perhaps its life might not in any case have been long since rust had eaten into the metal. Demolition left the huge concrete base on the south of the road from West Meon to East Meon which is likely to remain, a permanent reminder of the railway, for many years perhaps centuries to come. By 1958 the tracks had gone from the sections of the railway no longer in use.

North of the West Meon viaduct much has disappeared though not the embankments which remain features of the landscape. There are vestiges of two tunnels, both sealed to prevent entrance and several road bridges. One of the tunnels enjoyed a brief

86. Former Privett station now a private house. The stationmaster's house was the building on the left, centre was waiting room and ticket office and outside were lavatories (now demolished).

but spectacular after-life. The proposed channel tunnel was at first intended to be a road tunnel and was of the same dimensions as the tunnels on the Meon valley line. Cars were tested to destruction by fire to assess what might be the effect of a blaze in the proposed channel tunnel.[19]

There were a variety of suggestions for uses to which the line might be put. Could it be converted into a relief road for the already overloaded A 32? This was a suggestion supported by villages like Droxford, Corhampton and West Meon which needed relief but opposed by those which did not.[20] Three of the stations became private houses. In 1971 Wickham station was demolished to prevent further vandalism. Eventually the southern section of the railway from Knowle junction to West Meon was bought by Hampshire County Council and designated a nature walk. It provides a fascinating ten-mile walk for naturalists as well as industrial archaeologists who wish to view nostalgically 'overgrown platforms and ivy covered bridges'.[21]

For half a century the Meon Valley railway had served to draw together all but the most northerly and the most southerly villages – East Meon and Titchfield – in the Meon valley. Its loss, inevitable as it was, was felt as a deprivation by all for whom the railway had been a familiar backdrop to the valley scenery. As Edwin Course comments 'It was a delightful line to ride on but even the replacement bus service loses money'.[22]

19

Parish and Rural District Councils

THE CREATION OF PARISH COUNCILS in 1894 was the biggest revolution in local government in the countryside since parish vestries began to replace the manor court in the sixteenth century. Elected local government had come to the towns in 1835 and more recently to the counties where in 1888 county councils had replaced the government of justices of the peace in quarter sessions. The Parish Councils Act of 1894 provided for villages with a population of over 300 to elect a parish council of nine or more members depending on size. Smaller villages would hold parish meetings.[1] Both were to be represented on the Rural District Council (RDC). The Act even fixed the date on which meetings to elect the new councils were to take place – Tuesday 4th December 1894 – so on that date those living in all the villages concerned – men and women – were invited to meet in what ever halls were available.

The central part of the Meon valley came into the Droxford RDC which was based on the Droxford Poor Law Union set up in 1835. East Meon was in Petersfield RDC whilst Titchfield was at first part of the Fareham Rural District. In 1932 Fareham became an Urban District and its constituent parishes lost their parish councils. The new ecclesiastical parishes created during the nineteenth century could petition to become civil parishes: Swanmore and Shedfield were amongst those which did so, each becoming independent from Droxford whilst Crofton, Sarisbury and Hook-with-Warsash were carved out of Titchfield. At the other end of the valley Langrish was separated from East Meon.

Meetings to elect the first parish council were called by the Poor Law Guardians. Names were proposed and placed in alphabetical order. A vote by show of hands followed. The chairman of the meeting must then leave ten minutes during which anybody could call for a poll. If nobody did then those elected constituted the first council. One of the objects of the act was to free villages from the hierarchy headed by squire and parson who had dominated the unelected vestry. Many villages nonetheless remained profoundly deferential and naturally elected the same men to the new council. At Wickham for example John Carpenter-Garnier, squire and Lord of the Manor, was elected chairman and when he moved to London in 1897 he was succeeded by Colonel Harry Richards Farquhar another large landowner who lived at Park Place. He remained chairman until 1919. The clerk at Wickham was Henry James Brock the village postmaster who held the post for 26 years.[2]

East Meon's first council was rather more representative of the whole village. In addition to the rector T.H.Masters, it included a doctor, cattle dealer, hawker, undertaker and two farmers whilst the curate John Thomas Hindle was appointed clerk with an annual salary of £5.[3] In the combined parish of Soberton and Newtown over 100 villagers crowded into the National School and there were 21 candidates for the 11 places on the Council. The vicar William Morley was elected chairman, another example of *noblesse oblige*.[4]

At Droxford the meeting was held in the National School the only meeting place in the village. Unfortunately the early minutes of the council have not survived but the minutes of annual meetings and parish meetings were kept in a separate minute book and these are in the Hampshire Record Office.[5] At the first meeting the candidates were two blacksmiths, one painter, one plumber and one man who claimed both vocations, a labourer, a butcher, miller, hire carter and gardener. Francis Hurley who lived at the Mill gained 28 votes and was subsequently elected the first chairman. The minutes of early meetings of many of the new councils read as though cautious window shoppers enjoyed contemplating what they could buy if they had the money but decided with relief to keep the money and forego the additional amenity.

Two of the villages of the Meon valley were too small to merit a council. The first parish meeting at Corhampton was held in the schoolroom.and was attended by a total of ten people. The squire Colonel Campbell Wyndham of Corhampton House was elected chairman and when he stood down in 1901 the vicar succeeded him. In 1895 the parish meeting was attended by three people and it did not again reach double figures until 1913. Local democracy had arrived but it remained a sickly specimen in many villages unless a keenly felt local issue arose.

At Droxford lighting the village was raised as early as 1896 but when 30 years later Exton suggested that the Meon valley might be lit by electric light the Parish Council was in favour but 'more details were needed' – this usually meant procrastination on grounds of cost. In 1934 it was 'not opportune' to proceed. A recreation ground for Droxford was suggested as a possible project to mark the Diamond Jubilee of Queen Victoria in 1897 but the suggestion was rejected. It had still not been achieved in 1931 when there was a proposal to buy five acres of land: once more the proposal was turned down.

Water supply was a perennial problem. As early as 1895 it was pointed out that property owners were obliged under the recently passed Public Health Act to ensure a safe water supply to premises which they owned – a reminder that most properties were then rented not owned. The subject of piped water for the village of Droxford was not raised until 1929 when it was decided not to proceed. The matter did not appear again until March 1934 when it was decided to erect a parish pump. A year later the project of a parish pump was 'to await further discussion with Soberton, Meonstoke and West Meon.' The following year the Gosport Water Company said it would charge 11¼d per 1000 gallons and would require £25 towards the extension of the facilities at Mislingford. The company's terms were unanimously rejected. In 1935 the matter of water was again under discussion, no doubt inspired by the drought of the previous year. Mrs Wyndham Long of Corhampton House had offered to supply water from her artesian well at a fixed price for 1000 gallons of water. The meeting wondered if she would agree to a stand pipe with a meter for use in case of emergency. Mains water was not available in Droxford until 1955.

Refuse collection or ' scavenging' as it was called before the Second World War became important as a result of two developments – the disappearance of open stoves and the increasing use of tins and glass which could not easily be burnt. In 1928 cost appears to have been the obstacle to the adoption of a scheme at Droxford. Not until 1934 did the Parish Council agree to a voluntary scheme for three years. It worked well and they renewed it for a further three years. Cottagers paid 2/6 per year, house-holders 5/- and larger houses 10/-. A voluntary 'scavenging' arrangement seems to have been the favoured solution until the Rural District Council scheme was launched after the Second World War. At West Meon there was a farm locally known as 'Bedstead Farm' since the occupier marked his boundaries with bedsteads which he had collected as a result of holding the contract to collect rubbish in the village. William Haslet of Marldell Farm collected refuse in his horse and cart.[6]

*   *   *

The minutes of parish councils reveal the similarity of the problems each faced. Vandalism and unruly behaviour was a persistent problem. As early as 1907 the Parish Council of East Meon resolved to place a wire door with padlock over their notice board from which notices had been disappearing.[7] At Titchfield vandalism centred on the Recreation Ground where turf, fences, gates and the pavilion frequently caused problems. At Titchfield too the visit of gypsies during the strawberry season led to rowdy scenes, complaints about which reached the Parish Council. Cricket and foot-ball teams each wanted exclusive use of the recreation ground but there was insufficient space for the cricket square to remain sacrosanct during the winter, another fruitful cause of conflict.[8]

East Meon was concerned at its early meetings about the provision of allotments, flooding in the village and the state of the footpaths. The streets were lit by oil-lamps and the lamplighter was paid 5/- per week out of which he had to provide oil for the lamps. The council agreed to the Post Office's suggestion that before they installed the telegraph they should provide a guarantee of income.

East Meon had one of the earliest supplies of piped water in the Meon valley. In 1909 Lord Hotham provided a public water supply. Villagers would no longer have to rely on wells, rain water tanks or the river. Most householders did not however opt to have water connected to their houses. The reason can only have been the desire or perhaps need to keep the rates down. They preferred instead to make use of the stand-pipes shared by groups of householders each of whom had a key to the nearest stand-pipe from which water was drawn and carried home in pails.[9]

Even before the First World War all parish councils were concerned about the growing problem of motorcars (*sic*). Most roads in the countryside were not yet tarred and it is easy to imagine the state of the roads after rain. Motorcars generated dust in summer and mud in winter. The parish council frequently drew the attention of the Rural District Council to the state of the roads. The Motor Car Act of 1903 required the placing of notices indicating danger and each council had to decide on an appropriate place. In 1916 the Droxford Parish Council asked the Automobile Association to erect notices at both ends of the village drawing attention to the school.

After the war motorcars and charabancs appeared in increasing numbers and the state of the roads led to improvements. In 1938 a bypass for Droxford was proposed but rejected [10] In the 1970s a bypass for Wickham reached the planning stage but was abandoned on account of cost. By the 1970s the M27 was about to be completed and when a route for the projected Winchester by-pass was agreed the M3 would bridge the gap from Winchester to Southampton. The villages were assured optimistically that the pressure would be taken off the A32 up the Meon valley. It may have done briefly but the volume of traffic has continued to increase and remains a major concern of the villages through which it passes.

Women were eligible for membership of parish councils from the beginning but very few were elected – it was still a man's world. The First World War began the emancipation of women. They replaced men in many spheres and demonstrated their competence and so in 1918 they gained the right to vote in parliamentary elections – but only at the age of 30. Titchfield had an early woman parish councillor in the person of Agnes Hewitt elected in 1919 who was by all accounts an exceptionally able and energetic woman.[11]

The overwhelming impression of the work of parish councils until well after the Second World War is that they were determined, to keep the rates down and inevitably this meant preferring economy to amenity. The result was that the villages presented a striking contrast to the towns where comparable services had been taken for granted for many years. Two issues dominated all others – the supply of piped water and the provision of mains sewerage. In the twentieth century there were hot, dry summers in 1911, 1934 and 1975 (see pages 160–1). By 1975 piped water had been installed in all the villages but on the first two occasions they suffered drought.

After the Second World War there was an outburst of idealism. Surely the cooperation and camaraderie which had been evident during the war, for example in the Home Guard, could be continued afterwards. Each parish council had aspirations for enhancing village life. At Droxford in addition to a war memorial there should be a village hall and swimming pool as well as provision for mains water and sewerage which had not yet reached the village.[12]

Rationing lasted until 1954 and in recognition of the plight of the mother country the 'dominions and colonies' sent consignments of food in 1946 and again in 1947 which parish councils agreed to distribute. The Meonstoke and Corhampton Parish Council like others decided to allocate the food to those living alone since in their view the hardest hit by rationing were those who had only one ration book in the family. In 1946 they were able to supply provisions to old age pensioners whether or not they were living alone.

20

Late Victorian and Edwardian Villages

☙

T HE FIRST NATIONAL CENSUS of population took place in 1801 but it was not until 1841 that names first appeared. From then on a census has taken place every ten years except 1941 when we had other things on our mind. Data collected has gradually been refined. The 1881 Census of Warnford contains the names of 401 people who lived in the 80 houses in the village. Two houses in particular provided accommodation for large numbers. There were 17 people resident at Warnford Park and 13 at the Rectory and both households employed a large number of living-in servants.

Warnford Park was the home of Henry Woods (aged 58) who described himself as Magistrate. His wife was Henrietta (50) and they had two daughters at home, Catherine (15) and Henrietta (13). There were in addition no less than 12 living-in servants – butler, cook housekeeper, two ladies' maids, four housemaids, kitchen maid, scullery maid and two footmen. All were unmarried, aged between 19 and 39 and born in a variety of places – London, Norfolk, Dorset, Monmouth, Berkshire – so they were presumably recruited by advertisement. Marie Lewhardt from Steinfort in Germany was a private governess, probably employed to teach the girls. But that was not all. In the stable room were three young men who looked after the horses and in the garden bothy three gardeners, whilst in the garden house was the head gardener. All were young men and all unmarried. In addition Henry Ubsdale lived at the Lodge with his wife and two children.

Across the turnpike was the Rectory (now Abbey House) where lived John Wynne (aged 51, rector 1872–1903), his wife Elizabeth (48), son Louis (22) an undergraduate at Oxford and daughter Constance (16). They too had a substantial staff – footman, coachman, gardener, cook, ladies maid, house maid and kitchen maid – once more all young, unmarried and recruited from the south of England. Constance seems to have had a governess named Rose Martin aged 23.

Warnford was, like all others in the nineteenth century, a young village. The death rate was high and many did not survive to old age. The median age was about 22. There were 91 young people between the ages of ten and 19 but this narrowed to 64 in their twenties and only 25 in their sixties. The Census identifies 'scholar', by which is meant those, mostly between the ages of four and twelve, who were on the register of the village school. There were 70 but a further 18 are not named as scholar and we must assume that they were not to be found on the books of the school even in 1881 by which time the pressure was on to make education compulsory. Eliza Mandano (34) born at

87. The County Police Station, Droxford, built 1858.

Dalston in Middlesex was the teacher at the school and lodged in the village. Emily Newell (19) was pupil-teacher.

It was a farming village. Over 80 men are described as 'agricultural labourer' or some variant. There were for example 17 carters, six shepherds and three gamekeepers. The largest farm was Wheely Down Farm, its 476 acres farmed by 76 year old James Cousins who had moved with his family from Dorset and was now a widower. He was assisted by his sons – Henry (42), James (41) (who was deaf and dumb), Septimus (34) and Charlton (32) and by two daughters Elizabeth (40) and Fowler (36). All lived in the farmhouse, all were unmarried and they employed Eliza White a 15 year old, born at Micheldever, as servant.

In addition to those involved directly in agriculture were the village craftsmen who supplied essential services. Every village needed a blacksmith who not only shod the horses but made and maintained the farm carts. At Warnford in 1881 George Wells (65) was blacksmith assisted by his two sons James (31) and Henry (24) and by a kinsman Richard Wells (65). The village would include a carpenter and wheelwright whose expertise overlapped with that of the blacksmith – in Warnford in 1881 he was Willliam Moreton (21). Domestic crafts represented in the village included thatcher William Osgood (65), dairyman George Down (36) of Peak Farm Dairy, two shoemakers Truman Merritt (60) and William Windebank (61), grocer David Burch (56), inn keeper Thomas Turner (46) and beerhouse keeper Edgar Robinson (44).[1]

*   *   *

Daily life for working people at the end of the nineteenth century and the beginning of the twentieth had much in common not only in the Meon valley villages but throughout southern England. Frederick Standfield recorded the reminiscences of several villagers who were born in East Meon in the last decade of the nineteenth century and the first years of the twentieth and so spent their childhood in the village in the years before the First World War.[2]

East Meon was also predominantly an agricultural village and almost all the cottages were occupied by farm workers. At harvest time even the few who normally worked at other crafts would lend a hand, hay-making or hop picking for example. School holidays were determined by the needs of the harvest, enabling children to play their part whilst women would be employed to turn and scatter the hay using a long-handled rake. Clara Fisher (born 1902) accompanied her mother, walking four miles each way to Buriton where the hops were grown. Sheep shearing was an annual event when gangs of half a dozen men would leave the village very early in the morning wearing white corduroy trousers and, using only hand shears, could each shear 20 sheep in a day.

Houses were lit by oil lamps or candles. The lamplighter carrying ladder and can of oil would light and, late at night, extinguish the street lights. Farmers each ran a small dairy delivering cream, milk and butter directly to cottages in the village and selling the surplus at the market in Petersfield. The milkman visited each house, his pail of milk suspended on a yoke over his shoulder and filling the jugs of customers from half pint or pint measure hanging on the lip of the pail. Many villagers made their own bread and some made cheese. Most kept poultry, a pig or two and sometimes a goat. The pigs

88. River Meon at Meonstoke c.1900. *The Bucks Head* is advertising 'Good stabling and Accommodation for Cyclists'.

were fed on household scraps and barley meal bought from Frogmore Mill and in due course were slaughtered and the carcase cured and salted to be eaten during the winter.

Clara Fisher recalled that 'the village had four bakers, three grocers, a paraffin and hardware store, saddler, two butchers, two mills, wheelwright, farrier, a post office and a fish and chip shop.' Many shops were general stores which sold clothes, boots and shoes as well as grocery. There was no mains sewerage and the privy was emptied at night and the contents collected in a horse-drawn cart. Nor were there bathrooms; children were bathed once a week in front of the fire in a metal tub filled by kettles and saucepans heated on the fire. Cooking took place in a pot suspended over the open fire and the Sunday joint for a large family would be taken to the baker to be cooked.

Each village had a doctor. At East Meon Clara Fisher remembered Dr Jones who drove a gig or rode a bicycle until about 1910 when he became the proud owner of the first motorcar in the village. Clara remembered him extracting her tonsils at his house assisted by the Petersfield doctor as anaesthetist. In many rural communities there was no dentist and the doctor filled that role too. Clara sat in Dr Jones' chair while her tooth 'was yanked out without a pain killer'. If people were very ill straw would be put down in the street to deaden the sound of passing horse and cart.

John Macdonald, born in East Meon in 1894 was a member of the Rat and Sparrow Club, paid for collecting rats' tails and sparrow heads. They were taken to the blacksmith who would mark your card and throw the tails and heads into his fire to prevent them being counted twice.

Sunday was filled with church and Sunday School. You attended Sunday School first, then the morning service leaving before the sermon. Sunday School took place again in the afternoon and when you were old enough you went to church at night. You wore your best clothes and a family walk and Sunday dinner marked the day. Boys in the church choir were either 'penny' boys – the older ones paid 1d for each attendance at practice or service – or halfpenny boys – the younger ones paid ½d for each attendance.

Amusements were simple. For children 'crazes' followed each other without rhyme or reason – hopscotch, marbles, tops, skipping, hoops and of course conkers each autumn. Everybody would gather to watch the village blacksmith shoeing horses or the sparks flying as he fitted tyres to a wagon wheel. There were parties at Christmas organised by the Sunday School with a Christmas tree, games, tea and buns and oranges and crackers to take home. The summer party was held in the vicarage garden with games, races, scrambling for sweets and finally a large balloon warmed by methylated spirits lighted in a saucer and sent soaring into the air.

Travel outside the village was an adventure. Unless you walked or cycled you paid for a seat on the carrier's cart or hired a wagonette or dogcart perhaps to meet the train at Petersfield or after 1903 at West Meon. The carrier was George Noble White who travelled the 17 miles each way to Portsmouth on Tuesday, Thursday and Saturday. The main roads were gradually surfaced with tar in the years before the First World War. Clara Fisher recalled meeting 'a strange horse-drawn contraption' for tarring the road. A barrel of tar was hoisted over the centre frame of a tank, the bung was released and thick, black tar poured into a tank which was heated by a fire underneath. A big tap was turned on and the hot tar sprayed on to the road. It was spread with long handled brushes by workmen with sacking tied over their boots for protection and sand was then thrown on the road.

*   *   *

From the middle of the nineteenth century the strawberry industry played a major part in the economy of the southern end of the Meon valley. It was centred in the area between the Meon and the Hamble in the parishes of Titchfield and Wickham in the Meon valley and in the parish of Botley beyond it. The sale particulars of Rookesbury Park in 1928 claimed that the strawberry industry of south Hampshire was encouraged by the Garnier family and began on the Hundred Acre smallholdings on their estate as early as 1845.[3] Titchfield Common which became the centre of the strawberry industry was enclosed in 1859 and was then occupied by smallholder tenants. The light sandy and gravely soils of the Common were suited to the shallow rooting strawberry. It was reckoned that a family could make a reasonable living on two or three acres and that cultivation of double that acreage might with luck and good weather make a man passing rich during a season which lasted only five or six weeks. In June the gypsies would arrive to provide the needed casual labour first to straw and later to pick the fruit and would leave when the strawberry harvest was over in late July or August.

In the early days horse drawn carts took fruit to the markets in Portsmouth and Southampton. In 1888 the railway line from Fareham via Netley to Southampton was built and the new station at Swanwick was ideally situated to the needs of the industry. Other railway stations shared the boom years. Botley on the line from Eastleigh to Gosport was one and, when the Meon valley line opened in 1903, there were 'strawberry specials', whole trains devoted to strawberries, departing from Wickham station or Mislingford siding.[4] Strawberries were loaded soon after midnight in time to reach Covent Garden early in the morning. London was not the only destination: the towns of the midlands and north and even Glasgow bought Hampshire strawberries. Horse drawn carts took the strawberries to stations along crowded lanes. At the height of the boom in the years before and after the First World War 100,000 baskets were loaded on to the trains, over 3000 tons of fruit in 1913. In 1923 66,000 baskets left Botley in 64 freight vans.

The trade was always susceptible to the weather. In August 1885 the vicar of Sarisbury, frequently a pessimist it must be said, wrote: 'As we write, the strawberry crop is drawing to its close, leaving no little disappointment to many whose year's labour has been expended in its cultivation. Competition from places nearer to the great markets and the unusual dryness of the season … have so reduced the prices as to make them almost unremunerative to some growers. We have always regarded the crop as a dangerous one to depend on and we think that the experience of the last three years has proved this beyond doubt'.[5]

*   *   *

89. Tudor Cottage and Annie Hillier's Tea Rooms opposite *The White Horse*, Droxford showing Cyclists' Touring Club sign. Demolished 1960s.

90. An early motor car owned by William Woods of Warnford House c.1908.

The late Victorian period saw the arrival of the first democratic means of transport – the bicycle at least four times faster than walking. It caught on with both sexes and all classes and began the broadening of social life which had hitherto been confined largely to the village and its near neighbourhood. The first bicycles were 'penny farthings', precarious since the rider was perched over the front wheel. The 'safety bicycle', commercially viable by 1885, had better steering and brakes. Frames were heavy and until the 1890s bicycles were iron tyred.

The popularity of bicycles can be followed in Hampshire trade directories. The first mention of a 'Bicycle Manufacturer' occurs in White's Directory of 1878 when cab and fly proprietors were legion. By 1885 Kelly's Directory records no less than 18 'Bicycle and Tricycle manufacturers' though still only in the towns. By 1895 the 'Bi' is omitted and there are 47 cycle agents and dealers, 20 cycle makers and 14 repairers. By now the Meon valley had a Cycle Agent and Dealer in E.&W. Linter of Swanmore and by 1903 there were agents and dealers also at Wickham (Alfred Page) and Droxford (Edmund H. Jones).

Cycling clubs were founded in many villages and since Sunday was the only full day free from work it was the day for meetings. In 1899 the bishop of Winchester, Randall Davidson, devoted part of his address to the Diocesan Conference to the threat posed to church attendance by the bicycle. In reply churches laid on Cyclists Services. Meanwhile hotels and pubs recognised the existence of a new clientele. At Droxford Annie Hillyer's tea rooms carried the symbol of the Cyclists Touring Club as did *The Bugle* in Titchfield.[6] *The Bucks Head* at Meonstoke advertised rooms for cyclists and at

91. Traffic on the main road through Warnford c.1910 – later A32.

Warnford there was a pub renamed *The Cyclists Rest* in the hope of attracting customers. A new industry was born and cycle repair shops multiplied rapidly. Merington's Cycle Works in Mill Lane Droxford was founded in 1904 selling, repairing and rebuilding bicycles. The cost of cycling soon came down, by the mid-1890s you could buy a bicycle for as little as £4.10.0 or acquire a secondhand one for even less.[7]

Motorcars – 'horseless carriages' was the name by which the early ones were known – came rather later and were in any case in the early years the preserve of the rich. Outlay and maintenance put cars well beyond the purse of the average person until well into the twentieth century. The local doctor is often remembered as the first person in the village to replace pony and trap or a bicycle by a motor car. Gradually the coachman was replaced by the chauffeur, the coachhouse by the garage and the joiner by the garage owner. Merington's at Droxford put in a petrol pump and added motorcycle and motorcar maintenance and repairs to its cycle repair provision. Until the early years of the twentieth century motorcars had a tiller in place of a steering wheel and petrol was sold by chemists.

*   *   *

Cricket in Hampshire will always be associated with Hambledon and nationally with Thomas Lord. The earliest cricket match in the Meon valley of which there is a record took place in 1775 at Milldown on the Preshaw estate. A landscape painting owned by Sir Richard Pelly and probably the work of Dominique Serres, a Spanish visitor, shows a cricket match in progress at Millbarrow near to the present North Lodge. It includes a marquee erected to serve as pavilion as well as a gazebo, a finely painted coach as well as the match and in the distance Preshaw House. The cricket match is particularly interesting. There are two stumps, bowling appears to be underarm and the bat is shaped like a hockey stick. Seventeen seventy five was the year in which a third wicket was added to the stumps after the demon bowler Edward 'Lumpy' Stevens shot the ball three times through the two stump wicket, then in use.[8] Previously each wicket consisted of two stumps one foot high and twenty four inches apart. The height of wickets was increased to 22 inches. At about the same time the bat which until then had looked like a hockey stick was straightened.[9]

The Hampshire Chronicle provides tantalising glimpses of matches in the nineteenth century. In 1850 it records Droxford beating Winchester at a ground in Hyde Street, Winchester and in 1852 a team called Old Winchester beat West Meon at Twyford. Much later there is a photograph of men and women playing a mixed cricket match at Droxford in 1904.[10]

James Aylward one of the men who created the fame of the Hambledon Cricket Club at the end of the eighteenth century was born at Peak Farm, Warnford and later moved with his family to Corhampton. He was short and stocky, a left-handed batsman and occasional wicketkeeper and until 1779 he played for Hampshire. Between 5pm on Wednesday 18th, and 3pm on Friday 20th June 1777 in a match played at Sevenoaks he scored 167 runs in an innings, at that time the highest individual score achieved in a cricket match. On the scorecard he is shown batting at number ten; in fact he opened the innings. Names on scorecards were determined by rank not order of batting – gentlemen first then professionals and finally rustics – Aylward was a rustic. He became bailiff to Sir Horace Mann one of the pioneers of cricket and and played for Mann from 1780–84 when he became landlord of the *White Horse Inn*, though remaining both caterer and player into his 60s.[12] He died in London in 1827 and was buried in St John's Wood, not far from Lord's cricket ground. His two brothers John and Thomas also played cricket. Both are buried in the churchyard at Warnford, John at the age of 88.

Thomas Lord was born in 1755 at Thirsk in Yorkshire. After a period in Norfolk he moved to London and opened a cricket ground in 1787 in what is now Dorset Square where he himself played mostly as a bowler and where the Marylebone Cricket Club (MCC) was founded. In 1813 he acquired part of the land of what became Lord's cricket ground and lived in St John's Wood until 1830. He then retired to live at East End Villa, West Meon (now Home Paddocks) so came to be regarded as an inhabitant of the Meon valley. He lived there for less than two years dying at the age of 77 and was buried in the churchyard in January 1832. The MCC placed a new stone slab over his grave in 1951. On 6th August 1955 to mark the 200th anniversary of his birth a match was played between a team drawn from Warnford and West Meon Sports Club and the MCC – the latter won convincingly. In the same year *The New Inn* was renamed *The Thomas Lord* and began to collect and exhibit cricket memorabilia.[13]

Cricket was played with enthusiasm by the youth of the village in the parish of West Meon in the 1830s and 40s. Sunday was then the only full day available for cricket so men would conceal their cricket bats in the belfry until after morning service. The rector Henry Bayley was a keen sabbatarian and did not approve of Sunday cricket. He first persuaded local farmers to give their men time to play during the week and later gave a ground on which cricket might be played, but not on Sundays. It later became part of the parish recreation ground.[14]

Country house cricket in the Meon valley was represented by the Corhampton Club founded by the Wyndham-Longs. The club played on land which they owned on Corhampton Down. There continued to be a pavilion on what later became part of Corhampton golf club.[15]

*   *   *

The earliest recorded football club in Hampshire was founded in 1868. It was one of the earliest in the country and is still in existence. It was named the 'Fordingbridge Turks' to commemorate the fighting spirit of the Turks who had fought against the Russians in the Crimean War. Football caught on and the Hampshire Football Association was founded in 1887. By 1914 almost every village had its football club. Teams played 'friendly' matches against each other playing often on grounds on which

92. West Meon Football Club 1900.

93. West Meon and Warnford Football Club 1910.

cowpats had to be dodged, posts erected and kit and changing facilities improvised. In the 1890s Portsmouth Football Club transformed 'an area of cow grazing land into what became the impressive Fratton Park ground'.[16] A number of local leagues came into existence of which the Meon Valley Football League was one. It was founded at a meeting held at *The White Horse* at Droxford in 1906. In the first season six clubs took part and the challenge Shield was won by Wickham. In the early years the valley clubs which took part were Droxford, Wickham and Soberton which adopted the name 'Meon Valley'. The League was suspended during the First World War since many players joined the services and was resumed in 1919. Something similar happened during the Second World War when once again the league was suspended between 1940 and 1946.[17]

*   *   *

Scouting was an overnight sensation attracting boys from a variety of backgrounds as well as men of all classes who became its leaders and patrons. Scouting arrived in the Meon valley soon after Robert Baden-Powell held his first experimental camp on Brownsea Island in Poole Harbour in August 1907. At Droxford it was the village shoe repairer Mr Higgins who ran the Scout troop. The village aristocrats took a benevolent interest from the beginning contributing funds for equipment. Lance Padwick, one of the first members of the Droxford troop, recalled loading Scout gear on the troop handcart and pushing it to Hillhead for the annual camp.[18]

The Girl Guides came a little later, founded in 1909 with Baden Powell's sister Agnes as its first leader. Brownies came in 1914. Soberton Guides were founded in 1918 by Mrs Culley and Miss Sullivan of Droxford and was for some time a joint enterprise between the two villages.[19]

*   *   *

The Boer War was both cause and effect of an upsurge of military spirit which was sustained through the early years of the twentieth century and may help to account for the spontaneous enthusiasm with which the outbreak of the First World War was greeted. The popularity of the Scout movement was perhaps a sign. During the summers of the early years of the century contingents of army reservists came to Droxford and set up camp along the Hambledon Road, on Bushy Down and along the Droxford to Wickham Road. Kenneth Ward includes photographs of the Hampshire Carabiniers camp at Bushy Down in 1904 and the arrival at the newly opened Droxford station of Princess Beatrice's Own, a volunteer battalion of the Hampshire regiment. He recounts the remarkable story of the Hampshire Cyclists Battalion which went to India in 1915 and did not arrive back in England until December 1919 having covered 52,000 miles.[20]

*   *   *

94. A village wedding at Warnford c.1910.

95. Warnford Post Office and Store c.1900.

96. *The George Hotel* Warnford c.1900.

97. Old houses and St Nicholas' church, Wickham.

The years before the First World War were the last in which large houses, dependent on abundant living-in servants, were built. Two examples from the Meon valley were Soberton Towers built at the turn of the century and New Place, Shedfield designed for Annie Franklyn by Sir Edward Lutyens and completed in 1908.

Soberton Towers must rank as one of the oddest large houses built in the Meon valley at any period. It was begun in 1897, took seven years to build and was completed in 1904, after the death of its owner in 1902. Its builder and designer, though it would be an exaggeration to describe him as an architect, was Charles Brome Bashford (1839–1902). The house occupies a prominent site at the top of the hill close to Soberton church. Its battlements, round corner turrets and mullioned windows are impressive but David Lloyd writing in the Pevsner Buildings of England volume on Hampshire is nonetheless scornful of its dated pretentiousness. He describes it as 'the last gasp of Otranto and Fonthill… The plan is utterly unpicturesque'.[21] Members of the Bashford family had lived for much of the nineteenth century at Soberton when they were not serving in the army in foreign parts. Memorials and stained glass windows to members of the family fill the north aisle of Soberton church. By the time Soberton Towers was built Colonel Bashford was ADC to Queen Victoria and briefly to Edward VII and he may have built the house so that he could receive royal visitors there. It was a family house only briefly before it became a boys' preparatory school. During the Second World War it was a base for the Women's Royal Naval Service and in 1970 was sold and converted into nine self-contained houses.

*   *   *

New Place has an unusual origin: it was built to house material salvaged from a mansion in Bristol and named after a house in Stratford-on Avon which had been demolished as long ago as 1759. Henry William Franklyn was partner in a family tobacco business in Bristol. His wife Annie Sophie Allenby was a distant relation of Mary Arden, mother of William Shakespeare who had lived at New Place, Stratford on Avon. In 1875 Henry and Annie moved from Bristol to Shedfield Lodge where Henry died in 1884. Annie Franklyn meantime had inherited an early seventeenth century house in Bristol which had become a tobacco factory, deteriorated badly and was now due for demolition. In 1904 she commissioned the well-known architect Edwin Lutyens (1869–1944) to design a house to be called New Place to which the interior of the Langton mansion on the Welsh Back in Bristol could be transferred.[22]

The result was a house of great character, built of red brick with impressive chimneys facing the main road in Shirrell Heath. Ceilings and panelling, a magnificent stone fireplace and staircase were all transported by rail from Bristol to Wickham and from there by horse and wagon to Shirrell Heath and installed in the new house.[23] Annie Franklyn's son Henry Arden Franklyn married Emily Geraldine the great grand daughter of William Wilberforce in 1908 and Annie Franklyn gave them New Place as a wedding present. In the early years they employed no less than 18 servants caring

98. High Street Meonstoke c.1900.

99. New Place, Shirrell Heath designed by Edwin Lutyens built 1907.

for the house, its occupants and the extensive grounds. They moved to the Red House, Botley on 1956. Since then New Place has changed hands several times. From 1956 to 1978 it was a boys preparatory school. It has been enlarged and in various guises has since then been a management centre and hotel.[24]

21

The First World War

BRITAIN DECLARED WAR on Germany at 11pm on Tuesday 4th August 1914. There followed what has been described as the 'four bloodiest years in human history'.[1] Almost three quarters of a million men were killed on the western front in France and Belgium alone. But the war was also fought at sea, in Italy, the Balkans and the Dardanelles and in the Middle East. It was the first war in which civilians were involved thanks to the invention early in the twentieth century of aircraft, though not to the same extent as in the Second World War. It was the last war in which horses were involved at least on the western front. At Wickham horses were taken to fields between Droxford and Meonstoke where their suitability for service was assessed and those selected left for the France from Droxford station.[2] The war, it was at first believed, would be short – 'over by Christmas' it was widely held. Nobody anticipated the horror of the trenches nor the costly stalemate which was its consequence. In 1914 enthusiasm for war was everywhere evident and men in the Meon valley villages as men everywhere went off in huge numbers to join the services, some of them under age.

Henry Curtis Gallup, who owned Bereleigh, one of East Meon's substantial estates, had no previous military experience and was no longer a young man but nevertheless volunteered at once and took with him not only his horse but Mark Neil his gardener and George Knight his chauffeur to enlist at Larkhill on Salisbury Plain where they were trained as gunners. Henry's wife Marjorie Gallup and the vicar's wife Kate Masters joined up, serving as nurses at Greenhill Hospital. The vicar Thomas Heywood Masters was at first rejected for service as a chaplain on grounds of age and so took a Red Cross ambulance to France. By October 1915 the age limit had been lifted and he became a chaplain and later Assistant Chaplain General.[3]

Henry Gallup, Mark Neil and George Knight went together to join the British and Indian force fighting in Mesopotamia. They were amongst the troops forced to surrender to the Turks at Kut-el-Amara on the river Tigris, now in Syria (then part of the Ottoman Empire), after a siege lasting four and a half months during which the British and Indian troops endured horrific suffering. After the British capitulation the Turks separated officers from men, Henry Gallup among the former, Mark Neil and George Knight the latter. Many died from malnutrition and ill treatment. Mark Neil and George Knight were never heard of again. Henry Gallup survived but spent two and a half years in a Turkish prisoner of war camp and was a changed man as a result of his experiences.[4]

One of the first casualties of the war on the western front was John Carpenter-Garnier, Major in the Scots Guards and the eldest son of the squire of Wickham, who died in September 1914.[5] Two months later on 26th November *HMS Bulwark* was torpedoed at Sheerness and over 600 men were drowned including Harry Deadman who only eighteen months before had been a boy at Soberton school.[6] Men from the villages served in all theatres of war and many were decorated for conspicuous bravery. Amongst those from Soberton who volunteered Henry Cusdin won the Military Medal, Albert Coates served at Zeebrugggge and John Purser at the Battle of the Marne. Walter Cluer was a wireless operator with Admiral Beatty, whilst Fred Matthews was amongst those blinded on active service.[7] At East Meon two Coopers, two Pollards and two Titheridges were among the dead. At West Meon two members of the Douglas-Pennant family died, one a captain in the Grenadier Guards and one a Lieutenant in the Coldstream Guards.

Every village has heart-rending stories of suffering, loss of limbs, shell shock, devastating gas attacks, and horrific wounds. In many villages the names of two or more members of one family who fought and died appear on memorials. The most poignant memorial in the Meon valley is to be found in Soberton church, placed there by John and Mary Twynam of Soberton House. It commemorates four sons and a son-in-law, all killed during the war: William Hugh a Corporal in the 7th Battalion of the Canadian Regiment killed in France on 24th April 1915, John killed by a lightening strike while on duty as a Staff Sergeant in the South African Mounted Police on 3rd November 1914, Hugh who was a Lieutenant in the Royal Navy drowned in a submarine on 19th January 1917 and George a Lieutenant with the 11th Border Regiment killed in France on 12th November 1916. Their brother-in-law Geoffrey Culley a Captain in the Royal West Kent Regiment was killed also in France on 15th September 1916.

Charles Matthews, vicar of Titchfield, volunteered as a chaplain early in the war. He left England on 30th April 1915 and his first experiences were published in the Parish Magazine in June 1915.

> I arrived at a large seaside town about 40 kilometres from Calais on May 3rd and am in charge of No.11 General Hospital containing 530 beds. … Wounded men arrive by train from the front and are conveyed in motor ambulances at all hours. Here they are treated or operations are performed and they are forwarded to England on one of the hospital ships which daily cross the channel… I write letters for those who cannot do so themselves … to mothers and wives. I have had to write some very sad news to bereaved ones. … and I have accompanied several relatives to the cemetery … who had come over here hoping to see their dear ones alive… The funerals take place daily at 8am and the officers' funerals are at 2.30pm.[8]

We do not know exactly how many men from the villages served in the war as volunteers, or after 1916 as conscripts, but it may have been as many as 1500, mostly men in their twenties, some younger still and others older. Of those who went to war about 220

100. The War Memorial, West Meon.

did not return and many were buried in France or at sea. At Wickham there were almost 50 deaths, at Titchfield 41, at West Meon there are 30 names on the War Memorial. In the church in the small village of Froxfield, until 1870 part of the large parish of East Meon, an illuminated tablet contains the names of 99 men who served in the war of whom 14 were killed. In only one village were there no deaths. Warnford was one of the very few villages in the whole country where all those who had gone to war returned. The brief 20 years between the First and Second World wars were in many families years of prolonged mourning for sons, brothers, cousins, fathers and sweethearts who had been killed. The dead included men from all three services. (The Royal Air Force was formed in February 1918. Previously there had been air detachments in the army – the Royal Flying Corps – and the royal navy – the Royal Naval Air Service.) Men of all social classes died as did men of all ranks and in all theatres of war.

Women served but mostly at home taking over from the men who had joined the forces. Few names of women are to be found on village war memorials. At Wickham they were photographed at Park Place, then the home of Colonel Harry Farquhar, sitting at tables sorting nuts and bolts for reuse in the manufacture or repair of aircraft. Women could work at home and some did making shirts, gloves and balaclava helmets for men in the services. 'Dig for Victory' was a Second World War slogan but provision of home grown food was as vital in the First as the Second World War if the German blockade were to be defeated. Hitherto uncultivated plots were turned over to potatoes. The wounded came to Netley and to the Queen Alexandra hospitals and to convalesce in makeshift nursing homes in the big houses, *Mayburys* for example in Titchfield Square. At Wickham volunteers took the men out and provided tea in the Square.

German prisoners of war came to the Meon valley. There was a camp next to the Gosport Waterworks near Mislingford which was served by the Meon Valley Railway.

When at last at 11am on 11th November 1918 war ended there was general rejoicing and in many villages church bells were rung. Every village erected its war memorial on which were inscribed the names of those who had died. Almost all are in the church or churchyard of the parish still regarded by many as the heart of the village. No expense was spared in providing a worthy memorial. At Droxford it was unveiled by Admiral Sir Doveton Sturdee who lived at Meonlea. He had become a local hero after he had successfully avenged the German victory in the battle of Coronel off the Falkland islands in December 1914 by destroying the German squadron responsible. He was later to initiate the movement to restore *HMS Victory* and to install it in dry dock at Portsmouth.[9]

101. The Old Brewery, Wickham converted to the Victory Club as a First World War memorial.

102. Wounded servicemen in Wickham Square en route for Hambledon 1921.

At Wickham at the end of the war it was decided to commemorate the fallen by erecting a 15 foot high cross of Portland stone and to appeal for money to build the Victory Hall to accommodate local activities. The war memorial was duly erected and dedicated in a ceremony in the Square attended by 800 people by General Herbert Powell who was a relation of Robert Baden-Powell the hero of Mafeking in the second Boer War and the founder of the Scout movement. The Victory Hall was eventually opened but never quite met the aspirations of its originators.[10] At Shedfield in addition to the parish war memorial a second memorial was given by Annie Franklyn now living at Shedfield Lodge. It still stands at the end of St Ann's Lane and recalls the men who marched along the road to Botley for embarkation for France from Southampton. It reads

> Remember, O Lord, all who passed
> by this road on their way to
> the Great War, 1914–1918. Be
> gracious to all Wayfarers.[11]

Every village has its War Memorial on which the names of the fallen were inscribed. In the Meon valley and in most villages the parish church or its graveyard was the natural setting, the memorial often accompanied by Biblical text and imagery and forming the centre piece for ceremonies held on 11th November, Armistice Day, until another war began twenty years later. At Titchfield the war memorial was in the centre of the village but the names are to be found only in the parish church.

'Comrades of the Great War' was one of the organisations formed to help the many who had been wounded or suffered in some way from the war. It was founded by Lord Mount Temple and a branch was started in Droxford with Howard Rogers as Commandant and Edward Harriott the village butcher as secretary. In 1923 it merged with the British Legion which had been founded in 1921. Droxford's commemoration included the opening in 1920 of the Fred Bunning Memorial Hut. Fred Bunning, the son of the licensee of *The White Horse*, was killed in the war and the hut came from Netley Hospital and was re-erected in Station Road.[12]

	First World War	*Second World War*	*Total*
Titchfield	41	20	61
Wickham	49	12	61
Droxford	14	10	24
Meonstoke	24	8	32
Soberton	15	4	19
Newtown	10	10	20
Corhampton	5	1	16
Exton	10	with Corhampton	
Warnford	0	1	1
West Meon	30	9	39
East Meon	21	14	35
Total	219	89	308

Number of men from the villages of the Meon valley who died and are commemorated on the war memorials erected in each village.

22

The Inter-war Years

U<small>NTIL WELL AFTER</small> the Second World War facilities in the villages were inferior to those which had long been available in the towns. England was still a country of two nations, not only rich and poor and north and south but town and country. When the 25 year old Dorothy Warwick, recently married to Reginald Warwick, came from the northern town of Preston to live in the Square at Wickham in 1919 it took her several months to get used to the quiet life of the Hampshire village. She noted 'the small quaint shops with their tiny windows, the tall chimneys and large open spaces' and she wondered what she would find to do. 'Except for a few dogs lying around, a carriage or two and a horse drawn carrier's cart, the village seemed deserted. There was no such thing as a car, bus, motor vehicle of any kind in sight'.[1]

She had left behind a home where there was every comfort and a town with ample facilities – hot and cold water at home, public transport, theatres, libraries, excellent schools and museums in the town – and had come to live in a fairy-tale village, outwardly picturesque, with old-world charm, but without street lights, mains water, gas or electricity or any means of transport except two trains daily to London, no cooking facilities except oil stoves and coal and worst of all neither piped water nor sanitation.

> 'I had to pump the water I required from an old fashioned pump which had a handle, held together by a leather band …To have a bath was a major operation. I remember with horror the large tin tub, shaped like a coffin which took ages to fill. Each kettle of water had to be separately heated and the first was almost cold before the second one was added. It took a whole evening to get one uncomfortable bath.'.[2]

Those who lived in the cottages in Bridge Street had to draw water in buckets from the Dip Hole in front of the mill and carry it up the hill back home. The Dip Hole was not fenced in and Dorothy Warwick recalled a child of three falling in, being swept along the river and found drowned a mile downstream. Only houses whose owners had installed their own had electric light, the remainder were lit by oil lamps whose wicks needed careful adjustment if ceilings black with soot were to be avoided.

She found that strangers were only slowly accepted. Wickham like many villages was self-contained, families who had lived there from time immemorial, were related to each other and eyed strangers with suspicion. The village was self- supporting.

Horses were shod by the village blacksmith; a leather shop in the Square sold harnesses, bridles, stirrups and whips, the butcher in the Square slaughtered cattle on the premises, milk was delivered by horse drawn carts, dresses were made from material bought in the village. If you needed something which the village could not supply then the carrier would collect goods ordered from a shop in Fareham. Shop-keepers knew everybody and there was no chance of keeping scandal quiet.

Few people left the village for work. Girls had to be content with domestic work, employment in the shops or work on the land, most boys became farm labourers or village tradesmen. Wages were low and work was hard to get. Women earned between 6d. and 1/- per hour for cleaning, 8/- to 12/- per week for general domestic work, 20/- to 25/- for cooking and girls earned 10/- to 15/- a week. The average weekly wage of a farm labourer with a tied cottage was between 25/- and 35/- and shop assistants averaged £1.

In her early years in Wickham Dorothy Warwick recalled the rats.

> I have never seen more [rats] in my life than I did during my first years at Wickham. …these enormous ones terrified me. I used to look out of my bedroom window quite early in the morning to see what all the squealing was about. The first time I did this I saw dozens of large rats running across the Square and small groups of them eating scraps of food dropped there. Later, between 7am and 8am, men working in the Agricultural Machinery Foundry brought out wire cages containing two or three rats caught during the night. They made a large circle in the middle, opened the cage doors and let their dogs loose to kill them'.[3]

And what Dorothy Warwick noted by contrast with what she was used to in the town was also characteristic of villages elsewhere in the valley. May Watts was born in Titchfield before the First World War and grew up there in the 1920s. She too had vivid recollections. Few houses belonged to their occupiers, most were rented for 5/- per week or less with 2/- for rates. Some were still thatched. The poorest made a living by collecting cockles and whelks from the shore of the Meon. On leaving school girls still often went into domestic service, others worked at the laundry at Locks Heath or the jam factory on Titchfield Common. Many people in the village worked at the Tannery which remained open until 1955.

Most people shopped in the village. May recalled the mingled smell of bacon, paraffin, meat and groceries at Lankester and Crooks at the corner of the Square and West Street. Almost all needs could be met in the village – there were tailors, saddlers, two butchers one with a slaughter house next door, two shoe shops, drapers and a cycle shop whose proprietor would make up a bicycle from second hand parts for 5/-. In Mill Lane was the mill where Mr Russell was the miller. There were eight pubs and behind one of them, *The Red House* in South Street, a marquee was erected once a year and Joe Beckett a boxer took on all comers.

In Titchfield as in many other villages well-known personalities had nicknames, the product of long-standing residence, endearing peculiarities or professional roles.

'Oily Willy' was a lamp and oil dealer in South Street. Others included 'Josher 'Williams', Peppernose' Cross, 'Farm'Hewitt, 'Hoppy' Ford, 'Suety' Waters, whilst George Read was 'Whistling Baker'.[4]

At the other end of the valley Ruby Snell who was born in 1920 left West Meon school on Friday and began work at what was called 'the big house' (West Meon House) for Major Waudby on the following Monday. Her sister was already a house-maid there and her brother a gardener. She was paid 5/- per week and her keep and was provided with a uniform. She went home only on her day off. She came from a family whose local roots went back at least to the end of the eighteenth century. Her father-in-law was born in West Meon in 1873 and his father was buried in the churchyard at West Meon in 1883.[5]

Ann Baring's father bought Woodlands and Woodlands Farm in 1914 and Anne was born there in 1918. She recalled the staff – 24 men working on the farm, 11 in the house, four in the stables, five in the garden as well as two chauffeurs. She recalled how during the drought in 1921 Woodlands ran out of water which had to be brought by traction engine from the river at Warnford.[6]

* * *

Though the boom years might be over, the strawberry industry remained an important component of the economy of the villages of the southern part of the Meon valley in the 1920s and 30s. Competition was however growing from Kent and the Vale of Evesham and by the 1930s strawberries were coming from Europe. Cliff Burgess whose mother and father grew strawberries in Titchfield at Abshot and in St Margaret's Lane was taken on at 1/- per week for a six-day week when he left school at the age of 14 in 1927. He recalled the early years when his father hired a ploughman and horse though he later bought a pony and did his own ploughing. He hired casual labour at 8d per hour to spread straw and later pick the fruit. Trains from Swanwick station took the strawberries to Covent Garden or Brentford market sometimes involving a wait of up to two hours at Swanwick station in the queue for the train. After the season the plants were trimmed back, the straw raked out and used as bedding for pigs which in return provided manure for next year's crop.[7]

* * *

Until the coming of bus services you either walked from Titchfield into Fareham or travelled by carrier's cart which made the journey once a day and cost 6d. May Watts recalled paying 3d for a seat at the cinema in Fareham and 1d for a bun after the show. To go to the railway station in Fareham or Swanwick you walked or if you could afford it hired a horse-drawn Victoria from *The Bugle* for 2/6. The doctor, working from home, charged 2/6 for a visit, beyond the means of many people unless there was a dire emergency. Children with whooping cough would be wheeled to Hillhead where there was a flock of sheep – contact with sheep was believed to provide a cure. During the strawberry season gypsies arrived as seasonal labour, sold horses in the Square and bought cheap meat from the butcher.[8]

Amenities began to arrive in the villages between the wars. At Titchfield villagers had been obliged to use the wells or pumps built many years before, though some preferred to carry water from the flight of steps at the edge of the canal in Bridge Street or from the stream or village pump. By the end of 1923 most houses had been connected to mains supply.[9] Meanwhile a mains sewerage scheme was agreed in 1923 and installation was complete two years later. The sewerage works was then by the river Meon just south of the bridge. Electric light too was available from 1923. In some places the telephone was installed before the First World War but at first was only installed by the better off. The telephone did not reach Droxford until 1927.

Outings were no longer by horse-drawn carriage as they had been before the war. Instead motor driven charabancs made their appearance, single deck with open top though there was a hood which could be raised in case of rain. At Droxford by 1920 Tony Merington ran a monthly trip to the dance held in the Drill Hall at West Meon.[10]

Droxford had a small part in the early history of powered flight. On 18th May 1919 Kenneth Mackenzie-Grieve, son of the owner of Fir Hill, was navigator in a Sopwith plane piloted by Harry Hawker which took off from Newfoundland with the intention

103. Charabanc outing c.1920 – hats were essential headgear for all.

of being the first plane to cross the Atlantic. After a week there was no news and the aviators were given up for lost. The plane and its occupants had been obliged to land at sea after only 1000 miles. They were rescued and although the plane had failed in its attempt Kenneth was given a hero's welcome when later he returned to Droxford.[11]

*   *   *

After the First World War the Court House and Hall at East Meon had been long neglected and might easily have been replaced by modern premises. The south end of the Hall had become accommodation for farm workers, whilst the surrounding buildings included a cowbyre, midden and a not too savoury smelling pond. Salvation came in the person of Morley Horder an eminent architect with a particular interest in the restoration of old properties. He bought the hall and house and gradually transformed the building removing wallpaper and plaster so as to reveal the structure of the medieval walls as well as the remarkable roof beams. He lived in the house until his death in 1944 converting the farmhouse into a family home, which harmonised sensitively with the existing buildings and transforming the farmyard into a terraced garden. Morley Horder was also responsible for buying and restoring other houses and thatched cottages in East Meon which would otherwise not have survived much longer. He is a person who should be remembered with gratitude in the Meon valley as well as the village of East Meon.[12]

*   *   *

If Place House at Wickham was the first mansion to be built in the Meon valley, begun soon after the Norman Conquest, Leydene high up on the Downs south of East Meon at the northern extremity of the valley, was one of the last.[13] Leydene was the creation of Eleanor Williamson who, in 1899, married William Robert Wellesley Peel, the grandson of the nineteenth century Conservative Prime Minister Robert Peel and was himself a member of parliament until he became Viscount Peel in 1912. Even before her marriage Lady Peel was fabulously wealthy. She determined to build a country house of spectacular grandeur. The site she chose was near the summit of Hyden Hill two miles south of East Meon and 700 feet above sea level, sheltered from the north wind and with superb views to the Solent and the Isle of Wight. Work began on levelling and building foundations in the spring of 1914. The Peels meanwhile bought Coombe Cross, a nearby farm, from which they could supervise the building of the new house.

No sooner were levelling and foundations complete than war supervened and building was suspended until 1919. The Peels moved into Leydene in the autumn of 1924 but not until the end of 1925 were staff cottages, garages, tennis court, fruit and vegetable gardens, the drives and walks complete. The house had an impressive entrance hall from which issued a magnificent staircase. There were elegant reception

104. *The Shoe* Exton early 1930s before rebuilding on the opposite side of the road to reduce the risk of floods.

105. The Flood, Exton 1934.

106. Staff of the International Stores, Wickham 1924.

rooms with Georgian style ceilings and generous suites of bedrooms. No expense had been spared. The gardens were on the same scale. The Peels employed 14 gardeners who cultivated a seven-acre kitchen garden, and tended the orchard and greenhouses where grapes and nectarines as well as tomatoes, cucumbers and potted plants were grown.

From 1927 the Peels entertained on some scale, personal and parliamentary friends including, it is claimed, Winston Churchill – in the political wilderness during the 1930s. In winter there were pheasant shoots organised by Harry Dean the head game-keeper who employed local men and boys as beaters at 5/- per day plus bread, cheese and beer for lunch. Lord Peel however lived at Leydene only when he could be away from London where he had a house in Holland Park. Each year too the Peels would spend part of the time at Beaufort Castle, their house in Aberdeenshire, where they fished for salmon in the river Tweed.

Lady Peel was an eccentric, she was personally reticent and found contact with local people difficult. She cared nothing for elegant clothes and conducted a vendetta with the Petersfield Rural District Council over trivial sums of money. She kept a herd of Saddleback pigs, whom she knew by name and visited daily, feeding them bread and toast – reminiscent of Lord Emsworth the comic creation of P.G.Wodehouse. Lady Peel accumulated a huge estate and eventually owned over 10,000 acres in East Meon and the surrounding countryside.

The halcyon years at Leydene were brief, lasting only 12 years. Lord Peel died at Leydene at the age of 70 in 1937 and was buried at East Meon. Two years later just

107. Leydene House built 1914–25, requisitioned by the navy 1941, later *HMS Mercury* closed 1993.

before the Second World War Eleanor Peel bought Hendesyde, a house and 1600 acre estate in Scotland. She rebuilt the house and it was here that she died in November 1949 aged 77. She too was buried in East Meon churchyard. Leydene was never again a private house. It had been requisitioned by the Admiralty at the beginning of the Second World War and became *HMS Mercury* in 1941. In 1949 the Admiralty bought the house and four years later the remainder of the estate was sold in small plots mostly to local farmers. The last country house to be built in the Meon valley had flourished for less than 20 years. It was finally sold by the Admiralty when *HMS Mercury* was transferred to Portsmouth in 1993.[13]

*   *   *

In the course of the nineteenth century the huge medieval dioceses of the Church of England were reduced in size by the creation of new bishoprics. Winchester was one of the largest comprising the whole of Hampshire and Surrey including the Channel Islands and the Isle of Wight. In the east it extended as far as Southwark in south London. In 1877 eastern and mid-Surrey were taken out of Winchester and attached at first to Rochester and in 1905 were made part of the new diocese of Southwark. Winchester was still an unwieldy diocese with 570 parishes and 1000 clergy and included the growing towns of Portsmouth and Southampton.

There was discussion of dividing the diocese before the First World War but it was not until 1927 that the new dioceses of Guildford and Portsmouth were carved out of Winchester. The Meon valley was in the diocese of Portsmouth and so the link with the diocese of Winchester which went back to 660AD was broken. The first bishop of Portsmouth was Neville Lovett the father of Elizabeth Hulbert who lived at Fir Hill, Droxford. When Neville Lovett retired from Salisbury, of which he had been bishop since 1936, at the end of the Second World War he lived at Meonlea in Droxford and when he died in 1951 the south chapel of Droxford church was named the Lovett Chapel.

In the years after the First World War the Church of England took the first steps to free itself from parliamentary control by the creation of the Church Assembly and at parish level Parochial Church Councils (PCC). The pattern of services established at the end of the nineteenth century continued and the tradition of the deanery continued to be moderately evangelical. Leonard Etheridge (rector of Droxford 1926–46) was from the beginning aware of the strong Protestant traditions of the parish and determined to introduce only innovations which carried the approval of the PCC. Changes came gradually: fully sung services in 1926, lighted altar candles at first only at early morning Holy Communion. A robed choir was proposed and blue gowns and caps for women and black cassocks and white surplices for men were worn for the first time at Easter 1934; two members of the choir left in protest at the new practice.[14]

23

The Second World War

NOBODY ALIVE at the time will ever forget where they were when the lugubrious tones of the Prime Minister, Neville Chamberlain, announced at 11.15 on Sunday morning 3rd September 1939 that Britain was at war with Germany. Nor are they likely to forget the siren which sounded, for example at Titchfield, almost at once. Some were in church where the morning service had just begun and where arrangements had been made to convey the news at once to apprehensive congregations. Dorothy Warwick was at the offices of the Droxford Rural District Council in the Square at Bishop's Waltham. She had been elected its first woman member in 1938. 'I remember that strange bewildering moment and the silence that followed it very clearly; it was one of the most dramatic moments of my life', she recalled.[1] Den Marriner, a boy of nine, was told of the outbreak of war by a neighbour as he stood in the road outside the house where he and his family lived opposite the church in Exton. He too will never forget the moment.[2] Many remembered the First World War which had ended less than 21 years earlier and wondered if the conflict on which the country had now embarked would bring casualties on the same scale.

The Second World War cast a long shadow before it. War had been anticipated since at least 1935 and by 1938 was regarded as inevitable. The first circular about Air Raid Precautions was issued to local authorities in September 1935 and in April 1937 local councils were required to appoint Air Raid Wardens. In September 1938 in anticipation of imminent war ARP was mobilised, evacuation plans were published and gasmasks were issued: at Wickham from a room at the back of the King's Head.[3] Although by 27th September it seemed that war might be averted, at West Meon School trenches were being dug in Knapps Yard to provide protection for the youngest children if there were immediate air raids. Three days later the head reported in the Log 'Crisis passed – peace in sight'.[4] At the last minute war had been averted by the Munich settlement – but only for a year.

When in September 1939 war finally came there was almost a sense of relief. The Second World War involved the civilian population on a scale never before experienced; women as well as men, children and old people as well as those called up for what was called 'active service'. The threat of invasion, aerial bombardment and shortage of food affected all equally and are matters which all alive at the time still recall vividly.

Sirens were placed on prominent buildings in many villages but this was not always possible. At Soberton Air Raid Wardens were issued with wooden rattles to warn of raids since the nearest sirens were at Droxford and Wickham, only audible if the wind was in the right direction.[5] Prominent buildings were requisitioned. Rookesbury Park School at Wickham was evacuated to the west country and the army used the buildings and grounds of the school as a motor vehicle workshop for the duration of the war and incidentally laid on electricity and mains sewerage not previously available at the school. The maternity unit at Haslar hospital in Gosport was moved to Beverley a large private house in Wickham. Warnford Park was also requisitioned. Each parish was required to appoint a billeting officer – at Meonstoke John Stanning (rector 1905–43) undertook the task, at West Meon the billeting officer was Timothy Colebourne of Bank House.

*   *   *

The government made two assumptions about the approaching war, both of which turned out to be unduly alarmist. Poison gas had been used in Abyssinia in 1936 so in September 1938 gas masks were issued to all but fortunately were never used. Second, it was believed that the outbreak of war would be followed at once by the bombing of major cities causing heavy casualties so plans were made for the immediate evacuation of schools and of women and small children from the main towns. The country was divided into evacuation areas, reception areas and neutral areas. About 1½ million people were evacuated between June and the first week in September 1939, the largest mass movement of population ever attempted in the British Isles, but considerably less than the planned 3½ million.

The only large conurbations in the south of England apart from London to be evacuated were Portsmouth, Gosport and Southampton. All the villages in the Meon valley were in reception areas so the initial evacuation which took place on Friday 1st September meant the arrival in the Meon valley villages of children and their teachers mostly from Gosport though some came from the east end of London. At West Meon children from Elson Road Infants school Gosport arrived on Friday 1st September and the following day younger children with parents.[6]

All available accommodation was requisitioned. Fifteen people, mostly children but some mothers with young children, were billeted at West Meon House. School did not reopen until 12th September when Lord Northbrook made available the Woodlands hut for school use.[7] In some places local children worked in the mornings and evacuees used the same buildings in the afternoon. But not for long. Aerial bombardment did not take place nor was gas used. The novelty of country life soon gave way to boredom. Tension between hosts and evacuees sometimes developed and the drift back home began.

At Soberton evacuees found village life strange after the closely-knit community life and the familiar streets of the east end of London. Even the danger of bombs seemed preferable to a night visit to the outdoor earth closet at the end of the garden accompanied by the hooting of owls while bats swooped overhead. The absence of indoor water closets and a ready supply of tap water were obvious privations suffered by most families and felt particularly by children. Gas and electricity were taken for granted in the towns; in the villages cooking was by open fire and cottages were lit by candles or oil lamps.

All the villages have stories of families who arrived and departed days or even hours later. At Exton one of two brothers was billeted with the Marriner family and the other at the house next door. Both went to school at Meonstoke. After only a day or so both failed to return for afternoon school. They had colluded, left school together and walked back home to Gosport though the fact was only confirmed later since neither family was on the telephone.[8]

Large families presented problems to billeting officers. At Soberton one family of 12 refused to be separated and were eventually accommodated in a barn at Meonware, Woodend. In March 1940 the head of West Meon school noted that the evacuees were leaving Woodlands and returning to Gosport. He wondered whether they would return.[9]

Meanwhile at Wickham the two billeting officers responsible for meeting the evacuees and arranging their accommodation were both remarkable characters. Dorothy Warwick (1894–1979) who had lived at Wentworth House in the Square since 1930, emerged during the war as a person with boundless energy to whom the village owed much. A.E.Roberts (1888–1973) of Frith Farm was the other billeting officer and was described as 'a man with progressive ideas, colourful personality and wide interests' as well as being able to quell a recalcitrant evacuee with a look.[10]

The early months of war were an anti-climax and the country settled down to the 'phoney war'. Air raid shelters were built in gardens, some lined with bricks, some made of corrugated iron. A brick shelter was built outside Havelock House in the Square at Wickham for the use of people caught when shopping, but was rarely if ever used. It survived, an eye-sore, for many years after the war before it was demolished. Rationing of butter, sugar and bacon began in January 1940. The black-out was rigorously enforced and road casualties rose dramatically.

If the first evacuation in September 1939 was a false alarm later ones were certainly not. The phoney war ended abruptly in April 1940 and the Battle of Britain fought over the south of England from July to September 1940 gave the Meon valley its first taste of warfare. A second evacuation took place in June 1940. From November 1940 Portsmouth and Southampton were bombed heavily. By March 1941 less than half the population was still living in Portsmouth. In Southampton's first major raid on 23rd November 1940, 77 people were killed and several thousand made homeless. The town was a blazing furnace and the fires were visible from Wickham. After a series of sleepless nights, morale was low and many left the city, some altogether, others spent nights in the country and caught the bus back to work next morning, referred to as 'trekking'. By March 1941 only one third of the pre-war population was living in the city. The villages of the Meon valley provided a refuge for many and large houses were requisitioned. The Marriner family lived in a large thatched cottage opposite the school in

108. *Marriners*, Exton.

Exton (still called Marriners). They put up a family from Southampton where father and son cycled each day to work in Southampton. Later in the war a mother whose husband had been drowned when *HMS Hood* was sunk by enemy action came to live at Marriners with her children, a boy and girl as well as a baby.[11]

With the Battle of Britain raging overhead a further evacuation from Gosport to West Meon took place and the school had to accommodate an additional 15 children. But they were not safe even in the deep country of the Meon valley. On 25th September 1940 a bomb dropped close to Lippen Cottages, West Meon and in October a stick of eight bombs fell close to Brookwood Park. In May 1944 West Meon was on the edge of the area which could be reached by flying bombs and for a brief period the school was in a danger area. At Titchfield too stray bombs fell frequently. The main track of V1s ran just south of the village and one fell on a house at Meon.

* * *

The formation of what was initially called the Local Defence Volunteers (LDV) was announced by Anthony Eden on 14th May 1940 and there was an immediate rush to sign on. The LDV consisted of those too young or too old to join the forces and those in reserved occupations. At first there were no uniforms; volunteers wore an armband stamped with the letters LDV and drilled with improvised arms. In August 1940 the volunteers were renamed the Home Guard and became the force immortalised in the BBC's long running and oft repeated serial, *Dad's Army*. Every village had its detachment of the Home Guard. At Droxford the Home Guard was at first commanded by

109. Warnford Home Guard Unit commanded by Reginald Chester.

Lieutenant Jack Adams. A photograph of the unit shows 27 men and one woman, Jack's wife Ellen, the unit cook.[12].The men trained with the Royal Fusiliers at Fort Widley. At East Meon the unit's first commandant was the vicar the Revd C.H.Mylne and the first volunteer was the sexton and postman Frank Collier. A photograph of the contingent shows 29 men, many wearing stripes and medal ribbons earned in earlier wars.[13]

At Warnford the commanding officer was Reginald Chester and the unit photograph includes over 40 men, many of them his employees. At Wickham the commandant when the Home Guard was formed was General Herbert Powell, who had commanded Gurkhas in India during the First World War and until he retired. The unit was initially armed with pitchforks and scythes and even Gurkha knives. It was not until 1941 that a supply of rifles reached Home Guard units from the United States. There is a photograph of the Wickham contingent with some 30 or so members, their commanding officer incongruously resplendent in General's uniform with peaked cap. Is it imagination which makes him appear ill at ease, aware of the huge gap in rank between him and the villagers whom he commanded?[14]

One Home Guard recruit at East Meon was Edward Fitzroy Talbot-Ponsonby, a young man in his 20s who lived at Langrish House and was employed in a munitions factory next door. His membership of the Home Guard was a cover for clandestine activities to which he was recruited after the defeat and surrender of France in 1940. He joined the XII Corps Observation Unit, a body of 5000 men who would form the core of a resistance movement in the eventuality of a German invasion. Each cell consisted of six or seven men, whose peacetime occupations might include farmer, poacher, gamekeeper or burglar. Talbot-Ponsonby became a Lieutenant in the Home Guard as a cover for his activities as leader of 28 men in the Unit responsible for the parishes of Buriton, Froxfield, Steep and East Meon. They would disappear in the event of invasion and undertake sabotage and intelligence gathering.[15]

Each unit had its headquarters, often requisitioned for the purpose. At Titchfield the Home Guard met in the Drill Hall, now the Community Centre. At Droxford the unit was based in the loft of the coach house at Fir Hill. All units of the Home Guard had their lighter moments reminiscent of *Dad's Army*. One evacuee recalled the Soberton unit marching to the *Falcon Inn*, smartly dismissing and entering the pub as one man.[16] After D Day the Home Guard was no longer needed and on 6th September 1944 parades became voluntary. Two months later on 14th November 1944 the Home Guard was stood down and on 3rd December over 7000 members attended a final parade in Hyde Park.

*   *   *

Everyone contributed to the war effort. Members of the Droxford Women's Institute worked in the squash court of Studwell Lodge.[17] On weekday afternoons they prepared material for the wings, ailerons and rudders of trainer aircraft. They made camouflage netting in a barn in the Rectory garden, bottled fruit and made jam which was sold locally. What was referred to ironically as the 'Wickham Armaments Factory'

110 War workers at Droxford repairing aircraft wings.

111. Collecting waste paper with donkey cart during the Second World War.

worked throughout the war at Park Place, then the home of Commander Bird, director of the Vickers Aircraft factory at Southampton. Approaching 40 people, mostly women, sorted nuts and bolts for use in the armaments factory. At the Victory Hall in Wickham a baby clothes exchanges was organised.

Young people were mobilised too. Scouts and Guides in all the villages collected waste paper, gathered rose hips (from which rose-hip syrup was made) and removed docks from grazing fields.[18] School children were recruited to help on the land. In their last year at school boys and girls could opt to spend up to 20 sessions (ten full days) working on a local farm. (Prohibitions which would no doubt apply today were not then in operation: the school leaving age was 14, only the grammar schools took external examinations and Health and Safety legislation lay far in the future.) Sometimes the pupils already knew a farmer who was glad of extra labour but on occasion Droxford School for example recruited and supervised a gang of boys picking potatoes for Reginald Chester at Warnford Park.[19]

Everybody alive at the time of whatever age has his or her memories of the war years. The Meon Valley railway provided an identifiable target and one of the few land mines which fell left a huge crater near Droxford and blew out the east window of the parish church. Children became used to air raid warnings and quickly went to the shelters, provided at first in trenches dug in the fields. Village boys watched mesmerised when a dogfight took place overhead between a Spitfire and a Heinkel. They collected shrapnel and rushed to the site of a crashed aircraft in the hope of securing souvenirs such as spent cartridge cases. Fareham station was machine gunned from the air. A German bomber crew landed in the meadows south of Titchfield.

The Meon valley was in the front line throughout the war. Troops were stationed in the villages. Morale was maintained by regular dances wherever there was a venue – the Victory Hall at Wickham for example. A band came over from Hambledon twice a week to play for dances, with the Army Catering Corps responsible for refreshments.[20] Mobile cinemas were set up in the Square at Wickham and at Droxford to help pass the time while troops were waiting for D Day. They were popular with local youth since troops could be relied upon to supply comics, candies and chewing gum of which they appeared to have an abundance. Further up the valley troops from Warnford Park were entertained at the Queen Victoria Institute at West Meon.

At Titchfield Free French and American as well as British troops were billeted in the village and the old National School in West Street was the military headquarters. The best known unit was No.12 Commando under Lord Lovat. There was a small BBC radio station in Ranvilles Lane from which politicians, soldiers and reporters returning from France through Gosport were able to broadcast. The village also had an RAF camp on the Plessey site and a depot for barrage balloons from Portsmouth and Southampton. The coast was fortified and there were pill boxes all over the parish.[21]

*   *   *

Preparations for the invasion of Europe began in the summer of 1943 a full year before the invasion took place. Yvonne Downer was a member of the Women's Royal Naval Service (WRNS) and was posted to Warsash to work with the flotillas of landing craft preparing for D Day. Much time was spent in the Solent between Portsmouth, Southampton and the Isle of Wight. When Spring came in 1944 the number of troops built up and tanks and convoys of vehicles were everywhere in lanes round Warsash whilst the creeks in the Hamble river concealed landing craft. The men who were to take part in the invasion entrusted prized possessions to members of the WRNS. These often included a sealed envelope addressed to wife or girl friend, with instructions to post it if the soldier or sailor did not return. Then came D Day. Yvonne Downer describes her experience.

> Fantastically and suddenly the whole Solent filled with ships. One day there was the usual assortment of craft going about their business and the next time we left the river it was as if a curtain had been raised. A vast armada of ships rode at anchor. It seemed as if the entire Solent could be crossed by stepping from ship to ship… We had already carried boxes and boxes of ammunition, stores and equipment … out to the craft, refuelled and waiting on their buoys.

> I remember seeing a long column of khaki-clad men winding their way down the tow-path, past the Inn [at Warsash] which had once served shellfish teas… The French Commandos came first, French Canadian Commandos followed…

British Commandos were the last to embark, their quiet determination bordered on reserve.

On the seven o'clock news the following morning, the sixth of June, we heard the long awaited words ' the Allies have landed in France.'[22]

All along the south coast similar preparations were going on, masterminded from Southwick House which was the headquarters of General Eisenhower. Roads were widened, verges used and troops stationed in every possible location: there was for example a contingent of Canadian soldiers in Warnford Park The bridges were strengthened and the roads surfaced. By the beginning of June 1944 troops were camped along the roads in Titchfield, Wickham, Southwick, Droxford and many other places. Camouflaged tanks and trucks were everywhere. There were ammunition dumps in the woods and searchlights on the Downs.

Nobody can have doubted what was afoot. Just before D Day the War Cabinet, led by Winston Churchill with Commonwealth leaders and General De Gaulle, visited Southwick House and spent a night in a train in a siding close to Droxford station. In September 1946, after the war the event was commemorated by the 'D Day Seat' placed in the centre of the village inaugurated by Vice Admiral L.V.Morgan. Bishop Neville Lovett gave the Blessing.[23] 'After the invasion of France' says Kenneth Ward, ' the village was strangely quiet.'[24]

*   *   *

Once more there were many casualties in the armed services though not as many as there had been in the First World War. Members of the same family sometimes suffered in both wars in successive generations. At Wickham John Prideaux Carpenter-Garnier was one of the twelve who did not return. He was the son of the squire and was killed at Salerno in 1942 as his uncle had been killed in France in the First World War. A photograph of the church choir at Wickham in 1927 shows 14 boys aged about 12 all wearing school caps and all but one short trousers. They were the generation called up at the beginning of the war. Bob Davis was killed when the ship he was serving in was blown up and John Davis as an air gunner in the Royal Air Force. Three were taken prisoner, Bob Sadler at Dunkirk, Reg Higgins while serving in Egypt and Fred Dixon was a prisoner of war in Japan and so was Cliff Burgess (though not in the photograph).

At Droxford the dead included Gerard Hulbert whose father had bought Fir Hill in 1927. He was serving as a forward observation officer with the 11th Hussars when his regiment was overrun by Rommel's assault on the Sidi Rezegh ridge. The names of the fallen in the Second World War were added to the memorials which had been erected in the church or churchyard after the First World War this time more from convenience than out of Christian conviction. Remembrance Sunday replaced Armistice Day as the recognised national commemoration when wreaths were laid on

112. Choir boys of St Nicholas' Wickham c.1927.

113. War workers outside Park Place, Wickham before 'demobilisation' 1945.

the Cenotaph in Whitehall and on countless village memorials. It is still a solemn event in every village of the Meon valley over 60 years after the end of the Second World War. (For numbers of dead in each parish see page 202.)

24

Post-war Years

*‛*B RITAIN IN 1945. No supermarkets, no motorways, no teabags, no sliced bread, no frozen food, no flavoured crisps, no lager, no microwaves, no dishwashers, no formica, no vinyl, no CDs, no computers, no mobile phones, no duvets, no Pill, no trainers, no hoodies, no Starbucks… A land of orderly queues, hat-doffing, men walking on the outside, seats given up for the elderly, no swearing in front of women and children. Censored books, censored films, censored plays, infinite repression of desires…' This is how David Kynaston in his book *The Age of Austerity 1945–1951* characterised the immediate post-war years.[1]

The Second World War both delayed and accelerated change. Britain could not rely on food from abroad so it was essential to grow more at home. As a consequence, more land was ploughed, agriculture was mechanised and horses began to disappear from the familiar harvest scene. On the other hand there was no money to provide amenities such as mains water, sewerage, gas and electricity where those were not yet available. Improved roads too had to wait until well after the war. Only in the 1960s did awareness of change enter the consciousness of most people, not least those who lived in the Meon valley. The 1940s and 1950s were in many ways a continuation of the inter-war years.

*   *   *

Anthony Hulbert was born in 1940 and grew up at Fir Hill in Droxford in the late forties and early fifties. His father was in the regular army and was posted to Berlin in 1945 but left the army in 1947 and thereafter lived at Fir Hill. Anthony's recollections are of a village which resumed the even tenor of its life after the war.[2]

'The village was a cohesive unit with a vigorous village life. Opposite Fir Hill was a farm run by Mr Sylvester, an old style Hampshire farmer who sometimes wore a smock and always leather gaiters. There were tractors but horses were still used for ploughing and harvesting. Farmer Sylvester would perch me beside him on a hay turning machine drawn by a horse. He would crank a lever from time to time as the mown grass gathered and the horse plodded on. Down the hill [from Fir Hill] at what is now Taylors garage was a working blacksmith where Mr Grey shoed horses from a hot forge wearing a leather apron, the animals waiting their turn in the road. I can still hear the distinctive sound of the hammer on the anvil. Old Mrs Taylor ran a taxi service using a pre-war Austin 10 and wore large leather gauntlets and invariably a hat when she was driving.

Mr and Mrs Hobbs ran a wine and drinks shop next to the forge. They were a cheerful couple who had no children of their own but loved children. Ginger beer came in stone bottles with a levered fastener and my brother and I would be despatched to buy this. They wanted to know all the news and there were always sweets from under the counter (sweets were rationed until the 1950s). The Post Office was run by Mr and Mrs MacDonald, a Scotsman and his wife. Both were heavy smokers, friendly and efficient, always known as Mr & Mrs Mac. The shop attached to the Post Office sold 'Dinky' toys and to us was a great attraction.

Where the antiques shop is now there was a working bakery where bread was baked behind the shop. Then came a greengrocer and opposite that the telephone exchange. There was no automatic exchange in those days and Mrs Sparrow had to plug into a switch-board when a subscriber asked for a number so she was able to eavesdrop and as result was a mine of information on village life. She was garrulous and information gleaned in this way went rapidly round the village.

Next to the alley was a saddler and cobblers shop run by Mr Willsher and Mr Smith, craftsmen who made harness for working animals. In the Square was Harriots butcher. Meat was cut straight from the carcase on an old elm trunk and wrapped in newspaper. On the floor was abundant sawdust. Round the corner was Clarks, grocer and draper. That area of the village was full of people shopping, meeting, talking and gossiping. Opposite was a seat where the old men of the village sat and put the world to rights. Amongst them was Mr Cousins whose leg had been blown off in the London blitz. The story was that at the time his pockets had been full of loose change and there were still coins lodged in the stump.

The police station with its cells and magistrates' court next door was a hive of activity. At Studwell Lodge lived the Bruce family. Their boys were a handful and folk-lore had it that on occasion they had been put in the cells to cool off. The two pubs have been there from time immemorial. North of the village was Meringtons Garage where old Mr Merington had developed a car showroom. If you needed medical attention Dr Fraser's surgery was in his house next door to *The White Horse.* He had been a military doctor and had served in the Burma campaign. Like most doctors in those days his was a one man country practice with surgery and waiting room in his house. He took a lot of trouble on one occasion to get penicillin not then freely available and it saved the day. Traffic on the A32 was light and children could safely play in the square, ride bicycles or ponies through the village. There were of course impoverished homes and cottages in poor repair.

I remember the life of the village as secure, integrated and busy. Buses came and went frequently and people would gather at the bus stop talking animatedly. Many people then worked in the village as craftsmen, farmers or tradespeople. There was much common life centred round shops, businesses and trades. Doors were left unlocked and keys in the ignition of the few cars. It was possible to ramble, bicycle or ride almost anywhere without fear of danger. Miss King who taught me was a keen naturalist and taught us about the beauty of the countryside, the names of wild flowers, birds, rivers and hills.

In due course my father sold Fir Hill and went to live at the Old Mill which he had converted into a house of which he was immensely proud'.

* * *

Den Marriner was born in 1930 at Park Place, Wickham where his father was gardener.[3] When he was four his father became head gardener at The Grove, now Exton House and the family moved to Exton and lived in the gardener's cottage opposite to the former village school. When he reached school age Den went to Meonstoke school and at the age of eleven transferred to Droxford School. Life in Exton was basic – no gas, water from one of the deepest wells in the village, no mains sewerage and no telephone. Electricity had reached the village in 1934 and the Marriners possessed a wireless which required an accumulator. Den left school at the age of 14 (the school leaving age until 1947) and went to work for Mansfields, the baker in Droxford. He started work at 7am and his first job each day was to remove the bread from the oven where it had risen over night and load it on to the three wheeled cart which he then used for deliveries round the village. Meanwhile Mr Mansfield himself delivered bread by car to the surrounding villages – to Exton, Meonstoke and Soberton. Members of the Women's Royal Naval Service (WRNS) stationed at Soberton Towers collected the larger loaves baked specially for them.

Den's next job was at Exton Manor Farm. On the west of the A32 between Droxford and Beacon Hill Lane at Warnford the farms were all owned by members the Sylvester family. James Sylvester owned Northend Farm, where he lived, as well as Droxford Manor Farm and Sheep Pond Farm. He also operated Corhampton Mill, at that time still in operation producing crushed oats, the staple diet of the many horses on his and his sons' farms. Sidney Sylvester owned Exton Manor Farm, Percy Sylvester, another son, owned Exton Farm and Lower Barn Farm. Ernest Sylvester, also James's son, owned Corhampton Farm now known as Corhampton Lane Farm. All were mixed farms as were the great majority at that time. Exton Manor Farm had about 40 heifers, a bull and 'followers' – bull calves which were castrated and at about two years old sold for beef at the market in Fareham or Winchester.The milk was collected in churns by Portsmouth Cooperative Society. There were some fields of arable, mostly oats and wheat, as well as cattle, both dairy and beef. Oats – grain and straw – were fed to the cattle. During the war there had been a drive to grow more food and the Hampshire War Agricultural Committee was given Draconian powers to compel farmers to plough land which often had never been ploughed before. Until the war Exton Manor Farm had been mostly grass and it was during the war that land under arable was increased.

Den Marriner worked at Exton Manor Farm joining the cowman and his assistant.

During his last year at school he had worked at the farm part-time – after school, during the holidays and on Saturdays. At harvest time he had been a 'pitcher' loading sheaves of hay on to the cart where his partner would lay them flat so that the weight was evenly distributed. The horses were lead from field to rick but scarcely needed to be led since they soon knew the way. Den began work at 7am feeding the calves in the barn. When machine milking was complete 'stripping' took place – the last drops of milk were extracted by hand. In the winter loose hay from the ricks was spread round the field for the cattle after milking. Following afternoon milking the cattle would need straw spread in another field to ensure a good yield the next day.

On the larger farms silage was used to feed the cattle in winter. It was on the larger farms too that the first combine harvesters made their appearance and transformed agriculture. As F.G.Standfield writes 'Harvesting operations, spread over a period of months since time immemorial, are now completed so quickly that the morning's standing corn becomes, by evening, a grain mountain in barn or silo'.[4]

*   *   *

The strawberry industry of the lower Meon valley lasted until the 1980s. Cliff Burgess who had joined his father, a strawberry grower in Titchfield, in 1927 returned from war service in November 1945 and following his father's death shortly afterwards took on the strawberry fields just as change was beginning. Tractors were replacing horses, flame guns were substituted for hoeing, spraying was employed to control pests and smaller punnets superseded large two pound baskets. Trains gave way to road transport while lorries now collected the fruit from the growers. Competition came mostly from overseas and labour costs rose prohibitively. By the time Cliff retired in 1985 'Pick your own' was replacing commercial strawberry growing.[5] Today Titchfield Common is only a name on a map, the strawberry fields built over but still a powerful memory in the recollection of older people. A much bigger revolution has transformed the strawberry industry since then; the use of polythene tunnels, disease resistant plant strains, seasonal labour from eastern Europe, the extension of the season, are just some of the changes which have come over the strawberry industry. The number of growers has greatly reduced and most fruit is now bought by the supermarkets. Even 'Pick Your Own' is greatly reduced though still flourishing at Harris's in Titchfield. The Meon valley strawberry industry, once renowned, is no more.

*   *   *

In the nineteenth century the Church of England had achieved a resident parson in every parish even though in the smaller ones the result was rural isolation and under-employment. The second half of the twentieth century witnessed new pluralities. This time they were planned, the result of a reduction in the number of men ordained to the ministry of the Church of England and the realisation that a free for all had resulted in clergy disproportionately in the countryside and the south of England at the expense of the towns and the north of England. The first reorganisation in the Meon valley took place as early as 1926 when the small parish of Corhampton was united with Meonstoke whose church was a mere stone's throw from Corhampton. Soon afterwards the civil parishes were also united. No further reorganisation took place until the 1950s.

In 1953 Exton was joined to Meonstoke and Corhampton while the parishes of Soberton and Newtown shared a parson. In 1978 the three parishes of the centre of the Meon valley were joined by Droxford to make what has since become the Bridge Benefice, with one incumbent who now lives in a rectory built at Meonstoke. Early in the twenty first century Wickham no longer had its own parish priest but was joined with Shedfield whilst Soberton and Newtown rate only a half-time post. Further up the valley Warnford was added to West Meon in 1963 whilst East Meon assumed responsibility for Langrish. It is now rare in the country for a priest to have only one parish.

In the nineteenth century every parish had its own rectory or vicarage often built in the eighteenth century by a parson with private means whose house must be the equal of that of the squire. Meon valley parishes had a variety of substantial and handsome houses built in a period when families were large and living-in servants cheap and easy to come by. Wickham Rectory for example was built in 1698 with five bays, an elegant Doric pedimented porch and doorway and was described by David Lloyd as 'almost a mansion'.[6] It ceased to be the rectory in 1988 when a new house was built by the diocese next to the church. Droxford rectory also next to the church was another large, elegant house built in the eighteenth century. It ceased to be the rectory in 1964. The last old style Vicarage in the Meon valley, sold by the church in 2002, was the huge Victorian house in substantial grounds at Shedfield.

By the second half of the twentieth century the Church of England could no longer sustain such houses nor did it wish to be identified exclusively with the social class able to support such a life style. The large parsonages have been sold and every village now contains a substantial house often called the Old Rectory or the Old Vicarage. Some villages boast several such houses: West Meon recently built its fourth rectory whilst East Meon is on to its third. Meonstoke House was the rectory of Meonstoke and Soberton, half way between the two parishes until the two were separated in 1897 and the rectory was moved closer to the church at Meonstoke. But the new rectory was large and boasted extensive grounds. It was sold when Meonstoke ceased to have its own rector and was divided into two – the Old Rectory and Rectory Court. A modern house for the rector of the four parishes could still be built on part of what had once been a huge garden. Nor was Meonstoke parsonage the only one to be divided. Exton rectory for example is now three houses. Where a new parsonage is needed it may be built in the grounds of an earlier one as at both East and West Meon or it may be in a row of similar houses as at Titchfield and Shedfield.

Another change was the equalisation of the value of Church of England livings which took place as a result of the Glebe and Endowments Measure of 1976. Until then the value of livings depended on the amount of glebe and tithe attached to each church often stretching back to the middle ages and resulting in huge disparities of income. In future each diocese fixed the scale on which all its parish clergy were paid.

Until the mid-1960s the services of the Church of England remained as they had been for most of the twentieth century using the Book of Common Prayer. Holy Communion was at 8am, Morning Prayer with sermon at 11am and Evening Prayer with sermon at 6.30. All were reasonably well attended even if the clergy would like to have seen more people in church. In the afternoon there was Sunday School. As a boy Anthony Hulbert recalled the unreformed church of the 1940s. The rector of Droxford from 1946 to 1964 and the last person to live in the Old Rectory was Gerald Page, former chaplain to the King – bachelor, freemason and pipe- smoker. His sermons were long and indigestible, the choir large and the congregation substantial and there were few concessions to the children who were expected to attend afternoon Sunday School.[7]

In the mid-1960s all that began to change as the church embarked on reform of its services which led to the *Alternative Service Book* in 1980 and more permanently the adoption of the *Revised Common Lectionary* in the 1990s and *Common Worship* in 2000. Prayer Book services were phased out, remaining in use in many churches only for 8am Holy Communion ('The Early Service') though some country parishes stuck tenaciously to Prayer Book Morning Prayer once a month, attended mostly by the elderly. Otherwise the main Sunday service was Parish Communion. Evening Prayer declined as few people now attended church twice on a Sunday and young people's activities, no longer called Sunday School, were now held on Sunday morning. Congregations have dwindled. At West Meon there are about 30 regular churchgoers, at Droxford 40 and at Exton and Corhampton fewer. Only on special occasions – Christmas, Harvest Festival and Remembrance Sunday for example – can the village church expect its congregation to reach three figures.

In the last years of the twentieth century the Church of England had a variety of new types of ministry and from 1994 women were for the first time ordained priests. Shirley Henderson became priest in charge of Shedfield in 2003 and in 2005 Carolyn Headley was appointed to the parishes of Warnford and West Meon. They were the first women to hold paid posts in the parishes of the Meon valley. Elizabeth Groves was the first 'house-for -duty' appointment when she took up a post at Wickham in 2005 living in the new Rectory and Sandra Beavis became a half-time priest at Soberton and Newtown in 2010.

*   *   *

During the nineteenth century and until the Second World War Titchfield Haven was the haunt of wildfowlers some of whom came down from London to shoot. From 1920 Haven House was owned by Colonel J.S.Alston and was a hunting lodge whilst the gardener lived at Haven Cottage, long ago demolished. During the war the shore line was heavily defended and in the run up to D Day it was used by allied troops preparing for the invasion of France. Wild fowling was not resumed after the war, instead The Haven became a paradise for birds and parties of birdwatchers were often lead by Dr. Canning Suffern (1892–1978) after whom one of the hides is named. In 1972 Hampshire County Council bought the Haven consisting of 215 acres of natural marshland. A warden was appointed, the land was surveyed and partly drained and lagoons dug. Hides were built, paths laid and the Haven was fenced. Four years later it opened as a nature reserve. In 1995 it became a National Nature Reserve and in 1998 Haven House became the visitor centre retaining something of the ambience of the original house. Titchfield Haven has been developed to encourage the use of the marshes by migrating birds.[8]

*   *   *

Corhampton Golf Club is one of the oldest clubs in England. Founded in 1885, in the early years it made use of natural hazards rather than contrived bunkers which came later. The fairways were cropped by sheep and it was the duty of the groundsman to remove sheep droppings daily. During the First World War the club closed and was revived after the war by Edgar Mack of Swanmore and Herbert Clark of Droxford. New bunkers were made in 1929 and the course replanned in 1932. During the interwar years Wyndham's Cricket Club (so called because it had started life as an estate club at Corhampton House owned by the Wyndham-Longs) played in the middle of the Corhampton Golf Course and the remains of the cricket pavilion was for many years a reminder of those days.

During the Second World War golf once again ceased, part of the course was ploughed up and Canadian troops occupied Nissan Huts erected in the wood skirting the Corhampton to Bishop's Waltham road. Soon after the war the club bought the freehold of the ground from the estate of Mrs Wyndham-Long who died in 1948 and as a result the course was upgraded to 18 holes and a new club-house built. The club is one of the most popular in the neighbourhood and membership is higher than it has ever been. though no longer is there a substantial waiting list – high subscription and the preoccupations of younger people have taken their toll.[9]

*   *   *

If the Corhampton Golf Club flourishes, the Hambledon Hunt after 200 years is no longer an independent entity though it still meets and the kennels remain in the Meon valley. Despite its name the Hunt was throughout its life associated with the Meon valley and particularly Droxford. The first man known to hunt in the district was Mr Lord, who lived at Park House, Hambledon and hunted deer in summer and the fox in winter from 1756 until his death in 1791. The Hambledon Hunt was established at a meeting held in 1800, with a subscription of 10 guineas, then a substantial sum, and Thomas Butler of Bury Lodge Hambledon was its first Master.

Subsequently the Hunt was based at East Meon, Warnford, Preshaw or Droxford. Between 1841 and 1889 Walter Jervis Long and his son, also Walter Long, of Preshaw House were masters of the Hunt for a total of 27 years. During the Second World War hunting ceased. It was revived after the war and from 1949 John Hulbert of Fir Hill Droxford devoted his energies to the Hunt which met two or three times a week. The kennels were at the Halfway House between Droxford and Corhampton. John Hulbert's son Anthony recalled as a boy feeding time for the hounds and the smell and noise involved. He was fascinated by the cutting up of a cow's carcase which was then boiled in a huge copper and used to feed the hounds. As a boy Anthony followed the hounds as best he could and got to know some of those who frequented the hunt, 'the bicycle brigade' who came out from Fareham and Gosport and pedalled furiously to keep up with the mounted riders often taking short cuts to get ahead of the field. In 1978 the Hambledon Hunt united with the Hursley Hunt.[10]

25

The Changing Village

❧

I N APRIL 1966 the Planning Department of Hampshire County Council prepared
a report entitled *Village Life in Hampshire.*[1] The Council recognised that village life
was changing and asked whether it should encourage growth in all villages or should
select some for development. What sort of village should the Council try to provide –
should it be mainly for agricultural workers, commuters or people working in rural
industries? It needed factual information about what sort of people lived in the village,
where they worked, shopped and spent their leisure time. A comparison between the
way of life and outlook of villagers and townsmen (*sic*) was necessary.

Change had already begun to reach many villages though probably few realised how
far-reaching the change would be. The report noted that between 1951 and 1961 the
number of agricultural labourers had declined nationally by a third. Car ownership
was increasing. Of those aged between 16 and 24 no less than 85% already travelled to
work outside the village. In the country as a whole 15% owned a car, in Hampshire the
figure was 21% and in the villages it was 28%. The report noted little difference between
the activities of villagers and townspeople though those in the town were more likely
to watch television whilst villagers gardened more often.

The landscape changed too. Labour was no longer relatively cheap and easily available, so hedges were rarely layered, mechanical flails were much cheaper but also uglier.
Fields were larger to accommodate combine harvesters which had replaced horses on
bigger farms. Hedges were grubbed up to the detriment of wild life. There were fewer
trees and numbers of birds and small animals plummeted. Where there had once been
a bird's nest every 20 yards now they were rare. But there were gains too. John Hurst
(rector of West Meon and later Warnford as well) who had watched the change wrote
in the 1970s that the opening up of vistas has been all to the good. 'Photographs and
postcards of the villages at the beginning of the century astonish us with the size and
number of the trees', he wrote in 1978. 'Half the houses seem to have been buried under
big trees. I believe the wide and long views we get today make this corner of England
more beautiful than it has ever been in all the long years of its history'.[2]

Farming changed so rapidly and so completely as to justify the description of a revolution. Farms were larger, few were any longer family run. Instead they were owned by
syndicates and rented to tenants. Agriculture became an industry with fewer
employees. Yields of arable increased dramatically, the result of new technology and
the development of disease resistant strains. Hay was replaced by silage, compressed

grass which was more nutritious, less dependent on the vagaries of the weather and could be used at all seasons. In the inter-war years there were 150,000 milk producers many of whom delivered door to door. By the end of the century there were 15,000 milk producers and most milk was sold in supermarkets. Change came not only to the scenery but to the villages themselves. Since about 1970 the traditional village which had slowly evolved since Saxon times died and the commuter village was born. A series of social changes took place which together constituted a revolution. Only a village with a substantial population could withstand the transformation brought by motor cars (often more than one to each household) needed to provide all adult members of the family with the freedom which mobility brought.

That change was both cause and effect of the decline in population in the village. The age structure changed too – there were more older people and fewer young adults and children. Whilst the population of towns like Portsmouth, Fareham and Gosport increased dramatically in the second half of the twentieth century that of the villages did so only marginally or not at all. Between the censuses of 1951 and 2001 the population of Exton, East Meon and West Meon declined slightly whilst that of Droxford and Warnford increased only marginally. In the Meon valley the only place which showed significant growth was Wickham. In 1951 it was already by far the largest village in the Meon valley with a population of 3362 and by the early years of the twenty-first century there were 4055, an increase of just over 20%.[3]

People no longer shopped in the village. They preferred the supermarkets which arrived from the United States in the 1960s, diversified, grew in scope and size, were cheaper and more convenient and drove out the village shop. Only at Wickham is there a choice of shops in the Square but even there many are dry cleaners, hair dressers or cafes. The village has a primary school, modern and flourishing community centre and a group medical practice which caters for local villages.

There is now one shop in Droxford and one in Corhampton which has become a mini-supermarket. At West Meon there is a general store which provides post office facilities on two mornings a week and a butcher's shop. East Meon possesses a small supermarket. There are now no shops at all in Meonstoke, Exton or Warnford. When Bridge Cottage at Exton was decorated the owners decided to leave visible under a coat of paint a reminder of its previous status and the words 'Exton Post Office' framed by the words 'Provisions' and 'Groceries'. Despite attempts to save it the post office had closed in 1964.

Despite the popularity of the motor car there are fewer petrol stations. Going north on the A32 after Wickham you can now buy petrol in the Meon valley only at Merington's Garage on the outskirts of Droxford. A second garage at Droxford no longer sells petrol whilst garages at Corhampton and one between Warnford and West Meon and another in the village of West Meon had all closed by 2009.

Pubs found it hard to stay in business in part because alcoholic drinks were discouraged if you were driving and early in the twenty-first century smoking was forbidden in public places. All pubs now depend on the sale of food and feature Sunday lunch for the family.

Few of the big houses any longer employed living-in staff though some were still occupied by private owners – The Manor House, Fir Hill and the Old Rectory at Droxford, Meonstoke House and the recently built Manor House at Preshaw and Warnford Park. West Meon House and Hall Place at West Meon remained in private hands and so did the Court House at East Meon. Some were now weekends retreats used by people whose work required a flat in London during the week. Cottages remained but while the sixteenth or seventeenth century façade was retained sometimes concealed by a brightly painted exterior, the interior was often transformed. Council houses arrived in the Meon valley on the eve of the Second World War and many more were built in the late 1940s and 1950s. Meanwhile young people whose forbears had lived in the villages for many generations were unable to afford to live there. Rented houses were no longer available and purchase was prohibitive.

Farms diversified. Crops were still grown and animals kept. The fields were often bright yellow with oilseed rape. But at many farms arable was a minority interest. At Brooklands Farm, West Meon the henhouse now housed computer software, the fertiliser store was the office of a transport company, the erstwhile milking parlour was a cryogenic laboratory and in the calf house picture frames were made. Some now offered bed and breakfast, rented holiday cottages, or hosted caravans. Traditional village crafts described in trade directories up to about 1960 were no longer needed. Instead West Meon was home to a book-binder, calligrapher, maker of picture frames, a recruitment consultant, a psychotherapist, sculptor and a fashion designer. Many could now work from home making use of computer and the internet.[4]

*   *   *

Village meeting places were first built at the end of the nineteenth century often by the church or a sympathetic squire with the intention of keeping people out of the clutches of the pubs where alcohol was seen by many as one of the great social evils. Traditional meeting places now needed replacement. By the year 2000 almost all the villages had well-equipped and attractive village halls whose existence owed much to grants now available to enhance village life. One of the first village halls in the valley was the East Meon Reading Room, Library and Coffee House built in the 1880s and later called by the briefer name of the Church Institute. By the end of the Second World War it was badly outdated and was replaced by a modern Village Hall on the edge of the village opened in 1974.[5]

The Queen Victoria Institute was built at West Meon by public subscription at a cost of £400, on land given by the Touchet Trust to mark the Diamond Jubilee of Queen Victoria in 1897 and replaced a blacksmith's shop. It was intended for 'young men of labourer and artisan class for whom there was no room in which they might meet for amusement and instruction during the long winter evenings'. Like many such establishments it lacked toilet facilities: men used the adjacent hedge whilst for women a door was made to Number 1 Station Road where apparently there were chamber pots kept in readiness in the bedrooms upstairs.[6] The Queen Victoria Institute served the village for 80 years not least during the Second World War when evacuees had to be accommodated and the Institute became both classroom and canteen.

There was also in West Meon a Drill Hall built at the beginning of the twentieth century probably with a War Office grant and originally had a rifle range close by though that was soon abandoned. After the Second World War it was used by the British Legion. The Drill Hall was demolished at the end of the 1970s and five houses were built on the site opposite Floud Lane. The Queen Victoria Institute closed in 1976. By then West Meon had one of the best village halls in the valley due to the persistence of Robert Russell the headmaster of the village school for 32 years, parish councillor and leading light in the amateur dramatic society and John Hurst the rector from 1950–73 as well as others.[7] Opened in 1974 it was financed partly by a generous legacy and partly by the Heritage Lottery Fund and the Council for Rural Development. It was enhanced by the rebuilding of a rifle range, provision of a sports pavilion and children's playground. It was refurbished and extended in 1996 and is used by a large variety of activities and clubs.[8]

Droxford Parish Council recognised the need for a meeting place as early as the end of the nineteenth century but did not achieve its goal until 1955 when after protracted negotiations the purchase of the former school from the church was completed and adapted as a meeting place.

*   *   *

An example of what has happened in the last years of the twentieth century is provided by Droxford. From early times Droxford was the capital of the Meon valley. But in the latter half of the twentieth century the glory departed. In 1938 the headquarters of the Droxford Rural District Council moved to Bishop's Waltham though retaining the name of Droxford. In the 1990s the petty sessional court moved to Fareham and soon afterwards the police also abandoned their old headquarters and moved to a new police house at Bishop's Waltham. In 2000 the Methodists changed the name of the circuit from Droxford and instead called it the Meon Valley Circuit.

A walk through Droxford demonstrates what has happened. Reminders of former days are are to be found in the names of houses which were once shops: examples include Bakehouse Cottage, The Malt House, Brewery Cottage, the Old Bakery , the Old Stores and Millers Cottage. In Police Station Lane the building which once gave its name to the street is derelict, so is the erstwhile Methodist Chapel. The workhouse which was a well- known landmark for more than a century is commemorated in the name of the road in which it once stood, Union Lane and in Waltham Close the road where the houses which replaced the workhouse were built. But the building is no more. Though Droxford still has a parish council the Droxford Rural District Council was merged in 1974 with Winchester Rural District and Winchester City Council and local government is now based in Winchester. What is true of Droxford is true of other villages though in many aspects of traditional village life – sports, art exhibitions, plays and the parish church for example – are kept alive and sometimes flourish through the determination and public spirit of villagers.

26

Into the Third Millennium

THE THIRD MILLENNIUM started on the 1st January 2000 in a mood of euphoria. Perhaps we could turn our backs on the armed camps which in one form or another had dominated the twentieth century in Europe and had dragged in many other parts of the world. There was even the suggestion that history might have ended and we should all in future live in amity. It was a view cruelly and violently terminated by the attack on the Twin Towers of the World Trade Centre in New York on 11th September 2001 – quickly shortened to 9/11.

The mood is well caught by the entry in the West Meon School Log, 'A very black day for the whole world today. During the afternoon news began to filter through of the most awful terrorist attacks on both the World Trade buildings in New York and the Pentagon in Washington. Many thousands of people are feared dead after suicide pilots flew into the buildings. Everyone is just stunned by the horror of these events' (Log 11th September 2001). Three days later the head added her own gloss on events: 'A three minutes silence was observed in the country, Europe and America to remember those who died. I felt events were just too horrific to bring to the forefront of such young minds. Instead, I gave the staff the opportunity to observe the silence in their own way. It appears that the final death toll will never be known, but already it is running into several thousands' (Log 14th September 2001).

*   *   *

At West Meon the head reported when the Spring term began in the year 2000: 'We returned to school today. The parents led an assembly in the church to mark the new millennium. At the end of the Assembly every child was given a millennium medal struck by the Royal Mint' (Log 5th January 2000).

Meanwhile each village in the Meon valley, in common with most villages and towns in the British Isles and beyond, had celebrated the beginning of the new millennium in its own way. There were church services in many villages, some held at midnight on 31st December 1999 as the new Millennium was beginning. At Wickham there was a performance of Faure's Requiem.

West Meon's celebration, if not unique, was unusual. A book was written and published to which many villagers contributed, intended for their successors at the beginning of the fourth millennium. 'Why this small book?', they asked rhetorically and answered in the next sentence: 'The romantic answer is that as 2999 becomes 3000 the then inhabitants of West Meon will be curious to know about us and our time … So it is a book for present and future generations, which has modest social and historical significance'. They went on to inform their successors about how the village had celebrated the beginning of the third millennium. The arrival of the year 2000 had been marked by a huge street party held for the 700 people, some local and some visitors who had turned up.

> 'The High Street was closed to traffic for 24 hours and became a party zone. Lights, tents, a stage and a marquee transformed the place. A torch-light procession to the church started things off. There was street theatre, jazz, discos, Scottish dancing, a pig roast and the quaffing of wine and beer. It was a party for everyone – from two to 82… you could almost touch the spirit of friendship, goodwill and optimism. The year 2000 began to the broadcast chimes of Big Ben, a spectacular firework display and much hugging and kissing.'[1]

At the other end of the Meon valley at Titchfield a different sort of book was compiled and bequeathed to posterity as a record of the village at the beginning of the new millennium. It was entitled *Titchfield at the start of the Third Millennium* and subtitled *Domesday II*. A handsomely bound copy was to be kept with the archives of the History Society. It was a substantial A4 book containing 163 pages to which almost 50 villagers contributed, most of them members of the village History Society. It will increase in interest as the years go by though one is left to wonder whether paper and books will be as obsolete at the beginning of the fourth millennium as papyrus and scrolls were by the end of the second.

Three villages each made a Millennium Tapestry – Titchfield, Soberton and East Meon. The Titchfield Tapestry was the idea of Tessa Short conceived in September 1998 and inaugurated on 11th April 2000 by the Lord Lieutenant of Hampshire, Mary Fagan. Begun in October 1998 and completed less than 18 months later it hangs permanently in Titchfield Parish Room. The idea came from the Bayeux Tapestry, made 950 years before in the years following the Norman Conquest and the Overlord Tapestry in the D Day museum at Portsmouth, made after the Second World War.

The Titchfield Millennium Tapestry was designed by John Harper a local artist and historian and the six panels were based on the history of Titchfield from the Saxon settlement to the year 2000 respectively entitled: *Saxon Ticefelda 450–1066*, Norman *Ticefelle 1066–1154*, *Medieval Ticefeld 1232–1489*, *Wriothesley Tychfeilde 1542–1741*, *Delme Tichfield 1741–1894* and *Titchfield 1900–2000*. Each panel is a metre wide and just over a metre in height and framed in English ash. In its making a variety of techniques was used – embroidery, tapestry, collage, patchwork, beadwork, metallic thread work and metalwork among them. It was a painstaking labour of love in which at least 40 people, men and women, were involved and it is impossible to estimate the time taken to complete it.[2]

The Soberton and Newtown panel, the work of 34 named embroiderers, is displayed alternately in the churches of the two parishes. East Meon Millennium Embroidery was the last project to mark the millennium. Its planning and design began in the year 2000, the work started two years later and the embroidery undertaken by a team of 30 people was completed, mounted and displayed in 2008. Eleven feet long and four feet wide it shows 107 houses in the village as well as farms, church, school, village hall, woods, pubs, the river, roads, trees, bridges, fields, people and cars. The border includes roundels containing 26 birds and animals which can be found in the Meon valley. The separate pieces were made, assembled and stitched on to calico. It was then placed permanently in the North Transept of East Meon church protected by laminated glass with lighting designed to minimise the risk of the silks and other materials fading over years and centuries.[3]

Wickham's project was one of the most ambitious – the creation of the Water Meadows Millennium Green. It owed much to the persistence and hard work of Mike Gosney, at that time chairman of the parish council. The area south of the village through which the river Meon flows and which extended originally as far as the turn-pike road as rerouted (now the A32) was owned until the early twentieth century by the Lord of the Manor. Since it formed natural water meadows, as a result of the flooding of the river each winter, it had been used for as long as anybody could remember in early spring for grazing cattle. Sometime in the eighteenth century a side stream was constructed probably to provide a leat for the mill at the Wheatley works and to flood the meadows at Funtley further down the river.

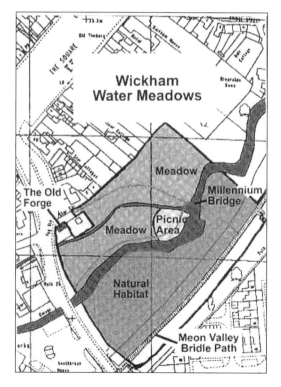

114. The Water Meadows – Wickham Millennium Project.

Then at the beginning of the twentieth century came the Meon Valley railway whose high embankment cut across the meadows and reduced their size. The meadows were still used as pasture for cattle until the 1960s after which they were abandoned to nature and quickly became a dense mass of impenetrable vegetation and were effectively lost to the village. In 1997 the recently established Millennium Commission came up with a scheme to mark the millennium with the provision of 250 greens around the country. Wickham meadows fitted the criteria for grant perfectly: they must have community support, be easily accessible and near another green space or right of way.

A great deal of hard work was involved in making the application and overcoming the technical problems. The application was successful and the purchase of the site was completed in July 1998. That autumn the area was cleared of vegetation including fallen trees by both volunteers and professionals. There was to be a new bridge across the Meon and timber edged pathways were built. The official opening by the Mayor of Winchester took place on Sunday 5th September 1999. In the following year routine cutting and maintenance began. To complete the project the Old Forge at the north east of the site was replaced by a new one which provided much needed income for the Trustees. The project evoked the enthusiasm of the whole village as the originators had envisaged.

The Millennium Window in the children's corner in the south aisle of Droxford church was the idea of Clare Hooper, at that time a member of the Parish Council, in 1998. There followed two years of hard work to realise the concept. The design, manufacture and installation of the window was entrusted to Vanessa Cutler, a young stained glass designer who had been at school at Waterlooville and studied at Swansea Institute of Higher Education. Permission for the installation of the window had to be sought from the Council for the Care of Churches and a faculty obtained from the Portsmouth Diocese. Money was raised – about £5,500 – much locally and in particular at a Millennium Ball held at the Meon Hall in July 1999. Children from Meonstoke Infant School and Droxford Primary School as well as members of the parish church Sunday School were invited to contribute ideas. The window is based on the story of Noah from the book of Genesis. It includes the figure of Noah in the ark set in choppy seas. Above is the rainbow and below a broad river which can be taken as the Meon. The whole symbolises appropriately hope for the future.

Encouraged by Hampshire County Council and aware that in recent years trees had often been the victims of road widening and the preference of farmers for larger fields, several parishes – Wickham, Exton and Meonstoke among them – planted commemorative trees to mark the Millennium.

*   *   *

When he wrote *The World We Have Lost* Peter Laslett had in mind the loss of pre-industrial England.[4] But his evocative title would apply equally to the Meon valley villages in the early years of the twenty-first century. Older villagers in particular were aware of change: the close knit community in which they had grown up, where for good or ill everybody had known everybody else, had been replaced almost imperceptibly but nonetheless quickly and irrecoverably, by a more anonymous and looser community. But this was not the only change which had taken place in the last years of the twentieth century in the villages of the Meon valley as well as elsewhere. There was much more – the full participation of women in employment and civic and cultural life for example and above all the upstairs-downstairs world of Victorian and Edwardian England which survived until the Second World War had perished for ever after 1945.

It was no doubt partly coincidence that the last thirty years of the twentieth century saw the publication of histories of each village. It was also symptomatic of awareness that the world was now very different from that recalled with nostalgia by those reaching retirement in the first years of the third millennium and of their desire to preserve the memory of earlier centuries. Interest was not however the monopoly of those who could recall a different village, it was enjoyed too by a younger generation and led to the founding of history societies to satisfy curiosity and increase knowledge of the past of the region. To that aim this book is intended as a contribution.

115. The river Meon entering the sea at Titchfield Haven.

Appendices

❦

A. Landmarks in the History of the Villages of the Meon Valley

National events mentioned in the text with a bearing on the Meon valley are in italics.

43–410	*Roman legions in Britain*
c.450	Saxon settlement in the Meon valley
c.450–600	Saxon cemetery at Droxford used for pagan burials
681–686	St. Wilfrid preaches in the Meon valley
685	The Meonware come under the rule of Wessex
c.690	Titchfield church built
786	First written reference to the river Meon
982	First mention of Titchfield (Ticcefelda) in a Saxon charter
c.1020	Corhampton church built in stone
1066	*William the Conqueror lands at Pevensey & wins battle of Hastings*
1080–1120	East Meon church built
1086	*Domesday Book compiled*
1120	Church dedicated to St Nicholas built at Wickham
1129–71	Henry of Blois bishop of Winchester
c.1150	Tournai font given to East Meon church by Bishop Henry of Blois
1168	First written reference to the Forest of Bere
1232	Titchfield Abbey (Premonstratensian Order) founded by Bishop Peter des Roches bishop of Winchester
1268	Charter given to the manor of Wickham to hold a market and fair: leads to new layout to the west of the river.
1282–1304	John of Pontoise bishop of Winchester – diocesan records available.
1324	Birth of William of Wykeham
1348–9	*Black Death in England*
1404	Death of William of Wykeham at Bishop's Waltham Palace
1537	Premonstratensian monastery at Titchfield dissolved and land obtained by Thomas Wriothesley, later first Earl of Southampton, who builds Place House
1538	*Thomas Cromwell orders each parish to keep registers of baptisms, marriages and burials*
1542	John Leland's *Itinerary of Hampshire*

1551	Lomer village deserted
1594	Wriothesley tomb in Titchfield church built
1611	Sea wall built closing off Titchfield Haven from the sea
1619	Building of the paper mill in Warnford – the first in Hampshire
1642	*Civil War begins*
1644	Bishop's Waltham Palace sacked, Bishop Walter Curll escapes to Soberton. Some clergy deprived of their livings.
1649	*Execution of Charles I (30th January)*
1660	*Restoration of Charles II (enters London 29th May)*
1662	*Book of Common Prayer reissued*
	Hearth Tax first levied (abolished 1689)
1685	Isaac Garnier arrives in England from France
1688	*Flight of James II*
1689	*Passing of the Toleration Act gives Protestant dissenters right to freedom of worship*
1719	Fire in Meonstoke High Street destroys 23 houses
1728	The Long family buys Preshaw estate
1758	Gosport to Chawton turnpike authorised by act of parliament (built via Shirrell Heath & Swanmore c.1770)
1765	George Garnier becomes Lord of the Manor of Wickham
c.1770	Turnpike from Gosport to Chawton built
1775	Henry Cort takes over the iron mill at Funtley
1781	Demolition of Place House Titchfield
1781–1820	Brownlow North, Bishop of Winchester
1793	Bridge over the Meon at Wickham built by subscription
1801	Turnpike from Curdridge Common to Corhampton authorised (B3035)
	First national census of population
1810	Cosham to Titchfield turnpike authorised and when built includes a new bridge over the Meon to allow the turnpike to enter Titchfield. Titchfield to Twyford turnpike authorised
1824	William Garnier begins the building of Rookesbury Park
1825	Winchester to Petersfield turnpike authorised (A272)
1826–44	Henry Vincent Bayley rector of West Meon (remains Archdeacon of Stow)
1827–69	Charles Sumner bishop of Winchester
1828	*Repeal of the Test and Corporation Acts gives Protestant dissenters civil rights*
1829	*Catholic Emancipation Act gives Roman Catholics some civil rights*
	Shidfield *(sic)* church built as chapel of ease in the parish of Droxford
c.1830	New section of Gosport to Chawton turnpike built from Wickham to Droxford following the Meon valley.
1837	Workhouse built at Droxford for union of parishes
1838	*Pluralities Act ends the holding of more than one living by clergy*
1841	*First national census to include names*

1845	St Barnabas church Swanmore built in the parish of Droxford
	William Garnier builds cottages at The Hundred Acres
1846	Opening of new church at West Meon dedicated to St John the Evangelist.
1851	*National Census of Church attendance (30th March)*
	Newtown church built in the parish of Meonstoke and Soberton
1852	Hampshire County Lunatic Asylum opened at Knowle Farm
	West Meon school opened
1863	John Carpenter becomes Lord of the Manor of Wickham and takes the name Carpenter-Garnier
1865	Meonstoke Primitive Methodist chapel opened (closed 1964)
1869–74	Samuel Wilberforce bishop of Winchester
1870	Woodlands chapel (Anglican) opened in the parish of West Meon (closed 1982)
1872	Warnford Primitive Methodist chapel opened (closed 1919)
1877	Privett church built by W.G.Nicolson; Privett becomes a separate parish.
1887	Droxford Primitive Methodist chapel opened (closed 1978)
1889	Woodland chapel built in West Meon parish
1894	*Parish Councils Act creates parish councils, parish meetings and Rural District Councils*
1897	Soberton separated from Meonstoke and becomes a parish.
1898	Walter Long sells the Preshaw estate
	Act of Parliament passed authorising the Meon Valley Railway
1901	Cross erected in West Meon in memory of Dr George Rogers village doctor for 40 years
1902	(February) Midlington House destroyed by fire
1903	(5th June) Opening of the Meon Valley Railway
1904	(November) Westbury House destroyed by fire
1905	Westbury House rebuilt
1910	(June) Fire at East Meon destroys six cottages
1914–18	*First World War*
1914	Building of Leydene House (East Meon) begun by Lady Peel – completed 1925
1920	Harold Pelly buys the Preshaw estate
1926	Westbury House becomes a preparatory school for 80 boys
	Hadow Committee recommends division of education at age 11 into primary and secondary
1927	Division of the diocese of Winchester – Meon valley villages included in the new diocese of Portsmouth
1929	National Health Act leads to the closure of the workhouse
	Rookesbury Park leased by the Carpenter-Garnier family and opens as a girls' school
1935	Roman villa found at Shavards Farm, Meonstoke

1937	Headquarters of the Droxford Rural District Council moved from Droxford to Bishop's Waltham
1939	*Fire Brigades Act requires local authorities to provide fire brigades*
1939–45	*Second World War*
1947	*School leaving age raised to 14*
1949	Leydene House, occupied by the navy during the war, bought by the Admiralty and becomes *HMS Mercury*
1955	Flood prevention scheme implemented at East Meon
	(5th February) The Meon Valley Railway closed to passenger traffic
	MCC versus West Meon Cricket Club to mark the 200th anniversary of birth of Thomas Lord. *New Inn* renamed *The Thomas Lord*.
1956	Demolition of the old house at Warnford Park
1973	Demolition of Waltham House (former workhouse) in Droxford
1961	Opening of Swanmore Secondary Modern School provides a separate secondary school for central part of the Meon valley
1974	*School leaving age raised to 15*
1976	Queen Victoria Institute at West Meon closed
	Long hot summer
1978	Westbury House, West Meon sold and becomes a private hospital
1982	Woodlands chapel in West Meon parish closed
1984	Corhampton House (Old Peoples Home) sold by Hampshire County Council and divided into self contained units
1987	(11th October) 'The Great Storm' uproots many trees throughout the Meon valley.
1996	Knowle Hospital closed
2000	All the villages celebrate the beginning of the Third Millennium

B. Population

The first National Census was taken in 1801 though names were not included until 1841. Since then censuses have been taken at ten yearly intervals except 1941. Before 1801 population figures are based on estimates made in a variety of ways, some likely to be more accurate than others. This Appendix lists a variety of figures for the villages of the Meon valley. See also Hearth Tax 1665 Appendix C.

Parish	1801	1851	1901	1931	1951	2008 (Estimate)[4]
Corhampton	120	225	131	87	With Meonstoke[5]	
Droxford	1199[2]	2005	498	505	567	636
Exton	224	283	299	266	239	243
East Meon	1026	1543	1058	908	1490	1187
Meonstoke	289	431	431	526	629	706
Soberton	672	1147	1189	1336	1400	1601
Titchfield	2949[1]	3956[1]	1569	2321	2960	[7350][6]
Warnford	272	414	277	142	200	239
West Meon[3]	536	901	950	700	740	711
Wickham	901	1049	1162	2588	2984	4204

Parish boundary changes make it difficult to ensure comparability from census to census but note the following:

1. *In 1801 & 1851 Titchfield includes Crofton, Sarisbury, Hook & Warsash.*
2. *In 1801 & 1851 Droxford includes Shedfield & Swanmore.*
3. *West Meon does not include Privett.*
4. *Population estimate made by Hampshire County Council for the year 2008.*
5. *In 1951 &2007 Corhampton & Meonstoke are counted together.*
6. *Estimate for Titchfield in 2008 is for Titchfield ward not Titchfield parish.*

Diocesan Population Returns 1603

Parish	Conformists	Recusants	Non-conformists	Estimated population
Warneford	160	0	0	267
Tichfeild	650	4	0	1090
Crofton	169	0	0	282
Wekeham	212	1	6	365
Corhampton	33	0	0	55
Estmeane	630	8	11	1082
Froxfeild	191	0	4	325
Stepe	209	1	0	350
Westmeane	150	0	0	250
Privett	40	1	0	68
Meene Stoke	120	3	0	205
Suberton	240	6	0	410
Exton	73	4	0	128
Droxford	293	5	0	497
Totals	3210	33	21	5440

There is no return for the Winchester diocese for 1563. The 1603 enquiry was part of Archbishop Whitgift's attempt to counter the Puritan criticism of the clergy that they were ignorant and inadequate and neglecting their flock.

Spelling and order of parishes as in the return. Places indented are dependent chapelries. The totals are adults so a multiplier of 5/3 is used to assess population.

There were few Roman Catholic recusants and few Protestant non-conformists in the Meon valley in 1603.

Source: Diocesan Population Return for 1563 and 1603 ed. A Dyer & D.M.Palliser 2005

Compton Census of 1676

The Archdeaconry of Winchester contained 10 Hampshire deaneries. The Archdeaconry of Surrey contained 3 Deaneries in Surrey (of which Southwark was one)

In the Droxford Deanery there were 13,526 conformists; 188 papists and 538 nonconformists. The Deanery contained 39 parishes and was the largest in the Archdeaconry of Winchester and included the parishes in Meon valley. (Andover had 38 parishes)

Parish	Conformists	Papists	Non-conformists	Estimated population
Corhampton	94	0	0	157
Droxford	345	2	20	612
Eastmeon	544	7	3	957
Exton	118	4	1	205
Meonstoke	143	2	4	248
Privett (cum West Meon)	61	1	4	110
Subberton (cum Meonstoke)	266	10	4	467
Titchfield(cum Capella de Crofton)	869	2	47	1530
Warnford	103	0	10	188
Wickham	259	2	0	435
Westmeon	225	–	16	402
Totals	3027	30	109	5711

Notes

1. There were Conventicles at Swanmore (Quaker) & Hill (Anabaptist) both in the parish of Droxford.

2. Spelling as in Census note Subberton, Eastmeon, Westmeon.

3. There had beeen a considerable increase in the number of Protestant nonconformists since 1603. The number of Roman Catholic recusants remained low.

4. Compton Census is of communicant: to convert adults to likely total population multiplier of 5/3 is used.

Source: The Compton Census of 1676: A Critical Edition ed. Anne Whiteman OUP 1986

*Population estimates made by clergy in reply to Visitation questions
compared with the Census of 1801*

Parish	1725	1788	1810	1801 Census
Corhampton	130	94	c.91	120
Droxford	c.568	NR	1200	1199
East Meon with	962	963	1050	1061
Froxfield & Steep	475	NR	450	401
Exton	180	221	224	224
Meonstoke	225	NR	289	289
& Soberton	460	500	672	672
Titchfeld & Crofton	1500	3000	3000	2949
Warnford	160	257	111	272
West Meon with Privett Chapel	403	NR	c.800–1000	536
Wickham	550	NR	1000	901

*Clergy were asked to estimate the population of their parishes before the Primary Visitations of 1725 and
1788 and in reply to a questionnaire of 1810. The 1810 figure for Warnford is wildly inaccurate. Some
of the 1810 figures are obviously drawn from the first census returns.*

NR – No Return

Source: ed. Vickers 1993

C. The Hampshire Hearth Tax 1665

	No. of Houses	T	Wi	D	M	C	E	Wa	WM	EM	Total houses
Poverty	1 hearth C	20	19	13	10	3	3	5	21	9	103
	1 hearth NC	25	29	26	46	2	12	4	28	23	195
	2 hearths C	23	7	19	16	3	2	1	9	7	87
	2 hearths NC	7	10	13	19	1	0	4	3	4	61
	Total houses	75	65	71	91	9	17	14	61	43	446
Middling	3–5 hearths	45	23	52	43	4	12	14	36	11	240
	6–9 hearths	8	1	6	4	1	4	3	2	5	34
	Total houses	53	24	58	47	5	16	17	38	16	274
Affluent	Houses with 10 + Hearths	3	1	2	1	2	0	1	0	0	10
Total houses	C	99	51	92	74	13	21	24	68	32	474
	NC	32	39	39	65	3	12	8	31	27	256
	Poor	75	72	54	65	9	51	44	61	73	61.1%
	Middling	53	27	44	34	5	48	53	38	27	37.5%
	Affluent	3	1	2	1	2	0	3	0	0	1.4%
	NC										35.1%
	Estimated Population	589	405	588	625	72	148	144	445	265	

Figures in column two are number of hearths.
C   Chargeable   NC   Not chargeable

T   Titchfield Barony &Titchfield
Wi Wickham Borough & Wickham
D   Droxford including tithings of Hill, Shedfield & Swanmore

M   Meonstoke with Soberton
C   Corhampton
E   Exton

Wa   Warnford
WM   West Meon & Privett
EM   East Meon (parish only)

Drawn from The Hampshire Hearth Tax Assessment 1665 ed. Elizabeth Hughes & Philippa White Vol. 11 Hampshire Record Series 1991.
The Hearth Tax for Titchfield Hundred was also published by the Titchfield History Society in 1985.
Estimated population is based on multiplier of 4.5 of number of households as suggested in Hughes & White p.xiv. Definitions of Poverty and Affluence are also based on Hughes & White p.xvi.

D. Parish Records

Parish	C	M	Bu	CW	V	Po.	Br
Corhampton	1665	1677	1695	1835	1844	–	–
Droxford	1635	1633	1633	1839	1763	–	–
East Meon	1560	1560	1560	1753	–	1727	–
Exton	1579	1579	1579	–	–	1805	1675–1720
Meonstoke	1599	1599	1599	–	1858	–	1804–1811
Soberton	1546	1538	1538	1658	1826	1729	–
Titchfield	1589	1589	1589	–	1672	1680	–
Warnford	1541	1604	1617	1732	1837	1773	1665–1688
West Meon	1542	1538	1536	1694	1871	1703	–
Wickham	1556	1556	1556	1803	–	–	1706–1751

Records are not always continuous from the time when they are first recorded.

C   *Christening*
M   *Marriages*
Bu   *Burials*
CW   *Churchwardens Records (various)*
V   *Vestry Book / Minutes*
Po.   *Overseers of the Poor before 1835 (sometimes includes settlement records, apprenticeship indentures, bastardy examinations, militia records)*
Br   *Briefs (see Page 51)*

Dates when records of Meon valley parishes were first kept or survive. They can be found in the Hampshire Record Office and are available for study on microfiche Some have been transcribed and are on the open shelves

Abbreviations

CUP	Cambridge University Press
DNB	Dictionary of National Biography
HCC	Hampshire County Council
HFCAS	Proceedings of the Hampshire Field Club and Archaeological Society
HRO	Hampshire Record Office
Log	School Log Book
Memoir	A Memoir of Henry Vincent Bayley. Printed for private circulation, 1846
Nd.	No date given
Np.	No publisher named
Npn	No page number
NMRC	National Monuments Record Centre, Swindon (English Heritage)
ODCC	Oxford Dictionary of the Christian Church
OUP	Oxford University Press
Op	Out of print
PCC	Parochial Church Council
PCM	Parish Council Minutes
PMM	Parish Meeting Minutes
P.Mag.	Parish Magazine
Registers	Parish Registers of Baptisms, Marriages, and Burials
RDC	Rural District Council
Treasures	Hampshire Treasures Survey Vol. 1 Winchester City District 1979 HCC
VCH	Victoria County History of Hampshire & the Isle of Wight, 5 volumes 1900–1914
WM 2000	West Meon 2000

Bibliography

UNPUBLISHED

This list includes works which are available only privately or through a copy deposited in HRO.

Borthwick A. & Chandler J. 1995 *The Preshaw Estate* 2 vols.

Etheridge L.S. 1926 *Memorabilia*. Handwritten notes about the parish church of Droxford held by the Rector of Droxford. Copy in HRO.

Garnier A.E. 1900 *The Chronicles of the Garniers of Hampshire*. Published privately. Copy in HRO.

Hampshire Water Meadows Survey 2000 Vol. 1 Report. Oxford Archaeological Unit HCC.

Hase P.H. 1975 *The Parish in Hampshire*. Unpublished Cambridge Ph.D thesis. Copy in HRO.

Hayward Keith 1998 *Titchfield Parish Register 1589–1634*. Titchfield History Society.

Hayward Keith 2006 *Titchfield Parish Register 1634–1678*. Titchfield History Society.

Hampshire Water Meadows Survey Vol. 1 Oxford Archaeology Unit 2000.

Headteacher [compiled by; no name] 1985 *Droxford School 1835–1985*. Np.

Hopkins Hilary 2002 *History of West Meon Primary School through the eyes of its headteachers*. Np.

The Restoration of Warnford Park 1988, updated 1995, 1998 & 2005. Np.

Sinclair Williams C.L. 1985 *The Hearth Tax Returns for the Parish of Titchfield*. Titchfield History Society.

PRINTED

Albert W. 1972 *The Turnpike Road System of England 1663–1840*. CUP.

Aston Michael & Lewis Carenza eds.1994 *The Medieval Landscape of Wessex*. Oxbow Monograph Number 46.

Bettey J.H.1986 *Wessex from AD 1000*. Longman.

Bettey J.H. 1987 *Church and Parish*. Batsford.

Blair John ed.1988 *Minsters and Parish Churches: the local church in transition 950–1200*. Oxford University Committee for Archaeology Monograph No.17.

Blair John 2005 *The Church in Anglo-Saxon Society*. OUP.

Burns Arthur 1999 *The Diocesan Revival in the Church of England*. OUP.

Bussby Frederick 1979 *Winchester Cathedral 1079–1979*. Paul Cave Publications.

Chandler John 1993 *John Leland's Itinerary*. Alan Sutton.

Chapman John & Seeliger Sylvia 1997(a) *A Guide to Enclosure in Hampshire 1700–1900.* Hampshire Record Series Volume 15 HCC.

Chapman John & Seeliger Sylvia 1997(b) *Formal and Informal Enclosures in Hampshire.* Hampshire Papers Number 12 HCC.

Collins Frances & Hurst John 1972 *West Meon Hampshire Some Chapters of its History.* Np.

Collins Frances & Hurst John 1978 *Meonstoke and Soberton Some Chapters of its History.* Winton Publications.

Course E.1974 *Railways of Southern England Vol. 2.* Batsford.

Cross F.L.& Livingstone E.A.eds. 1997 *The Oxford Dictionary of the Christian Church.* Third edition OUP.

Cunliffe Barry 1993 *Wessex to AD 1000.* Longman.

Davis V. 2007 *William Wykeham.* Hambledon Continuum.

Dyer A. & Palliser D.M. 2005 *Diocesan Population returns from 1563 & 1603.* OUP.

FitzHugh T.V.H. Fifth Edition 1998 *The Dictionary of Genealogy.* A&C Black.

Gardiner Juliet 2004 *Wartime Britain 1939–1945.* Headline Book Publishing.

Hampshire Treasures Survey Vol. 1 Winchester City District 1979. HCC.

Hare John 1999 *The Dissolution of the Monasteries in Hampshire* Hampshire Papers No.16. HCC.

Hart A.Tindal 1970 *The Curate's Lot.* John Baker.

Hope G.D.1980 (reprinted 2005) *800 years in Droxford.* Np.

Hoskins W.G. (1955) 1988 *The Making of the English Landscape new edition with introduction and commentary by Christopher Taylor.* Hodder & Stoughton.

Hughes E & White P. 1991 *The Hampshire Hearth Tax Assessment 1665.* Hampshire Record Series Vol. 11. HCC.

Hughes M. ed 1994 *The Evolution of the Hampshire Landscape: The Meon Valley* HCC. Archaeology Report No.1.

Hurst John C. and others 1969 *Warnford, Hampshire some chapters of its history.* Np.

Hurst John C.1980 *Corhampton and Exton, Hampshire.* Np.

Knight Frances 1995 *The Nineteenth Century Church and English Society.* CUP.

Kitching R.J. 2001 *No longer poor old Droxford.* Np.

MacCullough Diarmaid 2003 *Reformation: Europe's House Divided 1490–1700.* Allen Lane.

Mathews A.G. 1934 *Calamy Revised* Being a Revision of Edmund Calamy's Account of the Ministers and others ejected and silenced 1660–62. OUP.

Mathews A.G. 1948 *Walker Revised* Being a Revision of John Walker's Sufferings of the Clergy during the Great Rebellion 1642–60. OUP.

Moore Pamela ed. 1984 *A Guide to the Industrial Archaeology of Hampshire and the Isle of Wight.* Southampton University Industrial Archaeology Group.

Moore Pamela 1988 *The Industrial Archaeology of Hampshire and the Isle of Wight.* Phillimore.

Munby Julian ed. 1982 *Domesday Book 4. Hampshire.* Phillimore.

Page Mark 2002 *The Medieval Bishops of Winchester: Estate, Archive and Administration.* HCC.

Pendred Ann 1999 *The Story of Soberton and Newtown.* Soberton Parish Council.

Pevsner Nicholas & Lloyd David 1967 *Buildings of England: Hampshire & the Isle of Wight.* Penguin.

Rackham Oliver 2000 *The Illustrated History of the Countryside.* Seven Dials Cassell and Co.

Riall Nicholas 1994 *Henry of Blois, Bishop of Winchester.* HCC.

Smith Mark ed.2004 *Doing the Duty of the Parish* Hampshire Record Series Vol. 17. HCC.

Standfield F.G. 1984 *A History of East Meon.* Phillimore.

Stapleton Barry & Thomas James H. 1989 *The Portsmouth Region.* Alan Sutton.

Stone R.A. 1983 *The Meon Valley Railway.* Kingfisher Railway Publications.

Tappenden Bruce 2006 *A History of Wickham* Revised edition. Wickham History Society.

Tillman Denis 2003 *The Meon Valley Railway Revisited.* KRB Publications.

Wade R.& Watts G. eds. 1989 *Titchfield: A Place in History.* Ensign Publications.

Ward Kenneth Nd. *Droxford in the Meon Valley.* Np.

Ward W.R. ed. 1995 *Parson and Parish in Eighteenth Century Hampshire* Hampshire Record Series Vol. 13. HCC.

Warwick D.A. 1982 *Meon Valley Memories.* Rick Tomes.

Watkins Peter R. 2007 *Bishop's Waltham: Parish, Town and Church.* Swanmore Books.

Watkins Peter R. 2001 *Swanmore since 1840.* Swanmore Books.

Watts George ed. 1982 *Titchfield, a History.* Titchfield History Society.

Webb J, Quail S, Haskell P, Riley R. 1989 *The Spirit of Portsmouth.* Phillimore.

Whinney Richard 1981 '*All that capital messuage called Wickham Place*'. City of Winchester.

Whiteman Anne 1986 *The Compton Census of 1676.* OUP.

Wills K.C.A. 1977 *The Parish Church of St John the Evangelist West Meon.* Np.

Notes

Introduction

1. From Leland's Itinerary in England and Wales Vol. 1 Lucy Toulmin Smith London Centuar Press 1964 Vol. 1 Part 3 pp. 281–2. Punctuation as in the text. Square brackets indicate amendments made in subsequent editions. A modern version reads:' *The course of the Titchfield Water [river Meon]: Its source is near East Meon, ten miles north-east of Titchfield. From East Meon it flows five or six miles to a pleasant little town on its right bank called Wickham, where it breaks into two streams for a short distance and runs under two wooden bridges. Three or four miles lower it flows under another wooden bridge near Mr Wriothesley's house, and passes Titchfield on its right bank. Just below Titchfield is a timber bridge called Warebridge, and from this point the river is tidal. Less than a mile downstream it joins Southampton Water'.* Johm Leland's Itinerary ed. John Chandler 1993 John Sutton pp. 207–8. The southern section of the river has often been called the Titchfield river.
2. John Missing *Titchfield a Poetical Essay* 1749.
3. Pevsner & Lloyd 1967 p. 652.
4. Ib. p. 199.
5. Watts ed.1982. p. 7.

1. From Rainbow Bar to the Normans Pages 4–16

1. HFC Newsletters 42 & 50.
2. Leaflet published by English Nature May 2004 written by George Watts.
3. I.D. Margery *The Roman Roads of Britain* now updated see HFCAS Vol. 25 pp. 19–26.
4. Collins & Hurst 1972 p. 4. The site is shown on OS Explorer map 119 SU633244.
5. HFCAS Vol. 62 pp. 69–82.
6. HFCAS Vol. 36 pp. 153–60. For Roman East Meon see Standfield 1984 p. 9.
7. The suffix *ware* is found in the three areas settled by the Jutes – Kent, the Isle of Wight and southern Hampshire.
8. 'From the Jutes are descended the people of Kent and the Isle of Wight and those in the province of Wessex opposite the Isle of Wight are called Jutes to this day.' Bede Bk.1 c.15 also Bassett S. ed. 1989 *The Origins of Anglo-Saxon Kingdoms* Leicester University Press pp. 84–96.
9. *Yte* corresponds with Bede's *Jutae. Ytene* was the genitive plural of *Yte.*
10. Barbara Yorke in Mitchell K. and Wood I 2002 *The World of Gregory of Tours* Brill pp. 113–130.
11. *Excavations at Meonstoke 1984 & Excavations at Meonstoke 1985/6* HCC.
12. For an account of the opening of the new gallery by the Prince of Wales on 15th July 1997 by Gill Horn see *The Bridge* August –September 1997 p. 27.
13. HFCAS Vol. 5 pp. 173–7.
14. HFCAS Vol. 35 pp 93–182, Ward nd. pp. 5–6.
15. HFCAS Vol. 63 pp. 129–34.
16. See OS map 132 SU646255 to SU667255 also Collins & Hurst 1972 p. 5.
17. HFCAS Vol. 61 pp. 142 & 147–9 for details of Corhampton & Titchfield churches.

18. HFCAS Vol. 32 pp. 5–48 for the Anglo-Saxon church of St Peter, Titchfield.
19. HFCAS Vol. 61 pp. 142–3.
20. Jenkins S. 1999 *England's Thousand Best Churches* Allen Lane 1999 p. 244.
21. Guide to Warnford Church. Pevsner makes no mention of Saxon remains, Pevsner & Lloyd 1967 pp. 642–3.
22. Wulfric has sometimes been mistaken for Wilfrid. Adam is Adam de Port who held Warnford from 1171–1213.
23. Hope 1980 pp. 2–3 & conversations with Gordon Hope.
24. Grundy G.B. 1924 *Hampshire Charters and Place Names* quoted in Hope 2005 pp. 3–4 & Whinney nd. p. 5.
25. Hughes ed. 1994 pp. 15–9.
26. Coates 1989 p. 164.
27. Hase 1975 p. 61.
28. Hase 1994 *The Church in the Wessex Heartlands* in The Medieval Landscape of Wessex ed Aston & Lewis Oxbow Monograph No. 16.
29. HFCAS Vol. 7 pt. 2 p. 38. Bettey 1986 p. 11.
30. The Anglo-Saxon Chronicle quoted in Munby 1982 Introduction npn.
31. Collins & Hurst 1978 pp. 22–3.
32. Peter Ewence using dowsing found evidence of buildings which pre-date the present buildings on the site of many churches in the Meon valley.
33. Munby 1982, Watts in Hughes 1994 p. 47. Information about Domesday manors is summarised in Stapleton & Thomas 1989 pp. 47–8.
34. Riall 1994 p. 10. Page 2002.
35. Pevsner & Lloyd 1967 p. 642.
36. Bettey 1986 p. 77.
37. Jenkins 1999 p. 246.

2. The Later Middle Ages Pages 17–30

1. Coates 1989 p. 32.
2. Preston E. & Wallis S. 2006 *The Forest of Bere* Halsgrove.
3. Whinney 1980.
4. The market was assessed at £96 in the Lay Subsidy of 1334 compared with other markets in the Meon valley – Titchfield £111 and Meonstoke £68 (Granted a market in 1247) HFCAS Newsletter No.50 pp. 13–6.
5. This enlargement was usual e.g. New Alresford represented an enlargement of Old Alresford.
6. Hare 1999.
7. For St Norbert see Brooke 2006 *The Rise and Fall of the Medieval Monastery* pp. 184–5.
8. HFCAS Vol. 21 pp. 31–7.
9. Watts ed.1982 pp. 25–31.
10. HFCAS Vol. 21. p. 37.
11. Wade & Watts eds. 1989 pp. 17–22. HFCAS Vol. 7.
12. HFCAS Vol. 55 p. 11.
13. Wade & Watts eds. 1989 pp. 22–8.
14. HFCAS Vol. 55 pp. 11–3. The author was shown the house by the present owner Ken Groves in July 2009.
15. Beaumont James 1999 p. 23.
16. Standfield 1984 pp. 22–4.
17. Hope 2005 pp. 12–3.
18. Beaumont James 1999, Watts ed. 1982 p.39, Standfield 1984 pp. 22–4.
19. *Licence for Titchfield and Lomer to be served by canons of Titchfield*, 1283 HRO 5M53/183.

20. Hereditary surnames began to be used in 13th & 14th centuries. Until then the leading family was usually identified by the place from which it came.
21. Borthwick & Chandler 1995 Vol. 1 p. 47.
22. Ib. p. 48.
23. VCH Hampshire Vol. 3 pp.249–53, Collins & Oliver in HFCAS 1971 pp. 67–76, Hughes ed. 1994 pp. 20–32.
24. Borthwick & Chandler 1995 Vol. 2 Appendix 3. Chapel was the term used for a church which did not have parochial status.
25. The water table is now below 220 feet. The well at Lomer is comparable in depth with the well-known one at *The Milburys* (formerly *The Fox and Hounds*).
26. HFCAS 1971 pp. 67–76.
27. Borthwick & Chandler 1995.
28. Davis V. 2007 *William Wykeham* Hambledon Continuum.
29. His parents died before the late 1360s & were buried at Southwick Priory where William of Wykeham endowed a chantry to pray for their souls, Davis 2007 p. 107.
30. Parliament was opened in English rather than Norman-French for the first time in 1363.
31. Davis 2007 p. 29.
32. Hampshire Record Series Vol. 14 1996 & Vol. 16 1999.
33. VCH Hampshire Vol .2 p. 9.
34. Archaeological Journal 1993 pp. 456–81.
35. Collins & Hurst 1978 pp. 37–41.
36. Collins & Hurst 1972 p. 21.
37. Collins & Hurst 1978 pp. 37–40 & 136–9. For Bainbridge see ODCC & DNB.
38. For Droxford see Etheridge *Miscellanea* p. 7.

3. The Era of Reformation Pages 31–36

1. HFCAS Vol. 14 Part 1 pp. 63–85. The original is in the library of Corpus Christi College, Cambridge.
2. Op.cit.
3. Hart 1970 p.46.
4. *Liber Actorum* quoted in HFCAS Vol. 21 part 2.
5. Collins & Hurst 1978 pp. 43–46 & 139–140.
6. Hart 1970 p. 46.
7. Collins & Hurst 1978 p. 47.
8. His date of birth given as 1480 in DNB is incorrect. See M.St C.Byrne Vol. 1 pp. 364–5. who places his birth between 1462 and 1465.
9. Meonstoke, Droxford, Titchfield, Wickham, Segensworth and Soberton all appear in the Index to the Lisle Letters see Vol. VI.
10. See DNB & M.St.Clare Byrne ed. 1981 *The Lisle Letters* 6 vols. University of Chicago Press.
11. Funtley and Fontley are alternative spellings: 1086 Funtelei, 1242, Fonteleg, Coates 1989 p. 78.
12. See Mercer E. 1975 *Early Vernacular Houses* HMSO p. 106 & Plate 42.
13. 5M50/1875 quoted in HFCAS Vol. 51 p. 108.
14. Ib.
15. Warnford 1969 pp. 25.
16. Pevsner & Lloyd 1967 pp. 652–653; Tappenden 2006 p. 71.

4. The Wriothesleys of Place House Pages 37–43

1. For the Wriothesley family see DNB, Guide to Titchfield Church & Watts ed.1982 pp. 45–54.
2. Hare 1999 p. 20.

3. Chandler 1993 p. 207.
4. Pevsner & Lloyd 1967 p. 624.
5. HFCAS Newsletter 52 pp. 25–27.
6. Watts ed.1982 p .54.
7. The house was renamed Bedford House in 1734 and demolished in 1800.
8. DNB & Watts ed. 1982 pp. 45–50.
9. David Lloyd in Pevsner & Lloyd 1967 p. 620.

5. The Parish Registers Pages 44–52

1. Fearon W.A. & Williams J. F. 1909 *The Parish Registers and Parochial Documents in the Archdeaconry of Winchester.* Warren and Son, Winchester.
2. Collins & Hurst 1972 pp. 49ff.
3. Fearon & Williams 1909 op.cit. p. 3.
4. Ib.
5. Collins & Hurst 1972 c.8.
6. Hayward ed. 1998 & 2006. The methods employed are described in both volumes.
7. Titchfield Register August 1625.
8. Droxford Register 16th April 1624. In 1978 the Register was transcribed by Gordon Hope who kindly lent me his copy.
9. Quoted in Tate 1983 p. 67.
10. Hughes & White ed.1991 entries 21, 23, 30, 31.
11. Exton Register & Hurst 1980 pp. 34–36.
12. Fearon & Williams 1909 op.cit.
13. Quoted in Collins & Hurst 1978 p. 68.

6. From the Civil War to the Glorious Revolution Pages 53–56

1. Information from Margaret Ball who lives in the former school at East Meon.
2. Account based on Collins & Hurst 1972 pp. 32–37.
3. Hurst 1980 pp. 30–32.
4. Collins & Hurst 1969 p. 59.
5. Matthews 1934 *Calamy Revised* OUP p. 516.
6. Exton Register.
7. Frewen was one of only three bishops consecrated before the abolition of episcopacy who were available for appointment to bishoprics in 1660.
8. DNB & Hope 2005 p. 25.
9. DNB. Many of Isaac Walton's books are in the Winchestr Cathedral library.
10. Quoted in Hope 2005 p. 24.
11. Figures for the Meon valley villages are in Appendix C. See also Hughes & White eds. 1991 pp. xiv–xv.

7. The Poor Law to 1834 Pages 57–61

1. Tate 1983 pp. 188–241 for national legislation.
2. Standfield 1984 pp. 51–52.
3. Watkins 2001 p. 12.
4. Tappenden 1996 p. 98.
5. Collins & Hurst 1972 p. 44.

6. Collins & Hurst 1978 p. 96.
7. Standfield 1984 p. 50.
8. Collins & Hurst 1978 p. 98.
9. Ib.
10. Ib.
11. Ib.
12. Collins & Hurst 1972 p. 45.
13. HFCAS Vol. 44 1988 p. 109.
14. HFCAS Vol. 43 1989 pp. 237–254.
15. Calendar of Prisoners in the County Gaol at Winchester HRO 14M50/2.
16. Harrison J.F.C. 1971 *The Early Victorians* Weidenfeld & Nicolson p. 81.
17. Exton Parish Register 21.3.1832 & 24.3.1847.

8. Church and School in the Eighteenth Century Pages 62–66

1. Responses are printed in Ward 1995.
2. Ward 1995 pp. 130, 219.
3. Ib. p. xi.
4. Ib. pp. 169–239.
5. Willis 1964 *A Hampshire Miscellany II Laymans Licences 1675–1834.*
6. For John Baynes see Smith 2004 p. 47.
7. Hurst 1980 pp. 13 & 36–37.

9. Enclosure Pages 67–70

1. For enclosure in England see Hoskins c.6 for Hampshire see Chapman & Seeliger 1997a & 1997b.
2. Watts 1982 p. 43.
3. Borthwick & Chandler Vol. 2 App.4.
4. Maps of awards and details are in HRO.
5. Listed in Chapman & Seeliger 1997b pp. 20–21.
6. 21M65/F7/63/1–2, for Swanmore Watkins 2001 pp. 21–23.
7. HRO Q23/2/11/2.
8. Hoskins 1988 p. 142.

10. Workhouse, the Asylum and the Police Pages 71–79

1. Morrison K. 1999 *The Workhouse* RCHME. Despite the intention to abolish outdoor relief in 1846 there were still over 1.3 million paupers of whom only about 200,000 were in the workhouse.
2. Minute Book of the Guardians of the Droxford Union are in HRO PL/3/7/1–29.
3. Droxford Vestry agreed to join the new Union. HRO 66M76PV3, 21 & 29.1.1835.
4. Wade & Watts eds.1989 p. 83.
5. Standfield 1984 pp. 51–6.
6. The Droxford Vestry elected Robert Stares and James Warner of Steeple Court as its representatives. When Warner died he was replaced by George Habin Appleby.
7. The land was owned by the Marquess of Winchester.
8. HRO PL3/7/2 10.5.1836.
9. Ib. 4.10.1836.
10. White's *Gazeteer and Directory of Hampshire* p.579 & Census 1841.
11. Registrar of Births.

12. PLIII 7/2 17.10.1837.
13. PLIII 7/2 9.1.1838.
14. PLIII 7/2 13.2.1838
15. Droxford Census 1841.
16. The Revd J.A.G.Colpoys was appointed chaplain at a salary of £40 per year. HRO PL3/7/2 19.9.1837.
17. His wife lived until 1941 when she was 76.
18. *Hampshire Independent* October 1977 article by Barbara Burchill, grand-daughter of James Lindsay, HRO 217/84/65P2.
19. HRO PL3/7/29.
20. Letters exchanged with the County Council protesting about demolition of the workhouse without notice are in HRO 72M79/PX27.
21. White's *Gazeteer* op.cit.
22. Ib.
23. The former chapel was later a staff refectory.
24. I have drawn on *The Knowle Experience*, typescript in HRO, no author or date.
25. Midwinter 1968 *Victorian Social Reform* Longman pp. 39 & 43.
26. Ward nd. p. 34.

11. Roman Catholic and Protestant Dissent Pages 80–86

1. Collins & Hurst 1978 p. 77.
2. Ib. p. 79.
3. Dyer A. & Palliser D.M.eds. 2005 *Diocesan Population Returns 1563 & 1603* OUP.
4. Whiteman A. ed. 1986 *The Compton Census of 1676*. OUP.
5. DNB & Collins & Hurst 1972 pp. 67-68.
6. Collins & Hurst 1978 pp. 78-80. The author was shown the ceiling at Southend farm by the present occupant Arabella Edmonstone.
7. Watkins 2007 p. 149.
8. For Compton Census see Appendix B. Henry Compton was bishop of London from 1676-1714.
9. After 1852 a licence from the bishop was no longer needed but chapels had to be registered with the Registrar of Births, Marriages and Deaths.
10. Willis A.J. 1965 *Hampshire Miscellany Vol. III* & HRO 21M65F2/1-7.
11. Vickers 1993 p. 30.
12. Based on research on the Primitive Methodists of the Meon valley in Kitching 2001.
13. Kitching 2001 p. 4.
14. Vickers 1993 p. 141.
15. Kitching 2001 pp. 6-7.
16. Ib. p. 13.
17. The ministers were John Leach (1908-1911) & Walter Barnsley (Droxford Circuit 1900-1903) though he was stationed in Southampton at the time of his imprisonment.
18. A foundation stone of Warnford chapel is still to be found in the building which became first shop and post office & later a private house. It is now called the Old Chapel House.
19. Vickers 1993 p.145. It is described erroneously in the 1851 Census of church attendance as 'Soberton Heath Christian Catholic'. See also Pendred 1999 p. 25.
20. Kitching 2001 p. 30.

12. The Garniers of Wickham Pages 87–95

1. Much of this chapter is based on Garnier A.E.1900 published privately.
2. The presentation to the living of Wickham now belongs to Sir Richard Rashleigh of Menabilly in Cornwall.

3. Crook J.1984 *The Wainscot Book* Hampshire Record Series No. 6.

4. Etheridge *Miscellanea* p. 24.

5. Op.cit. p. 38. Droxford Rectory is next to the church, now called The Old Rectory. The last Rector to live there was Gerald Page (Rector 1946–64).

6. This is not the house next to the church now named The Old Rectory which was built by John Haygarth in 1832.

7. Smith 2004 pp. 37–9, 114.

8. Vickers 1993 pp. 193, 194.

9. Pevsner & Lloyd 1967 p. 656.

10. The tower was demolished in 1973 after it had been vandalised.

11. Preston & Wallis 2006 pp. 40–1; Tappenden 1996 p. 117 and conversation with Royston Pratt.

12. HRO 16M70.

13. DNB.

14. The second Oxford & Cambridge Boat Race did not take place until seven years later and not until 1856 did it become an annual event usually on the Thames from Putney to Mortlake.

15. Clark A. ed. 1974 *A Good Innings: the private papers of Viscount Lee of Fareham.* John Murray to which George Watts drew my attention. Also DNB.

13. The Village School Pages 96–109

1. For correspondence in 1840 & 1841 see HRO 31M86/A1.

2. Ib.

3. HRO 66M76/PJ9 dated 3.6.1860.

4. Standfield 1984 p. 63. For Charles Walters see Watkins 2007 p. 74.

5. Conveyance dated 10th August 1844 lent to me by Margaret Ball who lives at Park Hill House.

6. Standfield 1984 p. 63 ff.

7. Watts ed. 1982 pp. 103–104.

8. Collins & Hurst 1978 p. 102.

9. In 1955 the building was bought by Droxford Parish Council and became the parish room.

10. Hurst 1969 pp. 63–64. The school is now a private house.

11. Collins & Hurst nd. p.42.

12. Parish Magazine of Hook with Warsash October 1886.

13. Ib. July 1887.

14. Extracts from the Log Books of West Meon School were compiled by the present head Hilary Hopkins.

15. *Parish of West Meon for the year 1851*, a small manuscript book kept by the Rector and now in private hands.

16. Quoted in Sutherland 1971 p. 12.

17. *Parish of West Meon for the year 1851*, op.cit.inside cover.

18. HRO 67M81PJ1 15.12.1919.

19. Quoted in *Droxford School 1835–1985* no page numbers.

20. Ib.

14. The Church of England in the Nineteenth Century Pages 110–125

1. Crook J.ed.1984 *The Wainscot Book* Appendix A, Hampshire Record Series No. 9 App. A.

2. Collins & Hurst 1978 pp. 55–56.

3. *Hampshire Chronicle* 2.2.1895.

4. The return has been edited for Hampshire Record Series No.17, Smith ed. 2004.

5. Plaque in the chancel of St Nicholas' Wickham.

6. Smith ed. 2004 p. xxxvii & p. 121.

7. The story is told in Carpenter E Third edition 1997 *Cantuar* Mowbray pp. 257–58.
8. DNB. For the Ecclesiastical Commission see Chadwick 1966 pp. 126–141.
9. Collins & Hurst 1972 p. 71.
10. Banns 1828–64 kept in a small notebook now held privately.
11. *A Memoir of Henry Vincent Bayley printed for private circulation 1846.*[Cited below as *Memoir*].
12. Palmer B.1991 *Gadfly for God*, Hodder & Stoughton pp. 81–82. DNB. Collins & Hurst 1972 pp. 73–74.
13. *Memoir* p. 44.
14. *Memoir* p. 57.
15. *Memoir* p. 61.
16. *West Meon* 2000 p. 37.
17. 67M81/PW7 dated 6.5.1846.
18. Manuscript book kept by the rector of West Meon 1828–1871, held privately.
19. Pevsner & Lloyd 1967 p.497. For Colson see Poole B.2000 *John Colson: a Hampshire Architect of the Victorian Age* Hampshire Papers No. 20 HCC.
20. Watts ed.1982 p. 19.
21. William Nicolson built the church at Froxfield Green where there is a memorial to him.
22. Pevsner & Lloyd 1967 p. 471.
23. Founded in 1969 as the Redundant Churches Fund.
24. For the Pluralities Act see Knight 1995 pp. 119–22 & Jacob 2007 pp. 116–7.
25. Pretyman-Tomline died on 15.11.1827; Charles Sumner appointed 7.12.1827 HRO. 2M65/B.
26. Diocesan Calendar 1870.
27. Between 1856 and 1872 there was a Deanery of West Meon.
28. TOP Droxford 3/2. There is no date on the document but it is probably about 1860.
29. Vickers ed. 1993.
30 Ib. p. 29.
31. Held privately.
32. Notebook recording banns called in West Meon 1828–1864 held privately.
33. Pevsner & Lloyd 1967 p. 652.
34. Collins & Hurst 1978 pp. 27–28.
35. Hurst 1980 p. 10.
36. Chadwick 1970 pp. 426–427.
37. Titchfield Parish Magazine 12. 1888. Bound volume for 1885–88 lent by Brian Patten.
38. West Meon Parish Magazine 4. 1900.
39. Recently moved from the city of London.
40. West Meon Parish Magazine 11. 1900.
41. Hook Parish Magazine 1885.
42. Titchfield Parish Magazine 4. 1888.
43. Sarisbury Parish Magazine.
44. Hook Parish Magazine 3. 1885.
45. Sarisbury Parish Magazine 8. 1886.
46. For *The Wainscot Book* see Hampshire Record Series No.6. For Vaughan see Ward nd pp. 29–30, Bussby 1979 p. 289.

15. Mills and Water Meadows Pages 126–134

1. HFCAS Vol. 25 1968.
2. Watts ed. 1982 pp. 62–64.
3. Moore 1988 p. 35 & DNB.
4. *Chesapeake Mill, Wickham* Hampshire Mills Group nd. Copy lent to the author by Barrie Marson who also brought the author up-to-date on plans for the mill.
5. Ward nd. pp. 3–4.

6. Ward Ib. & conversation with Anthony Hulbert.
7. Rackham 2000 p. 142.
8. Bettey 1986 p. 133.
9. Droxford Vestry Minutes 66M76/PO3 7.4.1806 & 24.4.1810.
10. Ib. 24.4.1824.
11. Collins & Hurst 1978 p. 12.
12. Den Marriner in conversation with the author.
13. *Hampshire Magazine* September 1969 pp. 39–40 & Everard ed.2005 p. 38.
14. Shown to the author in February 2009 by John Larrett.
15. Observed by the author.
16. Everard op.cit. pp. 207–214.

16. Four Big Houses Pages 135–150

1. 5M76E1 ff.42–5 undated, quoted in Borthwick & Chandler Vol. 1 1995 p. 52. [Cited below as B.& C.].
2. HRO WR/3 p.193 quoted in B. & C. Vol. 2 1994 Appendix 4 Npn.
3. 1578BO60/1–2 inventory reproduced in B. & C. 1995 Vol. 2 Npn.
4. The claim is also made for Hinton Ampner House closer to the battlefield and also occupied by the Stewkely family.
5. Appendix C & Hughes & White p. 47.
6. HRO Photocopy 519.
7. B. & C.1995 Vol. 1 p. 58. The ice-house no longer exists.
8. Hurst 1980 pp. 51–3.
9. Ib. pp. 51–3.
10 DNB.
11. Hurst 1980 p. 47.
12. DNB & Pelly D. 2001 *Upton Connections 1732–1916* Pentland Books, copy lent to the author by Barbara, Lady Pelly. There is a Pelly Road in West Ham.
13. The house in St James's Place was bombed during the Second World War and not again occupied by the Pellys.
14. Based on *My Life in Service 1933–1938* an anonymous memoir of life at St James's Place and Preshaw. Typescript.
15. Pevsner & Lloyd 1967 p. 470.
16. HRO 38M82/15.
17. Source for information on Preshaw B.& C. 1995, a copy was lent to the author by Sir Richard Pelly. Also Sale Catalogue HRO38M82/15.
18. Hurst et al. 1969 c.3 & 4. I am also grateful for loan of *The Restoration of Warnford Park.* 2005 edition.
19. Place House was also the name used for the chief house in Titchfield after 1535 and for the manor house at Wickham.
20. Charles Millen in Collins & Hurst 1969 pp. 52–4.
21. Hampshire Industrial Archaeology Vol. 5 November 1968 article by Professor J.H.Thomas, also author's conversations with John Larrett, the present owner of Paper Mill Cottage.
22. VCH Hampshire Vol. 3.
23. The family name was Burke, changed to De Burgh to emphasise Norman origin of the family.
24. *Hampshire Treasures* Vol. 1 pp. 308–9.
25. Hughes 1984 *Hampshire's Countryside Heritage* 8 p. 24.
26. Catalogue of Sale 20, 21, 22 June 1939.
27. *Pig Production in Warnford* in Country Life 3.12.1938 pp. xxxvi–xxxviii lent to the author by Stephen Short.
28. For Westbury see Collins & Hurst 1972 pp. 56–62.
29. Letters from Jenifer Martin who grew up at West Meon House during the ownership of the

Waudbys. Also reminiscences of Ruby Small.

30. West Meon Burial Register 18.9.1635.
31. Collins & Hurst 1972 pp.28–31.
32. Keppel S. 1958 *Edwardian Daughter* pp.53–4. Copy lent to the author by Joy Prideaux.
33. Alice Keppel's elder daughter was Violet (1894–1972) who although married to Denys Trefusis in 1919 is better known for her lesbian relationship with Vita Sackville-West which began many years before when they were both children. The story of Alice and her daughter Violet is told in Southam D. 1996 *Mrs Keppel and her Daughter* Harper Collins.
34. For example *Who's Who 1931*.
35. Catalogue of Sale April 1987.
36. *West Meon* 2000 p.127. Minnie Montagu kindly showed the author the house and gardens in March 2009.

17. Roads, Bridges, Flood and Fire Pages 151–163

1. Coates p. 175.
2. See for example Watts in HFCAS Vol. 21 Part 1 1958 p. 35.
3. Collins & Hurst 1969 pp. 55–58 & 1972 pp. 63–64.
4. HRO Q26/3/942.
5. Albert 1972 lists turnpike acts passed 1663–1840 in Appendix B pp. 202–223. Chawton Pond was filled in in the 1930s.
6. The Act of Parliament of 1758 had the title ' An Act for repairing and widening the Roads from Chawton Pond, in the parish of Chawton in the County of Southampton, through Rumsdean Bottom, Westmean, Warnford, Exton, Bishop's Waltham, and over Sherrill Heath, and through Wickham and Fareham, to the Town of Gosport; and from Exton aforesaid, through Droxford, to the East end of Sherrill Heath in the said County.' (orignsal spelling and capital letters). We do not know why the direction of travel was reversed in the later version. The version above is confusing and suggests that it is a compilation of a number of suggestions for turnpike roads. I owe this information to Martin Morris in a letter to the author.
7. The words *hut* or *hutt* are associated with droving.
8. HRO Q26/3/25.
9. The Cold Harbour turnpike cottage was located on the north-west side of Titchfield Lane.
10. HRO 36M72A1.
11. I have found no documentary proof of the date.
12. HRO Q26/3/353 is a file of correspondence about the proposed road.
13. A map in the Rookesbury Estate Office shows the road proposed by the writers of this letter.
14. Pendred 1999 p. 94.
15. Watts ed.1982 pp. 84–85. I owe information about proprietary roads round Southampton to Martin Morris.
16. HRO 4M51/394.
17. HRO 66M76/T57/1.
18. HRO Q26/3/1.
19. John Ekins in *Eyewitness Account* 2007 pp. 167–74 Titchfield History Society.
20. Hurst 1969 p. 55.
21. Watts ed.1982 p. 66.
22. Tappenden 2006 pp. 90–91.
23. Hurst 1980 p. 36 & Exton Parish Register.
24. Standfield 1984 p. 106.
25. Ib. p.107.
26. Hurst 1980 photographs (iii) following p. 32.
27. Ward nd. Inside front cover.

28. Bosworth J. 1991 *Bishop's Waltham Fire Brigade Centenary* 1891–1991.
29. Collins & Hurst 1978 p. 110.
30. Ward nd. pp. 39–40.
31. Standfield 1984 pp. 104–106.
32. Ib. pp. 102–104.
33. Droxford Parish Meetings.

18. The Meon Valley Railway Pages 164–175

1. Course 1974 pp. 228–236, Stone 1983, Moore 1988 p. 82, Hughes 1994 pp. 56–61, Tilman 2003.
2. Moore 1988 p. 82.
3. Course 1974 p. 232.
4. Stone 1983 pp. 8–11.
5. Ib. pp. 18–19.
6. Tillman 2003 p. 37.
7. Tappenden 2006 p. 121.
8. George Watts' grandfather for example.
9. Collins & Hurst 1972 pp. 65–66.
10. West Meon School Log 12.3.1901.
11. Collins & Hurst 1972 p. 66.
12. West Meon 2000 p.73. *The White Horse* is now a private house named *White Horse Cottage.*
13. West Meon School Log & letter from Jenifer Martin.
14. I owe this reference to George Watts.
15. Hulbert op.cit.
16. Letter & telephone conversation June 2009 with Norah Blyth who now lives in Suffolk.
17. See Stone 1983 pp. 95–101 where the closure is described with quotations from local papers.
18. Stone 1983 p.102.
19. *West Meon 2000.*
20. Collins & Hurst 1978 p. 124.
21. Stone 1983 p. 108.
22. Course 1974 p. 236.

19. Parish and Rural District Councils Pages 176–180

1. Poole & Keith-Lucas 1994 cc. 1–2.
2. Tappenden 2006 p. 120.
3. Standfield 1984 p. 92.
4. Pendred 1999 pp. 122–124.
5. Droxford Parish Council Minutes from 1959 in HRO.
6. *West Meon* 2000 p. 26.
7. Standfield 1984 p. 93.
8. Wade & Watts eds. 1989 pp. 103–105.
9. Standfield 1984 p. 93.
10. HRO 72M79/PX9 3.5.1938. The number of vehicles in the United Kingdom increased from 873,700 in 1921 to 2,768,606 in 1936 – 216% – but mileage of roads increased by only 1.3% HFCAS Newsletter 52 p. 15 Note 2.
11. HRO 37M73APX 1–9.
12. HRO 72M74/PX9 24.3.1945 & 9.5.1945.

20. Late Victorian and Edwardian Villages Pages 118–196

1. Census Warnford 1881.
2. Standfield 1984 pp. 94–97.
3. HRO 47/M63/166.
4. Stokes 2007 p.115, Stone 1983 p. 42.
5. Parish Magazine Sarisbury August 1885.
6. Ward nd. p. 37.
7. Derry & Williams 1960 *A History of Technology* OUP pp. 390–393, Ward nd. p. 5.
8. Simons J.A. *A History of Cricket in Hampshire 1760–1914* Hampshire Papers 4 1993 p. 2; Major J. 2007 *More than a game* Harper Collins p. 95.
9. Major op cit.
10. Simons op cit p. 23.
11. Major op cit p. 70.
12. Collins & Hurst 1972 pp. 68–69.
13. Ib.
14. *Memoir of Henry Vincent Bayley* 1846.
15. For another country house cricket club see Watkins 2001 pp. 46–48.
16. Gannaway N. *Association Football in Hampshire until 1914* Hampshire Papers No. 9 p. 19. Goal posts with cross bars only became obligatory in 1882 and nets behind the goal in 1892.
17. Tull J.E.(compiled by) 2008 *Meon Valley Football League 1906–2006*.
18. Ward nd. p. 53.
19. Ib. p. 52.
20. Ib.pp. 55–57.
21. Pevsner & Lloyd 1967 p. 508.
22. Lutyens was the architect of New Delhi and of the Cenotaph in Whitehall. He was knighted in 1918.
23. Lloyd in Pevsner & Lloyd 1967 p. 497.
24. Pamphlet entitled *New Place History*, No author, date or publisher.

21. The First World War Pages 197–202

1. Nicolson V.2007 *Singled Out* Viking p. 11.
2. Tappenden 2006 p. 129.
3. Standfield 1984 p. 112.
4. Tappenden 2006 p. 132.
5. Pendred 1999 p. 104.
6. Ib.
7. Ib.
8. I am grateful to Brian Patten who lent me the Titchfield Parish Magazine for June 1915.
9. Ward nd. p. 22.
10. Tappenden 2006 pp. 134–6.
11. Emery 1991 *Some of the History of Shedfield Parish* Paul Cave Publications p. 63.
12. Ward nd. p. 25.

22. The Inter-war Years Pages 203–211

1. Warwick 1982.
2. Ib. pp. 6–8.

3. Ib. p. 10.
4. Wade & Watts 1989 p. 111.
5. *West Meon* 2000 & conversations with Ruby Clay.
6. Ib.
7. *Eyewitness Account* nd. pp. 13–16.
8. Wade & Watts 1989 pp. 118–121.
9. Ib. p. 116.
10. Ward nd.pp 46–47.
11. Ib.p.35.
12. *Country Life* 8th May 1937 & Standfield 1984 pp. 124–125.
13. Standfield 1984 pp. 125–130.
14. A bell form HMS Mercury was presented to East Meon church and erected with a plaque to commemorate 52 years association.
15. Etheridge *Memorabilia.*
16. Ib.

23. The Second World War Pages 212–222

1. Warwick 1982 p. 21.
2. Den Marriner in conversation with the author.
3. *Wickham in Wartime: the Home Front.*
4. West Meon School Log 30.9.1938.
5. Pendred 1999 p. 106.
6. West Meon School Log 4.9.1939.
7. Ib. 12.9.1939.
8. Den Marriner op.cit.
9. West Meon School Log 20.3.1940.
10. Warwick 1982 pp .40–44.
11. Den Marriner op.cit.
12. Ward nd. p. 59.
13. Standfield 1984 Fig. 47.
14. Tappenden 2006 p. 127.
15. Standfield 1984 p. 116 & Lampe David *The Last Ditch.*
16. Pendred 1999 p .106.
17. Ward nd. p. 61.
18. Ib.
19. Den Marriner op.cit.
20. Ward nd. p. 60.
21. Watts ed. 1982 p. 132.
22. *Eyewitness Account* pp. 45–50.
23. Ward nd. pp. 8 & 60.
24. Ib. p. 60.

24 Post-war Years Pages 223–230

1. Kynaston 2008 *The Age of Austerity* Bloomsbury pp. 19 & 38.
2. The following paragraphs are based on a memoir of life in Droxford in the 1950s written at the request of the author by Anthony Hulbert.
3. Conversation with Den Marriner 2009.
4. Standfield 1984 p. 74.

5. *Eyewitnes Account* 2007 pp. 13–16.
6. Pevsner & Lloyd 1967 p. 653.
7. Watts ed.1982 pp. 135–136 & information at Titchfield Haven.
8. Hulbert op.cit.
9. Hurst 1980 pp. 57–58 & conversations with Brian Lewis & Rob Cooper.
10. Hurst 1980 pp. 49–53 which includes a list of Masters from 1800–1978 & Hulbert op cit.

25. The Changing Village Pages 231–235

1. HRO 72M79PX8.
2. Collins & Hurst 1978 p. 12.
3. Census 1951 & 2001. See Appendix B.
4. *West Meon 2000.*
5. Standfield 1984 photos pp. 51 & 54.
6. *West Meon 2000* p. 59.
7. Robert Russell, headmaster of West Meon School 1932–1963, died 29.1.1977. West Meon School Log.
8. *West Meon 2000* pp. 157–158.

26. Into the Third Millennium Pages 236–240

1. *West Meon 2000* p. 5.
2. Details in *Eyewitness Account* pp. 215–218 & *Titchfield at the Start of the Third Millennium* pp. 141–156.
3. East Meon Embroidery: a leaflet to accompany the embroidery contains the names of contributors & a key to places included.
4. Laslett Peter 1983 *The World We have Lost – further explored.*

Index

The index covers the text of the book but not appendices, bibliography or notes. The pages on which illustrations appear are in bold type. Not all personal names are included in the index.